2014 Congressional Budget Justification

Table of Contents

CONTENTS

TABLES

TABLE OF CONTENTS

FIGURES

Executive Summary

EXECUTIVE SUMMARY

The mission of the U.S. Nuclear Regulatory Commission is to license and regulate the Nation's civilian use of byproduct, source, and special nuclear materials to ensure adequate protection of public health and safety, promote the common defense and security, and protect the environment.

The U.S. Nuclear Regulatory Commission (NRC) is an independent Federal agency established to license and regulate the Nation's civilian use of byproduct, source, and special nuclear materials (SNM) to ensure adequate protection of public health and safety, promote the common defense and security, and protect the environment. The NRC has formulated its fiscal year (FY) 2014 Congressional Budget Justification to support the agency's Safety and Security strategic goals and objectives.

The NRC's Safety goal is to ensure adequate protection of public health and safety and the environment. The agency's safety program outcomes are to prevent the occurrence of any nuclear reactor accidents, inadvertent criticality events, acute radiation exposures, or significant releases of radioactive materials. The Security goal is to ensure the secure use and management of radioactive materials. The security program outcomes are to prevent any instances in which licensed radioactive materials are used in a hostile manner in the United States and prevent unauthorized public disclosures of classified or safeguards information through quality measures.

The NRC's critical functions are to ensure the safe and secure use of byproduct, source, and SNM in the United States and to protect both the public and workers from radiation hazards that could result from the use of radioactive materials. The NRC's principal regulatory functions are to establish regulatory requirements and conduct confirmatory research to support requirements; issue licenses to facility owners, possessors, and users of nuclear materials; inspect these licensees to ensure they are in compliance with NRC requirements and that they operate safely and securely; and take appropriate enforcement action for violations of regulatory requirements.

Following the Fukushima Dai-ichi accident, the NRC established a task force (Near-Term Task Force, or NTTF) to conduct a systematic and methodical review of the NRC's processes and regulations to determine whether the agency should make additional improvements to its regulatory system and to make recommendations to the Commission for its policy direction. The NTTF identified near-term actions that the agency should consider to enhance safety. In FY 2014, the NRC will conduct Commission-approved activities associated with the near-term recommendations, as well as evaluating safety improvements identified as part of the longer term effort.

The NRC regulates every aspect of the civilian use of nuclear materials, from the processing of uranium ore to the disposal of radioactive waste. This includes all the steps and the facilities involved in the nuclear fuel cycle: (1) extraction of the uranium from ore, (2) conversion of the uranium into a form suitable for enrichment, (3) enrichment of the uranium to a level and type suitable for nuclear fuel, and (4) fabrication of the enriched uranium into fuel assemblies for use in reactors. The fuel assemblies are used in nuclear reactors; when they are no longer efficient for reactor operations, they are removed from the reactors and stored as waste.

Since October 2007, the NRC has received 18 applications (including Watts Bar, Unit 2) to construct and operate new nuclear power reactors. Five different reactor designs are referenced in these applications. The NRC has issued two design certifications (DCs) and is currently reviewing three design applications for certification. Approved DCs reduce the time required to approve a power reactor license application when a previously certified reactor design is used. If and when new power reactors are brought on line, they will substantially increase U.S. electrical generating capacity. The resurgence of interest in the construction of new nuclear power plants also has resulted in applications to construct and operate facilities for the manufacturing of nuclear fuel (e.g., uranium milling and enrichment). The NRC will perform safety, security, and environmental reviews of enrichment facilities, a uranium deconversion facility, and uranium recovery facilities.

The NRC ensures safety and security by licensing and overseeing nuclear waste and spent fuel storage facilities, certifying storage and transportation containers, and responding to events, as well as through decontamination and decommissioning activities. Additionally, security plans, emergency preparedness, and security testing are a major part of the licensing, oversight, and other regulatory activities that provide high assurance of physical security for nuclear facilities and materials. The NRC further enhances its regulatory program through coordination and cooperation with other Federal agencies, States, and international organizations and governments.

OVERVIEW OF THE FY 2014 NRC CONGRESSIONAL BUDGET JUSTIFICATION

The NRC's FY 2014 Congressional Budget Justification provides the necessary resources for the Nuclear Reactor Safety and Nuclear Materials and Waste Safety Programs to carry out the agency's mission and to achieve the stated goals and desired outcomes for the American public. The NRC's proposed FY 2014 budget is $1,055.0 million, including 3,919 full-time equivalents (FTE), which represents an increase of $16.9 million, including a decrease of 57 FTE, when compared with the FY 2012 enacted budget.

The Nuclear Reactor Safety Program increases by $12.3 million, including a decrease of 40 FTE; the Nuclear Materials and Waste Safety Program increases by $4.4 million, including a decrease of 11 FTE, when the FY 2014 request is compared with the FY 2012 enacted budget. Collectively, the Nuclear Reactor Safety and Nuclear Materials and Waste Safety Programs have an overall funding increase of $16.7 million, including a decrease of 51 FTE, when compared with the FY 2012 enacted budget.

The Office of the Inspector General's (OIG's) component of the FY 2014 proposed budget is $11.1 million, and it includes resources to carry out its mission to independently and objectively conduct audits and investigations to ensure the efficiency and integrity of NRC programs and operations and to promote cost-effective management.

Under the provisions of the Omnibus Budget Reconciliation Act of 1990, as amended, the NRC's FY 2014 budget provides for 90-percent fee recovery, less the amounts appropriated for (1) Waste Incidental to Reprocessing Activities under Section 3116 of the Ronald W. Reagan National Defense Authorization Act for Fiscal Year 2005 and (2) generic homeland security activities.

Total NRC Budget Authority by Appropriation (Dollars in Millions)				
	FY 2012 Enacted	*FY 2013 Annualized CR	FY 2014 Request	Delta FY 2014–FY 2012
NRC Appropriations	$M	$M	$M	$M
Salaries and Expenses (S&E)				
Budget Authority	1,027.2	1,033.0	1043.9	16.7
Offsetting Fees	899.7	905.0	920.7	21.0
Net Appropriated S&E	127.5	128.0	123.2	(4.3)
Office of the Inspector General				
Budget Authority	10.9	11.0	11.1	0.2
Offsetting Fees	9.8	10.0	10.0	0.2
Net Appropriated OIG	1.1	1.0	1.1	0.0
Total NRC ($M)				
Budget Authority	1,038.1	1,043.0	1,055.0	16.9
Offsetting Fees	909.5	915.0	930.7	21.2
Total Net Appropriated	**$128.6**	**129.0**	**$124.3**	**($4.3)**

(Numbers may not add due to rounding. *FY 2013 Annualized CR is estimated based on OMB MAX which is rounded)

	Budget Authority and Full-Time Equivalents					
	FY 2012 Enacted		FY 2014 Request		Delta FY 2014–FY 2012	
Major Programs	$M	FTE	$M	FTE	$M	FTE
Operating Reactors	534.7	2,100.4	571.9	2,120.0	37.2	19.6
New Reactors	265.4	924.6	240.5	865.5	(24.9)	(59.1)
Nuclear Reactor Safety Subtotal	**$800.1**	**3,025.0**	**$812.4**	**2,985.5**	**$12.3**	**(39.6)**
Fuel Facilities	56.1	228.4	60.2	237.7	4.1	9.3
Nuclear Materials Users	93.0	344.7	86.9	318.7	(6.1)	(25.9)
Spent Fuel Storage and Transportation	40.8	155.1	45.4	160.7	4.6	5.6
Decommissioning and Low-Level Waste (LLW)	37.3	142.1	39.0	142.1	1.8	(0.0)
Nuclear Materials and Waste Safety Subtotal	**$227.1**	**870.4**	**$231.5**	**859.2**	**$4.4**	**(11.1)**
Inspector General	10.9	58.0	11.1	58.0	0.2	0.0
Subtotal	**$10.9**	**58.0**	**$11.1**	**58.0**	**$0.2**	**0.0**
Reimbursable FTE		22.9		16.4		(6.5)
Total	**$1,038.1**	**3,976.3**	**$1,055.0**	**3,919.1***	**$ 16.9**	**(57.2)**

Numbers may not add due to rounding.
*The total FTE reported in this document is correct whereas the FTE total for FY 2014 shown in the President's Budget Appendix reflects an NRC data entry error that does not include the reimbursable FTE.

Accordingly, $930.7 million of the FY 2014 budget will be recovered from fees assessed to NRC licensees. This will result in a net appropriation of $124.3 million, which is a decrease of $4.3 million in net appropriations when compared with the FY 2012 enacted budget. In accordance with the requirements in Section 51.2 of the Office of Management and Budget (OMB) Circular A-11, "Requirements for Program Justification," the NRC is providing the full cost of its programs.

The NRC's FY 2014 budget request includes a 1-percent provisional estimate of the pay raise for January 2014. The FY 2014 budget contains FTE savings in office support functional areas of administrative services, human resources, information management, information technology (IT), and financial management (including contract management). The FTE savings are possible because the NRC is implementing cost-conscious business solutions to eliminate duplicative processes in agency support functions.

NUCLEAR REACTOR SAFETY

	Nuclear Reactor Safety (Dollars in Millions)					
	FY 2012 Enacted		FY 2014 Request		Delta FY 2014–FY 2012	
Business Line	$M	FTE	$M	FTE	$M	FTE
Operating Reactors	534.7	2,100.4	571.9	2,120.0	37.2	19.6
New Reactors	265.4	924.6	240.5	865.5	(24.9)	(59.1)
Total	$800.1	3,025.0	$812.4	2,985.5	$12.3	(39.6)

Numbers may not add due to rounding.

The Nuclear Reactor Safety Program encompasses the NRC's efforts to license, regulate, and oversee civilian nuclear power, research and test reactors in a manner that adequately protects public health and safety and the environment. This program also provides high assurance of the physical security of facilities and protection against radiological sabotage. This program contributes to the NRC's Safety and Security goals through the activities of the Operating Reactors and New Reactors Business Lines that regulate existing and new nuclear reactors to ensure their safe operation and physical security.

Overall resources requested in the FY 2014 budget for the Nuclear Reactor Safety Program are $812.4 million, including 2,985.5 FTE. This funding level represents an overall increase of $12.3 million, including a decrease of 39.6 FTE, when compared with the FY 2012 enacted budget.

An explanation of the changes between the FY 2014 and FY 2012 enacted budget levels is provided in the program chapters of this budget for each business line.

OPERATING REACTORS

The Operating Reactors Business Line supports the licensing, oversight, rulemaking, international activities, research, generic homeland security, and event response associated with the safe and secure operation of 104 civilian nuclear power reactors and 31 research and test reactors (RTRs). The FY 2014 budget request for Operating Reactors is $571.9 million, including 2,120 FTE. This funding level represents an overall increase of $37.2 million, including 19.6 FTE, when compared with the FY 2012 enacted budget. Resources increased to support the implementation of the Fukushima Near-Term Task Force (NTTF) recommendations that included a shift from New Reactors to Operating Reactors. Other increases support National Fire Protection Association Standard 805 (NFPA 804) license amendment request (LAR) reviews, license renewals, implementation of the congressionally mandated Force-on-Force program, replacement of the agency's Reactor Program System, and Commission-directed medium priority rules. The major activities that the requested resources will support include the following:

U.S. Operating Commercial Nuclear Power Reactors

Licensed to Operate (104)

REGION I	REGION II	REGION III	REGION IV
CONNECTICUT Millstone 2 and 3	**ALABAMA** Browns Ferry 1, 2, and 3 Farley 1 and 2	**ILLINOIS** Braidwood 1 and 2 Byron 1 and 2 Clinton Dresden 2 and 3 LaSalle 1 and 2 Quad Cities 1 and 2	**ARKANSAS** Arkansas Nuclear 1 and 2
MARYLAND Calvert Cliffs 1 and 2	**FLORIDA** Crystal River 3 St. Lucie 1 and 2 Turkey Point 3 and 4		**ARIZONA** Palo Verde 1, 2, and 3
MASSACHUSETTS Pilgrim		**IOWA** Duane Arnold	**CALIFORNIA** Diablo Canyon 1 and 2 San Onofre 2 and 3
NEW HAMPSHIRE Seabrook	**GEORGIA** Edwin I. Hatch 1 and 2 Vogtle 1 and 2	**MICHIGAN** Cook 1 and 2 Fermi 2 Palisades	**KANSAS** Wolf Creek 1
NEW JERSEY Hope Creek Oyster Creek Salem 1 and 2	**NORTH CAROLINA** Brunswick 1 and 2 McGuire 1 and 2 Harris 1	**MINNESOTA** Monticello Prairie Island 1 and 2	**LOUISIANA** River Bend 1 Waterford 3
NEW YORK FitzPatrick Ginna Indian Point 2 and 3 Nine Mile Point 1 and 2	**SOUTH CAROLINA** Catawba 1 and 2 Oconee 1, 2, and 3 Robinson 2 Summer	**OHIO** Davis-Besse Perry	**MISSISSIPPI** Grand Gulf
			MISSOURI Callaway
PENNSYLVANIA Beaver Valley 1 and 2 Limerick 1 and 2 Peach Bottom 2 and 3 Susquehanna 1 and 2 Three Mile Island 1	**TENNESSEE** Sequoyah 1 and 2 Watts Bar 1	**WISCONSIN** Kewaunee Point Beach 1 and 2	**NEBRASKA** Cooper Fort Calhoun
VERMONT Vermont Yankee	**VIRGINIA** North Anna 1 and 2 Surry 1 and 2		**TEXAS** Comanche Peak 1 and 2 South Texas Project 1 and 2
			WASHINGTON Columbia

- Continue implementation and review of Fukushima NTTF recommendations for Tier 1, 2, and 3.
- Complete 900 licensing actions (200 Fukushima-related), including reviewing approximately 11 extended power uprates and approximately 22 National Fire Protection Agency Standard 805 ongoing reviews.
- Complete 500 other licensing tasks and related activities, including assistance to the regions, interactions with vendors, industry and owners' groups, and 20 technical topical report reviews that resolve generic issues and reduce the topical reports backlog.
- Continue inspection activities for the 104 operating nuclear power plants.

- Conduct 14 active high-priority rulemakings (including 3 high-priority rulemakings related to the Fukushima event), review an estimated 22 active petitions for rulemaking (PRM), and close 8 PRMs. Develop regulatory bases activities and regulatory analysis guidance updates, and support rulemaking infrastructure.
- Support the replenishment of potassium iodide tablets in States where they are due to expire in FY 2013.
- Conduct research associated with digital instrumentation and control systems and electrical research.
- Evaluate areas of steam generator tube integrity to include (1) inspection reliability, (2) inservice inspection technology effectiveness, and (3) steam generator tube corrosion and degradation evaluation.
- Conduct research on irradiation-assisted corrosion cracking to shorten the amount of time required to obtain all necessary data and to support long-term operation efforts.
- Conduct research on materials degradation, particularly as it relates to license renewal.
- Develop implementation strategy for use of probabilistic risk-assessment tools to support the Reactor Oversight Process and other risk-informed agency decision processes.

NEW REACTORS

The New Reactors Business Line supports the licensing, oversight, rulemaking, international activities, and research associated with the safe and secure development of new power reactors from design, site approval, and construction to operational status. The FY 2014 budget request for New Reactors is $240.5 million, including 865.5 FTE. This funding level represents an overall decrease of $24.9 million, including 59.1 FTE, when compared with the FY 2012 enacted budget. The decrease is primarily due to a shift in resources from the New Reactor Business Line Licensing to the Operating Reactor Business Line to support Fukushima NTTF, and, reduced activity related to combined operating licenses (COLs) and DCs as the result of improved projections based on historical workload data. The major activities that the requested resources will support include the following:

- Provide licensing and hearing support for eight COLs) under Title 10 of the *Code of Federal Regulations* (10 CFR) Part 52, "Licensing, Certifications, and Approvals for Nuclear Power Plants," licensing reviews for Watts Bar, Unit 2, and Bellefonte under 10 CFR Part 50, "Domestic Licensing of Production and Utilization Facilities."
- Complete the review of two DCs, continue review of one DC and one DC renewal, and start the review of one DC renewal and two small modular reactors.
- Continue review of two large, light-water reactors and begin the review of one advanced reactor early site permit (ESP).
- Continue advanced reactor pre-application activity for one construction permit, two DCs, and for one ESP application.
- Continue work to address the impact of findings from the Fukushima NTTF recommendations for new reactor designs.
- Continue oversight activities at six reactors under construction.
- Provide support to mitigate schedule impacts to multiple COL applications by ensuring the availability of staff support for mandatory hearings.
- Provide support for inspections and for the closure of Inspections, Tests, Analyses, and Acceptance Criteria closure.

NUCLEAR MATERIALS AND WASTE SAFETY

| | Nuclear Materials and Waste Safety (Dollars in Millions) | | | | | |
Business Line	FY 2012 Enacted $M	FY 2012 Enacted FTE	FY 2014 Request $M	FY 2014 Request FTE	Delta FY 2014–FY 2012 $M	Delta FY 2014–FY 2012 FTE
Fuel Facilities	56.1	228.4	60.2	237.7	4.1	9.3
Nuclear Materials Users	93.0	344.7	86.9	318.7	(6.1)	(25.9)
Spent Fuel Storage and Transportation	40.8	155.1	45.4	160.7	4.6	5.6
Decommissioning and LLW	37.3	142.1	39.0	142.1	1.8	(0.0)
Total	$227.1	870.4	$231.5	859.2	$4.4	(11.1)

Numbers may not add due to rounding.

The Nuclear Materials and Waste Safety Program encompasses the NRC's effort to license, regulate, and oversee nuclear materials and waste in a manner that adequately protects public health and safety and the environment. This program provides high assurance of physical security of the most risk-significant materials and waste and protection against radiological sabotage, theft, or diversion of nuclear materials. Through this program, the NRC regulates uranium processing and fuel facilities; nuclear fuel research and pilot facilities; nuclear materials users (medical, industrial, research, and academic); spent fuel storage; spent fuel storage casks and transportation packaging; decontamination and decommissioning of facilities; and low-level and high-level radioactive waste. The program contributes to the NRC's Safety and Security goals through the activities of the Fuel Facilities, Nuclear Materials Users, Spent Fuel Storage and Transportation, and Decommissioning and Low-Level Waste Business Lines regulating byproduct, source, and SNM.

Overall resources requested in the FY 2014 budget for the Nuclear Materials and Waste Safety Program are $231.5 million, including 859.2 FTE. This funding level represents an overall increase of $4.4 million, including a decrease of 11.1 FTE, when compared with the FY 2012 enacted budget.

FUEL FACILITIES

The Fuel Facilities Business Line supports licensing, oversight, rulemaking, international activities, research, generic homeland security, and event response associated with the safe and secure operation of various operating and new fuel facilities, such as conversion, enrichment, fuel fabrication facilities, and nuclear fuel research facilities. The FY 2014 budget request for Fuel Facilities is $60.2 million, including 237.7 FTE. This funding level represents an overall increase of $4.1 million, including 9.3 FTE, when compared with the FY 2012 enacted budget. The major activities that the requested resources will support include the following:

- Conduct licensing actions for 14 major fuel cycle facilities and 17 minor facilities licensees under 10 CFR Part 70. Provide inspection oversight for approximately 8 existing facilities and 4 new facilities either under construction or operation. Complete approximately 80 new licenses, license renewals, license amendments, and safety and safeguard reviews for fuel cycle facilities annually.

- Review license amendments for AREVA Eagle Rock Enrichment Facility (AREVA), General Electric-Hitachi Laser Enrichment Facility (GE-Hitachi), and International Isotopes Deconversion Facility (INIS) before initial operations.
- Conduct inspection efforts for new facilities at the Mixed-Oxide Fuel Fabrication Facility, AREVA, GE-Hitachi, and INIS.
- Develop and test a risk-informed Fuel Cycle Oversight Process to enhance the oversight infrastructure development.
- Engage in rulemaking activities related to security at fuel facilities

NUCLEAR MATERIALS USERS

The Nuclear Materials Users Business Line supports the licensing; oversight; rulemaking; international activities; research; generic homeland security; event response; and State, Tribal, and Federal Program activities associated with the safe and secure possession, processing, handling, and use of nuclear materials for the many and diverse uses of these materials. The FY 2014 budget request for Nuclear Materials Users is $86.9 million, including 318.7 FTE. This funding level represents an overall decrease of $6.1 million, including 25.9 FTE, when compared with the FY 2012 enacted budget. The major activities that the requested resources will support include the following:

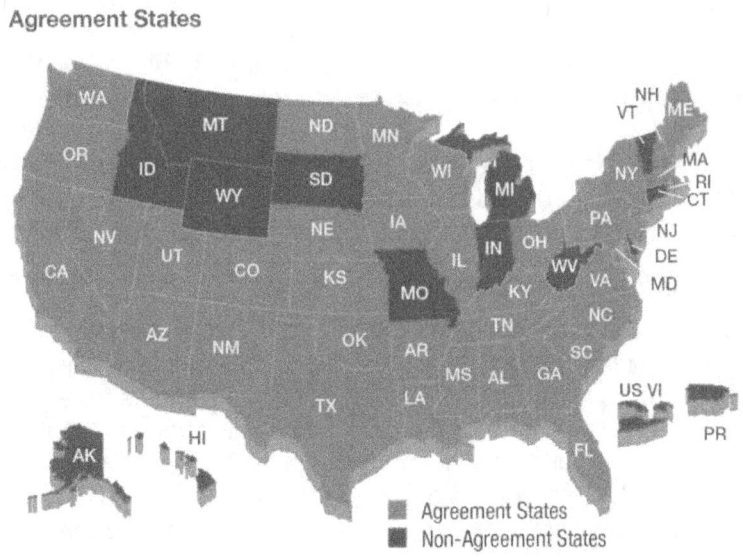

Agreement States

- Conduct licensing, inspection, event evaluation, research, incident response, allegation, enforcement, import and export authorizations, rulemaking activities, and major IT systems to maintain the regulatory safety and security infrastructure needed to process and handle nuclear materials.
- Complete approximately 2,300 materials licensing actions and 1,000 routine health and safety inspections and conduct security inspections of Agreement State licensees.
- Continue work on approximately four to six materials rulemakings.

- Continue development of the Integrated Source Management Portfolio to integrate the three systems that license and track sources and radioactive materials under one management mechanism. This development effort is vital to forming a comprehensive national materials license repository.
- Conduct materials oversight for Agreement States, including program reviews, technical assistance, regulatory development, and cooperative efforts. Funds also provide for Agreement State staff training and travel.

SPENT FUEL STORAGE AND TRANSPORTATION

The Spent Fuel Storage and Transportation Business Line supports the licensing, oversight, rulemaking, international activities, research, and generic homeland security associated with the safe and secure storage and transportation of spent nuclear fuel (SNF). The FY 2014 budget request for Spent Fuel Storage and Transportation is $45.4 million, including 160.7 FTE. This funding level represents an overall increase of $4.6 million, including 5.6 FTE, when compared with the FY 2012 enacted budget. The major activities that the requested resources will support include:

- Conduct safety inspections of transportation packages, storage cask vendors and fabricators, independent spent fuel storage installation (ISFSI) operations, security inspections of SNF ISFSIs, and transportation and route surveys.
- Participate in a U.S. cask demonstration and monitoring program of extended dry cask storage with high-burnup fuel and perform a security assessment scoping study to identify additional regulatory and technical needs for an extended storage and transportation security framework.
- Develop an environmental impact statement (EIS) to support a revised Waste Confidence decision rule. This EIS will address the Court decision to vacate the Waste Confidence decision and rule.
- Continue research on technical issues associated with very long-term dry spent fuel storage; such as concrete degradation; weld corrosion; impacts of high-burnup and mixed-oxide fuels; climate change effects on cask performance; transportability of fuel after long-term storage; and the need for an improved hazards assessment, including the potential impact of long-term storage on eventual disposal.
- Perform analysis, data collection, and modeling for future alternate strategies for disposal of spent fuel and high-level waste, including laboratory studies and field investigations needed to understand key technical issues and risk insights, technical inputs to resolve regulatory gaps, use of a performance assessment scoping tool for risk insights, and continued coordination of alternative disposal strategies with other aspects of the back end of the fuel cycle.
- Monitor national level developments stemming from the January 2012 report of the Blue Ribbon Commission on America's Nuclear Future and the Department of Energy response.

DECOMMISSIONING AND LOW-LEVEL WASTE

The Decommissioning and Low-Level Waste Business Line supports the licensing, oversight, rulemaking, international activities, and research associated with the safe and secure operation of uranium recovery facilities, removal of a nuclear facility from service and reduction of residual radioactivity to a level that permits termination of the NRC license, and the disposition of low-level radioactive waste from all civilian sources. The FY 2014 budget request for Decommissioning and Low-Level Waste is $39.0 million, including 142.1 FTE. This funding level represents an overall increase of $1.8 million, and the FTE remains level, when compared with the FY 2012 enacted budget. The major activities that the requested resources will support include the following:

- Support project management, financial, technical, safety, and environmental reviews for the licensing of new and existing uranium recovery facilities; the decommissioning of power reactors, RTRs, complex materials sites, and inactive uranium recovery facilities; and interfaces with licensees, applicants, Federal and State agencies, the public, other stakeholders, and Native American Tribal Governments.
- Monitor certain DOE waste determination activities and plans consistent with the NRC's responsibilities in the Ronald Reagan National Defense Authorization Act for Fiscal Year 2005. This Act requires DOE to consult with the NRC on its waste incidental to reprocessing determinations for facilities in South Carolina and Idaho, as well as the NRC's monitoring activities at those sites.
- Regulate and oversee LLW activities, including interactions with, and technical assistance to, DOE and the States on LLW regulatory issues.
- Provide analytical assistance on complex licensing cases, such as application of codes for decommissioning reviews and site cleanup at sites with uranium contamination and in situ uranium recovery facilities.

OFFICE OF THE INSPECTOR GENERAL

OFFICE OF THE INSPECTOR GENERAL GOALS

In accordance with the Inspector General Act of 1978, as amended, the Office of the Inspector General's (OIG's) mission is to (1) independently and objectively conduct and supervise audits and investigations related to NRC programs and operations, (2) prevent and detect fraud, waste, and abuse, and (3) promote economy, efficiency, and effectiveness in NRC programs and operations. The OIG carries out its mission through its Audits and Investigations Programs. The NRC OIG Strategic Plan will be updated; however, it currently features the following three strategic goals that guide the activities of its Audits and Investigations Programs and generally align with the agency's mission:

- Strengthen the NRC's efforts to protect public health and safety and the environment.
- Enhance the NRC's efforts to increase security in response to an evolving threat environment.
- Increase the economy, efficiency, and effectiveness with which the NRC manages and exercises stewardship over its resources.

	Budget Authority by Program					
	FY 2012 Enacted		FY 2014 Request		Delta FY 2014–FY 2012	
Summary	$M	FTE	$M	FTE	$M	FTE
Program Support	1.276		1.245		(0.031)	
Program Salaries and Benefits	9.584	58	9.860	58	0.276	
Total	$10.860	58	$11.105	58	$0.245	0

Numbers may not add due to rounding.

OIG's proposed FY 2014 budget is $11.105 million, including 58 FTE staff. In accordance with OMB requirements, OIG is providing the full cost of its programs, in that the budget identifies OIG's management and operational support costs and distributes these costs proportionately to the Audits and Investigations Programs.

AUDITS PROGRAM

With these resources, the Audits Program will conduct approximately 22 audits and evaluations. For FY 2014, the Audits Program will focus on agency programs involving the major management challenges and risk areas facing the NRC to include those agency programs concerning new reactors and spent fuel storage and transportation. Areas for OIG audit emphasis in FY 2014 include the following:

- NRC oversight of operating reactors and the licensing and construction of new and advanced reactors.
- NRC oversight of the safety of nuclear materials.
- NRC oversight of licensee security programs and management of internal NRC security.
- NRC oversight of the interim storage of HLW, increased quantities of spent fuel at reactor sites, and the safe management of civilian LLW disposal.

OIG also will conduct other performance audits to review the NRC's administrative and program operations, to evaluate the effectiveness and efficiency with which management responsibilities are carried out, and to determine whether the programs are achieving their intended results. Financial audits also will be conducted to attest to the reasonableness of the NRC's financial statements and to evaluate the agency's financial programs.

INVESTIGATIONS PROGRAM

The Investigations Program will initiate approximately 60 investigations and event inquiries. Areas for OIG investigative emphasis in FY 2014 include the following:

- Monitor NRC activities and gather stakeholder information to identify potential gaps in the agency's regulatory oversight.
- Review NRC and licensee reports and engage interested stakeholders to identify issues of concern in the NRC's oversight of nuclear material held by its licensees.
- Examine the effectiveness of NRC efforts to address stakeholders' concerns about LLW and HLW storage issues.
- Address NRC's efforts to oversee licensee responsibilities in effectively securing licensed facilities and nuclear materials.
- Investigate internal and external cyber breaches of the NRC's IT infrastructure.
- Examine allegations of misuse of the NRC's corporate resources pertaining to human resources, procurement, financial management, and IT.

Proactive investigations are also conducted when indications are raised about potential systematic violations, such as theft of Government property or contract fraud. In addition, OIG periodically conducts event inquiries to identify staff actions that may have contributed to the occurrence of an event.

Proposed FY 2014
Appropriations Legislation

Proposed FY 2014 Appropriations Legislation

The NRC's proposed appropriations legislation for FY 2014 is as follows:

SALARIES AND EXPENSES

For necessary expenses of the Commission in carrying out the purposes of the Energy Reorganization Act of 1974, as amended, and the Atomic Energy Act of 1954, as amended, including official representation expenses (not to exceed $25,000), $1,043,937,000, to remain available until expended: *Provided*, That revenues from licensing fees, inspection services, and other services and collections estimated at $920,721,000, in FY 2014 shall be retained and used for necessary salaries and expenses in this account, notwithstanding 31 U.S.C. 3302, and shall remain available until expended: *Provided further*, That the sum herein appropriated shall be reduced by the amount of revenues received during FY 2014 so as to result in a final FY 2014 appropriation estimated at not more than $123,216,000.

OFFICE OF THE INSPECTOR GENERAL

For necessary expenses of the Office of the Inspector General in carrying out the provisions of the Inspector General Act of 1978, as amended, $11,105,000, to remain available until September 30, 2015: *Provided*, That revenues from licensing fees, inspection services, and other services and collections estimated at $9,994,000, in FY 2014 shall be retained and be available until September 30, 2015, for necessary salaries and expenses in this account, notwithstanding 31 U.S.C. 3302: *Provided further*, That the sum herein appropriated shall be reduced by the amount of revenues received during FY 2014 so as to result in a final FY 2014 appropriation estimated at not more than $1,111,000.

ANALYSIS OF PROPOSED FY 2014 APPROPRIATIONS LEGISLATION

The analysis of the NRC's proposed appropriations legislation for FY 2014 is as follows:

SALARIES AND EXPENSES

1. FOR NECESSARY EXPENSES OF THE COMMISSION IN CARRYING OUT THE PURPOSES OF THE ENERGY REORGANIZATION ACT OF 1974, AS AMENDED, AND THE ATOMIC ENERGY ACT OF 1954, AS AMENDED:

42 U.S.C. 5841 et seq.

The NRC was established by the Energy Reorganization Act of 1974, as amended (42 U.S.C. 5801 et seq.). This act abolished the Atomic Energy Commission (AEC) and transferred to the NRC all of the AEC's licensing and related regulatory functions. These functions included those of the Atomic Safety and Licensing Board Panel and the Advisory Committee on Reactor Safeguards; responsibilities for licensing and regulating nuclear facilities and materials; and conducting research for the purpose of confirmatory assessment related to licensing, regulation, and other activities, including research related to nuclear materials safety and regulation under the provisions of the Atomic Energy Act of 1954, as amended (42 U.S.C. 2011 et seq.).

2. INCLUDING OFFICIAL REPRESENTATION EXPENSES:

47 Comp. Gen. 657, 43 Comp. Gen. 305

This language is required because of the established rule restricting an agency from charging appropriations with the cost of official representation unless the appropriations involved are specifically available for such purpose. Congress has appropriated funds for official representation expenses to the NRC and its predecessor, the AEC, each year since FY 1950.

3. TO REMAIN AVAILABLE UNTIL EXPENDED:

31 U.S.C. 1301 provides that no regular, annual appropriation shall be construed to be permanent or available continuously unless the appropriation expressly provides that it is available after the fiscal year covered by the law in which it appears.

4. REVENUES FROM LICENSING FEES, INSPECTION SERVICES, AND OTHER SERVICES AND COLLECTIONS SHALL BE RETAINED AND USED FOR NECESSARY SALARIES AND EXPENSES IN THIS ACCOUNT, NOTWITHSTANDING 31 U.S.C. 3302, AND SHALL REMAIN AVAILABLE UNTIL EXPENDED:

Under Title V of the Independent Offices Appropriation Act of 1952, the NRC is authorized to collect license fees. Pursuant to 31 U.S.C. 9701, any person who receives a service or thing of value from the Commission shall pay fees to cover the NRC's cost in providing such service or thing of value.

Pursuant to 42 U.S.C. 2214, the NRC is required to assess and collect annual charges from NRC licensees and certificate holders, with the exception of the holders of any license for a federally owned research reactor used primarily for educational training and academic research purposes. In accordance with amendments to 42 U.S.C. 2214, enacted in the Energy Policy Act of 2005, and this appropriations request, the aggregate annual amount of such charges shall approximate 90 percent of the Commission's budget authority, less amounts appropriated to the Commission to implement Section 3116 of the Ronald W. Reagan National Defense Authorization Act for Fiscal Year 2005 and amounts appropriated to the Commission for generic homeland security activities.

Section 3116 of the Ronald W. Reagan National Defense Authorization Act for Fiscal Year 2005, Public Law (P.L.) 108-375, assigns new responsibilities to NRC for waste determinations and monitoring of waste disposal actions for material stored at the U.S. Department of Energy (DOE) sites in South Carolina and Idaho. Section 3116(b)(4) requires that, beginning with the FY 2006 budget, the Commission include in its budget justification materials submitted to Congress the amounts required, not offset by revenues, for performance of its responsibilities under Section 3116. The $1,392,000 requested to implement Section 3116 is excluded from NRC's fee recovery requirements.

Section 637 of the Energy Policy Act of 2005, P.L. 109-58, modifies NRC's user fee legislation in 42 U.S.C. 2214 to exclude from license fee recovery the amounts appropriated to the Commission for homeland security activities, except for reimbursable costs of fingerprinting and background checks and the costs of conducting security inspections. The $19,522,000 requested for generic homeland security activities is excluded from NRC's fee recovery requirements.

The aggregate amount of license fees and annual charges to be collected for FY 2014 approximates 90 percent of the Commission's budget authority, less amounts requested to implement Section 3116 of the Ronald W. Reagan National Defense Authorization Act for Fiscal Year 2005 and amounts requested for generic homeland security activities pursuant to Section 637 of P.L. 109-58.

31 U.S.C. 3302 requires the NRC to deposit all revenues collected to miscellaneous receipts of the Treasury unless specifically authorized by law to retain and use such revenues

5. THE SUM HEREIN APPROPRIATED SHALL BE REDUCED BY THE AMOUNT OF REVENUES RECEIVED:

Pursuant to 42 U.S.C. 2214, the NRC is required to assess and collect annual charges from NRC licensees and certificate holders, with the exception of the holders of any license for a federally owned research reactor used primarily for educational training and academic research purposes. In accordance with amendments to 42 U.S.C. 2214, enacted in the Energy Policy Act of 2005, and this appropriations request, the aggregate annual amount of such charges shall approximate 90 percent of the Commission's budget authority, less amounts appropriated to the Commission to implement Section 3116 of the Ronald W. Reagan National Defense Authorization Act for Fiscal Year 2005 and amounts appropriated to the Commission for generic homeland security activities.

OFFICE OF THE INSPECTOR GENERAL

6. FOR NECESSARY EXPENSES OF THE OFFICE OF THE INSPECTOR GENERAL IN CARRYING OUT THE PROVISIONS OF THE INSPECTOR GENERAL ACT OF 1978, AS AMENDED:

P. L. 95-452, 5 U.S.C. app., as amended by P. L. 100-504

P. L. 100-504 amended P. L. 95-452 to establish an Office of the Inspector General in the NRC effective April 17, 1989, and to require the establishment of a separate appropriation account to fund the Office of the Inspector General.

7. TO REMAIN AVAILABLE UNTIL SEPTEMBER 30, 2015:

31 U.S.C. 1301 provides that no regular, annual appropriation shall be construed to be permanent or available continuously unless the appropriation expressly provides that it is available after the fiscal year covered by the law in which it appears.

8. REVENUES FROM LICENSING FEES, INSPECTION SERVICES, AND OTHER SERVICES AND COLLECTIONS SHALL BE RETAINED AND BE AVAILABLE UNTIL SEPTEMBER 30, 2015, FOR NECESSARY SALARIES AND EXPENSES IN THIS ACCOUNT, NOTWITHSTANDING 31 U.S.C. 3302:

Under Title V of the Independent Offices Appropriation Act of 1952, the NRC is authorized to collect license fees. Pursuant to 31 U.S.C. 9701, any person who receives a service or thing of value from the Commission shall pay fees to cover the NRC's cost in providing such service or thing of value.

Pursuant to 42 U.S.C. 2214, the NRC is required to assess and collect annual charges from NRC licensees and certificate holders, with the exception of the holders of any license for a federally owned research reactor used primarily for educational training and academic research purposes. In accordance with amendments to 42 U.S.C. 2214, enacted in the Energy Policy Act of 2005, and this appropriations request, the aggregate annual amount of such charges approximate 90 percent of the Commission's budget authority, less amounts appropriated to the Commission to implement Section 3116 of the Ronald W. Reagan National Defense Authorization Act for Fiscal Year 2005 and amounts appropriated to the Commission for generic homeland security activities.

31 U.S.C. 3302 requires the NRC to deposit all revenues collected to miscellaneous receipts of the Treasury unless specifically authorized by law to retain and use such revenue.

9. THE SUM HEREIN APPROPRIATED SHALL BE REDUCED BY THE AMOUNT OF REVENUES RECEIVED:

Pursuant to 42 U.S.C. 2214, the NRC is required to assess and collect annual charges from NRC licensees and certificate holders, with the exception of the holders of any license for a federally owned research reactor used primarily for educational training and academic research purposes. In accordance with amendments to 42 U.S.C. 2214, enacted in the Energy Policy Act of 2005, and this appropriations request, the aggregate annual amount of such charges approximate 90 percent of the Commission's budget authority, less amounts appropriated to the Commission to implement Section 3116 of the Ronald W. Reagan National Defense Authorization Act for Fiscal Year 2005 and amounts appropriated to the Commission for generic homeland security activities.

Nuclear Reactor Safety

NUCLEAR REACTOR SAFETY

NUCLEAR REACTOR SAFETY STRATEGIC GOALS
Safety—ensure adequate protection of public health and safety and the environment.
Security—ensure adequate protection in the secure use and management of radioactive materials.

The Nuclear Reactor Safety Program encompasses U.S. Nuclear Regulatory Commission's (NRC) efforts to ensure that civilian nuclear power and research and test reactors are licensed and operated in a manner that adequately protects public health and safety, protects the environment, and provides high assurance of the physical security of reactor facilities. This program contributes to the NRC's Safety and Security goals through activities of the Operating Reactors and New Reactors Business Lines that license and regulate existing and new nuclear reactors to ensure their safe operation and physical security. The Atomic Energy Act of 1954, as amended, and the Energy Reorganization Act of 1974, as amended, are the foundations for the NRC's regulation of the Nation's civilian nuclear power industry.

Nuclear security is a high priority for the NRC. Throughout the agency's history, effective regulation and strong partnerships with a variety of Federal, State, and local authorities have ensured security at civilian nuclear reactors across the country, especially power reactors. The NRC recognizes the need for continuous improvement to ensure the safety and security of nuclear power plants. In recent years, the NRC has undertaken comprehensive enhancements to bolster the security of our Nation's nuclear facilities and radioactive materials.

Nuclear Reactor Safety (Dollars in Millions)						
	FY 2012 Enacted		FY 2014 Request		Delta FY 2014–FY 2012	
Business Line	$M	FTE	$M	FTE	$M	FTE
Operating Reactors	534.7	2,100.4	571.9	2,120.0	37.2	19.6
New Reactors	265.4	924.6	240.5	865.5	(24.9)	(59.1)
Total	**$800.1**	**3,025.0**	**$812.4**	**2,985.5**	**$12.3**	**(39.6)**

Numbers may not add due to rounding.

PROGRAM RESOURCE SUMMARY

The fiscal year (FY) 2014 proposed budget request for the Nuclear Reactor Safety Program is $812.4 million, which includes $334.7 million in contract support and travel and $477.7 million in salaries and benefits to support 2,985.5 full-time equivalents (FTE). This amount funds activities in the Operating Reactors and New Reactors Business Lines. It represents an increase of $12.3 million, including a decrease of 39.6 FTE, from the FY 2012 enacted budget. This increase primarily supports implementation of the Fukushima Near-Term Task Force recommendations and regulatory activities associated with locating, licensing, and overseeing new and operating nuclear power plants, and an agencywide effort to reduce overhead resources through increased efficiency and effectiveness.

OPERATING REACTORS

	Operating Reactors by Product Line (Dollars in Millions)					
	FY 2012 Enacted		FY 2014 Request		Delta FY 2014–FY 2012	
Product Line	$M	FTE	$M	FTE	$M	FTE
Licensing	89.5	477.3	101.4	479.1	11.9	1.8
Oversight	157.3	888.6	163.6	878.3	6.2	(10.3)
Rulemaking	13.3	60.9	17.7	72.5	4.3	11.6
International Activities	2.3	13.5	2.4	14.2	0.1	0.7
Research	66.1	171.0	67.8	177.1	1.7	6.1
Generic HLS	6.5	25.1	3.8	18.9	(2.8)	(6.2)
Event Response	14.3	55.8	16.8	55.1	2.5	(0.6)
Subtotal	**$349.4**	**1,692.1**	**$373.4**	**1,695.1**	**$24.1**	**3.0**
Corporate Support	185.4	408.3	198.5	424.9	13.1	16.5
Total	**$534.7**	**2,100.4**	**$571.9**	**2,120.0**	**$37.2**	**19.6**

Numbers may not add due to rounding.

The Operating Reactors Business Line encompasses the regulation of 104 operating civilian nuclear power reactors and 31 research and test reactors (RTRs) in a way that adequately protects the public health and safety, protects the environment, and provides high assurance of physical security. Under the U.S. Nuclear Regulatory Commission's (NRC's) regulatory oversight, the amount of safe electrical power generated from the 104 domestic nuclear power plants now contributes approximately 20 percent of the Nation's electrical production.

The NRC establishes regulatory requirements for the design, construction, operation, and security of nuclear power plants and RTRs in accordance with the provisions of the Atomic Energy Act of 1954, as amended. Through Operating Reactors Business Line activities, the NRC ensures the fundamental tenets of its Safety and Security goals in protecting the public and workers from the radiation hazards of nuclear reactors. To ensure that plants are operating safely within these requirements, the NRC licenses the plants to operate, licenses the personnel who operate the plants, and establishes technical specifications for each plant's operation. The NRC also ensures nuclear safety through rulemaking and research efforts, enforcement, and international activities. The NRC oversees civilian nuclear reactors and verifies operator adherence to the NRC's rules and regulations.

The NRC has undertaken comprehensive enhancements to bolster the security of our Nation's nuclear facilities. Nuclear power plants must be able to defend successfully against a set of hypothetical threats that the agency refers to as the design-basis threat (DBT). These hypothetical threats challenge a plant's physical security, personnel security, and cyber security. The agency continuously evaluates this set of hypothetical threats against real-world intelligence to ensure that it remains current and prepared.

The budgetary resources will enable the NRC to continue licensing and regulatory activities to ensure the safe and secure operation of these civilian nuclear reactors. The NRC has developed product lines for operating reactors that best support safety and security strategies that affect strategic outcomes as they relate to existing civilian reactors. The resources requested support the Operating Reactors Business Line within the following seven product lines: Licensing, Oversight, Rulemaking, Research, International Activities, Generic Homeland Security (HLS), and Event Response. The outputs of the product lines under this business line contribute to the scoring of the NRC Safety and Security Performance Measures and their contribution to the achievement of its Strategic Outcomes.

CHANGES FROM FY 2012 ENACTED BUDGET

Resources increased to support the implementation of the Fukushima Near-Term Task Force (NTTF) recommendations that included a shift from New Reactors to Operating Reactors. Other changes include an increase in the Licensing Product Line to support activities related to an increase in scheduled workload for license renewals, medical isotope application reviews, National Fire Protection Association Standard 805 (NFPA 805) license amendment request (LAR) reviews, and reduction of the backlog of topical reports. Oversight Product Line resources increased to support the implementation of the Force-on-Force program and the replacement of the agency's Reactor Program System. Rulemaking Product Line resources increased to support Commission-directed medium priority rules. The Research Product Line increased to support the update of nuclear power plant risk analysis to include a broader scope of events, severe accident analysis methods, and materials degradation research.

LICENSING

STRATEGIC GOAL STRATEGIES SUPPORTED BY LICENSING
Safety—develop, maintain, and implement licensing and regulatory programs for reactors.
Security—review security plans and changes for consistency with security requirements.

For FY 2014, the NRC requests $101.4 million, including 479.1 full-time equivalents (FTE), for licensing activities. This funding level represents an increase of $11.9 million, including 1.8 FTE, when compared with the FY 2012 enacted budget. Resources increase to support the implementation of the Fukushima NTTF recommendations. Other changes include an increase in scheduled workload for license renewals, medical isotope application reviews, NFPA 805 LAR reviews, and reduction of the backlog of topical reports.

The Licensing Product Line supports licensing activities that the NRC uses to establish requirements to ensure the safety of operating nuclear power reactor licensees, RTRs, medical isotope production facilities, and requests for license renewals. Other changes provide an adequate margin of safety and security consistent with the NRC's rules and regulations.

The NRC licenses civilian nuclear power reactors and nonpower reactors to ensure that they are operated in a way that adequately protects the public health and safety, protects the environment, and provides high assurance of physical security.

In FY 2014, the NRC will continue licensing activities for 104 power reactors. The NRC anticipates that the licensing workload will include completing 900 licensing actions (200 related to Fukushima), including the review of approximately 11 power uprates and approximately 22 ongoing NFPA 805 reviews for the approximately 35 reactors that will be transitioning to a risk-informed, performance-based set of requirements.

Reviews will continue for 11 license renewal applications for operating reactors. The NRC expects to review two new applications. The resources will support the development, maintenance, and implementation of the license renewal infrastructure, process assessments, improvements, and activities related to developing infrastructure for potential applications for license renewals.

The NRC will continue licensing reviews, issuing license amendments, and performing project management activities for the existing 31 licensed operating nonpower reactors. The agency will ensure that operators are qualified and licensed to perform their duties. In addition, the NRC will review applications for medical isotope production facilities and information that licensees submitted to support conversion of nonpower reactors from high-enriched to low-enriched uranium fuel. The NRC will complete 500 other licensing tasks and related activities, including assistance to the regions; interactions with vendors, industry, and owners' groups; and 20 technical topical report reviews that will resolve generic issues and will reduce the topical reports backlog. In addition, the NRC expects to complete approximately 55 operator licensing examinations and 4 generic examinations for reactor operators.

Resources also support licensing activities, such as the review of licensing amendments associated with the security plan changes; cyber security; emergency preparedness reviews; and license renewal activities and associated adjudication, legal advice, and representation. The NRC will continue Federal interactions with the American Society of Mechanical Engineers (ASME) on coating guidance, grid stability, and digital instrumentation and control.

OVERSIGHT

STRATEGIC GOAL STRATEGIES SUPPORTED BY OVERSIGHT
Safety—continue to oversee the safe operation of existing plants and licensee safety performance through inspections, investigations, enforcement, and performance assessment activities.
Security—evaluate licensee security and emergency preparedness programs; use Force-on-Force inspections to test security.

For FY 2014, the NRC requests $163.6 million, including 878.3 FTE, for oversight activities. This funding level represents an increase of $6.2 million, including a decrease of 10.3 FTE, when compared with the FY 2012 enacted budget. Resources increase to support the implementation of the Fukushima NTTF recommendations. Other changes include an increase to support the Force-on-Force Program and the replacement of the agency's Reactor Program System offset by a decrease because of an agencywide effort to reduce overhead resources through increased efficiency and effectiveness.

The Oversight Product Line supports the activities and methods the NRC uses to oversee the safe and secure operation of existing nuclear reactors, to better identify significant performance issues, and to ensure that licensees take appropriate actions to maintain acceptable operating performance to adequately protect public health and safety and the environment.

The NRC performs continuous oversight of plants through its Reactor Oversight Process (ROP), which verifies that the 104 currently licensed nuclear power reactors are operated safely and securely in accordance with the NRC's rules, regulations, and license requirements. The NRC has full authority to take action to protect public health and safety and can demand immediate licensee action, up to and including a plant shutdown. The ROP uses NRC inspection findings and performance indicators from licensees to assess the safety performance of each plant within a regulatory framework of seven cornerstones of safety and security: (1) frequency of potential accident-initiating events; (2) availability, reliability, and capability of mitigating systems, (3) integrity of radiation barriers, such as fuel cladding, reactor coolant system, and containment boundaries, (4) emergency preparedness, (5) protection of the public from radiation releases, (6) occupational radiation safety, and (6) physical protection against the DBT for radiological sabotage.

The ROP recognizes that not all issues are equally significant. The ROP structure initiates more NRC engagement and oversight for more significant events. Plants are expected to address issues through their corrective action programs for less significant events. In this way, the oversight workload directly supports the Safety and Security goals and related strategic measures and outcomes.

As a condition of their licenses, nuclear power plant operators develop and maintain effective emergency preparedness plans to protect the public. The NRC inspects plants to ensure that they are meeting the requirements for emergencies and to evaluate the implementation of those requirements. In addition, the agency monitors certain performance indicators related to emergency preparedness.

Generally, the NRC performs two types of inspections: baseline and plant-specific. The FY 2014 budget request includes resources for planned baseline and anticipated plant-specific inspections. Historically, the resources required for these inspections have been fairly constant. A portion of the baseline inspection program is conducted on a 3-year cycle, including approximately 22 fire protection and 22 component design-basis inspections per year. Baseline inspections focus on plant activities, especially those that performance indicators do not measure adequately. Resources also support plant-specific inspections that typically include 20 reactive inspections, 75 inspections related to performance or specific changes (e.g., inspections at independent spent fuel storage installations, digital control room inspections), and approximately 100 generic issue inspections that address areas of emerging concern (e.g., cyber security or areas where recurring problems have occurred). Security resources support the NRC's security inspection and assessment program with a number of key elements. These include baseline, tri-annual Force-on-Force, and special inspections; and development of the annual report to Congress. For 2-years, there will be an increase in regional work for target set and protective strategy inspections as a result of the new 10 CFR Part 73 rule.

The ROP also includes the Industry Trends Program through which the NRC collects, analyzes, displays, and trends industrywide reactor performance data to determine whether the data show statistically significant adverse industry trends in reactor safety performance.

Resources also support assessment of licensee performance and evaluation of input data (i.e., performance indicators, the significance determination process, and determination of any necessary followup actions resulting from enforcement processing related casework and project and contract management oversight of the Alternative Dispute Resolution (ADR) Program). The NRC conducts performance-based evaluations of licensee security and emergency preparedness programs and assesses their effectiveness. The NRC will perform emergency preparedness baseline and special inspections that will include outreach activities with State and local Governments, Tribal organizations, and interstate organizations.

Resources also support legal review, communications to internal and external stakeholders, and audits associated with the ROP, license renewal inspections, investigations and early ADR program activities, security issues, performance assessments, and development of enforcement guidance.

Resources will support event evaluation, generic communications, and the review of industry operating experience (screening of approximately 3,000 national and international operational events per year). Approximately 150 to 200 issues per year receive additional detailed evaluations. Resources support independent evaluation and trending of operational events and funding of human factor event evaluations.

Resources also support enforcement, allegation activities, and investigations of alleged wrongdoing. Enforcement is used to deter noncompliance with NRC requirements and to encourage prompt identification and correction of violations.

The ROP includes an assessment process, which integrates inspection findings with other objective measures of performance that licensees submit quarterly for each power reactor site. Results from this assessment process are used as feedback to determine appropriate NRC actions for the reactor sites.

Resources will support the replacement, maintenance, and operation of the Reactor Programs System (RPS), which is used to plan and schedule inspection activities and capture and report inspection findings. Replacement of the current system is required since it was developed from 1995 to 1998; the system is now obsolete. RPS is critical to supporting the oversight and inspection of the 104 nuclear power reactors and 31 nonpower reactors. This agencywide tool supports 47 uranium recovery sites and 9 major fuel cycle facilities. The resources also will support simulator hardware and software maintenance for reactor technology training and Web development.

RULEMAKING

STRATEGIC GOAL STRATEGIES SUPPORTED BY RULEMAKING
Safety—use sound science and state-of-the-art methods to establish, where appropriate, risk-informed and performance-based regulations.
Security—use a framework of rules and regulations to guide the security activities of the agency.

For FY 2014, the NRC requests $17.7 million, including 72.5 FTE, for rulemaking activities. This funding level represents an increase of $4.3 million, including 11.6 FTE, when compared with the FY 2012 enacted budget. Resources increase to support the implementation of the Fukushima NTTF recommendations. Other changes include an increase to support medium-priority and Fukushima NTTF rules.

The Rulemaking Product Line includes the development and update of regulatory basis rules and regulatory guidance documents that promote licensee compliance with underlying safety principles and security requirements.

The regulatory framework guides the safety activities of the agency and its licensees. The NRC's rules and regulations contribute to the Safety and Security goals and related strategic measures and outcomes because they form the foundation for the safety and security activities of the agency. NRC regulations are contained in Title 10 of the *Code of Federal Regulations* (10 CFR), "Energy."

The FY 2014 workload includes 14 high-priority rulemaking activities and 3 medium-priority rulemaking activities directed by the Commission, including policy development activities related to the NRC regulatory framework after the Fukushima Event. Examples of high-priority rulemaking activities include 3 rulemakings from the Fukushima NTTF recommendations and a rulemaking implementing the new statutory authority from the Energy Policy Act of 2005 on the use of enhanced weapons.

NUCLEAR REACTOR SAFETY

Resources also provide support for approximately 22 petitions for rulemaking (PRMs), assuming receipt of 6 PRMs each year and the issuance of 8 closure packages. Additionally, resources will support legal advice for rulemakings, petitions, and regulatory basis development efforts.

Resources for rulemaking support the development of technical assessment and regulatory bases needed to prepare and issue new or amended regulations and to develop supplemental regulatory guidance directly related to new and amended rules. Resources also allow the NRC to maintain rulemaking and regulatory analysis guidance documents based on lessons learned and process improvements and enhancements. In addition, resources support updates of reports such as the Regulatory Agenda.

INTERNATIONAL ACTIVITIES

STRATEGIC GOAL STRATEGIES SUPPORTED BY INTERNATIONAL ACTIVITIES
Safety—use domestic and international operating experience to inform decisionmaking.
Security—work with international counterparts to exchange information.

For FY 2014, the NRC requests $2.4 million, including 14.2 FTE, for international activities. This funding level represents an increase of $0.1 million, including 0.7 FTE, when compared with the FY 2012 enacted budget, which does not represent a significant change in workload.

The International Activities Product Line supports the NRC's international work, which assists decisionmaking, awareness of and responses to emerging technical issues, and promoting best practices in realizing the Safety and Security goals and related strategic measures and outcomes. Additionally, the NRC participates in the development and evaluation of international standards to ensure that they are soundly based and to determine whether substantial safety improvement can be identified and implemented domestically. The NRC also must perform certain legislatively mandated international duties. These include licensing the import and export of nuclear materials and equipment and participating in activities supporting U.S. compliance with international treaties and agreement obligations. The NRC has bilateral programs to provide assistance or cooperation with 41 countries and Taiwan. In addition, the NRC actively cooperates with multinational organizations, such as the International Atomic Energy Agency (IAEA) and the Nuclear Energy Agency, as part of the Organization for Economic Co-operation and Development.

The International Activities Product Line workload includes periodic exchanges of information important to the safe operation of nuclear power plants, visits to operating domestic nuclear power plants, assistance to foreign regulatory bodies through the NRC Foreign Assignee Program, and the review and decisions on applications for the export and import of nuclear equipment. The NRC assists the IAEA and individual countries through its bilateral agreements and participates in multilateral activities with other nations, such as the Convention on Nuclear Safety, the Joint Convention on the Safety of Spent Fuel Management and the Safety of Radioactive Waste Management, and IAEA's Integrated Regulatory Review Service and International Physical Protection Advisory Service missions.

The NRC supports activities associated with safety, security, and conversion of nonpower reactors and participates in international cooperative research programs that provide access to operating experience from foreign reactors to augment NRC programs in areas such as plant aging and materials degradation, fire risk, and pressurized thermal shock. Analysis of this experience contributes to the NRC's knowledge base, improves assessments of plant risk, and improves the development of risk-informed approaches to regulation.

The NRC works with international counterparts to exchange information, expertise, and operating experiences; to participate in ongoing research to recognize and respond to emerging technical issues; and to promote best safety and security practices. This international cooperation promotes nuclear safety and security worldwide.

RESEARCH

STRATEGIC GOAL STRATEGIES SUPPORTED BY RESEARCH
Safety—improve the NRC's regulatory programs and apply safety-focused research to anticipate and resolve safety issues.
Security—use research to inform the security activities of the agency.

For FY 2014, the NRC requests $67.8 million, including 177.1 FTE, for research activities. This funding level represents an increase of $1.7 million, including 6.1 FTE, when compared with the FY 2012 enacted budget. Resources increase to support implementation of the Fukushima NTTF recommendations. Other changes include an increase to update nuclear power plant risk analysis to include a broader scope of events, severe accident analysis methods, and materials degradation research.

The NRC's research program mission is to evaluate and resolve safety issues for nuclear power plants and other facilities and materials that the agency regulates. Tasks under this mission include evaluating existing and potential safety issues; supplying independent expertise, information, and technical judgments to support timely and realistic regulatory decisions; reducing uncertainties in risk assessments; and developing technical regulations and standards. Research programs cover all technical areas of the NRC's regulations.

In FY 2014, research will be performed in various technical areas to ensure the continued safety and security of operating reactors. These areas include (1) research to address recommendations from the lessons learned evaluation of the Fukushima accident, (2) fire safety, (3) digital and electrical systems, (4) materials degradation, (5) reactor safety code development and analysis, (6) radiation protection, (7) probabilistic risk assessment (PRA), and (8) evaluation of hazards from natural events.

Research will address recommendations from the lessons learned evaluation of the Fukushima accident, including PRA of seismically induced flooding and fire and analysis of filtered venting.

Fire safety research will continue to support the transition to a risk-informed, performance-based set of requirements in response to NFPA 805 and the current licensing basis for plants. This work includes cable fire testing, spurious circuit actuation testing, fire risk-assessment training, and fire modeling.

Research on digital systems will include the review of current and future applications of digital instrumentation and controls, a failure mode and reliability assessment of software and digital systems, an assessment of the aging of components and equipment, and the security aspects of digital systems. Research associated with electrical systems will be conducted in equipment qualification for subsequent license renewal, assessment of the aging of electrical insulation materials, battery performance, the impact of smart grids on nuclear power plants, and assessment of failure of onsite power sources.

Research will continue to further understand and manage potential degradation associated with reactor pressure boundary components, vessel internals, containment liners, and neutron-absorbing materials used in spent fuel pools. This research includes assessing the effectiveness and reliability of various inservice inspection techniques, performing residual stress and nondestructive examination studies on retired components, evaluating the behavior of various components under severe accident conditions, developing a probabilistic code for assessing piping integrity, and studying the embrittlement of reactor vessel pressure boundary materials. Research is also being performed in material engineering to evaluate plant life extension for subsequent license renewal.

The NRC uses computer codes to perform PRAs and evaluate thermal-hydraulic conditions, severe accidents, fuel behavior, and reactor kinetics during various operating and postulated accident conditions. Research in this area will continue to support decisionmaking for risk-informed activities, the review of licensees' codes and performance of audit calculations, and the resolution of other technical issues. Code development is directed toward improving the realism and reliability of code results and making them easier to use.

Research efforts will provide technical support in radiation protection, dose assessment, and assessment of human health effects for licensing, emergency preparedness, and nuclear security activities. This research will support recommendations on health physics policy. Research activities also will provide technical support for the development of environmental regulatory guidance to support regulatory needs.

Research efforts will include development of plant-specific standardized analysis risk models and maintenance of the Systems Analysis Programs for Hands-On Integrated Reliability Evaluations PRA code to support the ROP and other risk-informed agency decision processes. Resources also support the development of improved methods and tools for risk-informing regulatory programs, including the development of new PRA methods, models, and tools, and the development of a site Level 3 PRA to incorporate insights from advances in PRA technology and pilot draft guidance for using expert judgment in areas, such as human reliability and severe accident analysis.

The NRC will conduct research to improve its understanding of earthquake occurrences and ground motion at nuclear power plant sites in the central and eastern sections of the United States and the performance of structures, passive components, and other issues related to earthquake engineering. Research efforts will include evaluation of hazards from natural events, including seismic hazards, flooding, and tsunami events. The agency will use these research results to inform licensing decisions and to update risk assessments.

GENERIC HOMELAND SECURITY

STRATEGIC GOAL STRATEGIES SUPPORTED BY GENERIC HOMELAND SECURITY
Safety—effectively respond to events at NRC-licensed facilities and other events of national interest, including maintaining and enhancing the NRC's critical incident response and communication capabilities.
Security—support Federal response plans that use an approach to the security of nuclear facilities and radioactive material that integrates the efforts of licensees and Federal, State, local, and Tribal authorities.

For FY 2014, the NRC requests $3.8 million, including 18.9 FTE, for generic HLS activities. This funding level represents a decrease of $2.8 million, including 6.2 FTE, when compared with the FY 2012 enacted budget. The NRC reviewed the activities under the definitions for the Generic HLS product and shifted some resources to non-Generic HLS products in order to more accurately align resources to the planned workload.

In FY 2014, the Generic HLS Product Line workload includes the entire scope of threat assessment activities (intelligence information assessment, internal and external communications, and information assessment team activities); intergovernmental coordination on national HLS priorities; integrated response planning and coordination; and emerging technology analysis and evaluation. The workload also includes developing and enhancing the ability to make risk-informed analyses of accident progression and radiological releases to the environment in response to accidents and malevolent attacks.

EVENT RESPONSE

STRATEGIC GOAL STRATEGIES SUPPORTED BY EVENT RESPONSE
Safety—effectively respond to events at NRC-licensed facilities and other events of national interest, including maintaining and enhancing the NRC's critical incident response and communication capabilities.
Security—support Federal response plans that use an approach to the security of nuclear facilities and radioactive material that integrates the efforts of licensees and Federal, State, local, and Tribal authorities.

For FY 2014, the NRC requests $16.8 million, including 55.1 FTE, for event response activities. This funding level represents an increase of $2.5 million, including a decrease of 0.6 FTE, when compared with the FY 2012 enacted budget. Resources increase to support the replenishment of potassium iodide tablets in States where they are due to expire in FY 2013.

The Event Response Product Line supports the NRC's incident response and emergency preparedness activities to ensure that the agency can respond effectively to events at its licensees' sites and ensure adequate protective measures can be taken by licensees to mitigate plant damage and minimize possible radiation exposure to members of the public. The NRC's program for emergency preparedness and event response is focused on ensuring its licensees are capable of implementing adequate measures to protect public health and safety in the event of a radiological emergency.

Resources are included to ensure the NRC Headquarters Operations Center (HOC) is staffed around the clock and is able to collect and disseminate event response information and coordinate the agency's response, consistent with its responsibilities as the coordinating agency for events involving NRC-licensed material under the National Response Framework. In addition, resources are included to support drill and exercise preparation and participation, NRC regional office event response readiness and Incident Response Centers, critical incident response communications tools (including the Emergency Response Data System and the HOC Information Management System), accident assessment tools (such as the Radiological Assessment System for Consequence Analysis (RASCAL) Radiation Dose Assessment Code), intergovernmental coordination and communications tools, and maintenance of the response program infrastructure (e.g., response manual procedures and associated guidance). Resources also support replenishing potassium iodide tablet supplies that will expire in FY 2013 for States with a population within the 10-mile emergency planning zone of operating nuclear reactors.

SIGNIFICANT ACCOMPLISHMENTS IN FY 2012

In 2011, the Nation's nuclear power plants were operated within the NRC's safety and security requirements. The performance measures for the Safety goal confirm that nuclear power plants were operating safely. In addition, the safety indicators for nuclear plants showed no adverse trends.

After the accident at Fukushima Dai-chi, the Commission directed the NRC staff to conduct a systematic and methodical review of NRC processes and regulations to determine whether the agency should make additional improvements to its regulatory system and to provide recommendations to the Commission for its policy direction. The NRC's NTTF developed recommendations related to lessons learned from the Fukushima Dai-ichi event. The NRC staff prioritized the recommendations. Additionally, the staff published advance notices of proposed rulemaking to solicit comments on modification of the NRC's station blackout regulation and the development of a new regulation concerning the integration of emergency operating procedures. The staff provided the Commission with its plans for implementing longer term activities associated with lessons learned from the Fukushima Dai-ichi event. The plans are to provide a roadmap for what actions or study the NRC should complete to be able to make an informed decision to either pursue further regulatory action or to conclude that the current regulatory approach is sufficient.

The NRC completed 770 reactor licensing actions in FY 2012 and 95.8 percent of the licensing actions in the agency's inventory within 1 year of receipt.

The NRC approved seven plant-specific power uprates in FY 2012, which added an additional 2,407 megawatts thermal or 802 megawatts electric to the Nation's electrical grid.

The NRC approved two license renewals in FY 2012. The NRC has renewed licenses for 73 units at 42 sites since the license renewal program was established. The NRC is currently reviewing applications to renew the licenses for 13 units at 9 sites. The agency expects that all licensees of currently licensed units eventually will apply to renew their licenses.

The NRC modified its regulatory inspection plan within the Reactor Oversight Process at both San Onofre Nuclear Generating Station and Crystal River Nuclear Generating Plant due to extended shutdowns to address technical issues. The NRC has continued to monitor and inspect both Crystal River and San Onofre in accordance with NRC Inspection Manual Chapter 0351, "Implementation of the Reactor Oversight Process at Reactor Facilities in an Extended Shutdown Condition for Reasons Other Than Significant Performance Problems."

The agency published a final rule to correct amendments involving ASME Codes and new and revised ASME Code cases. In addition, the agency published a final rule to amend its regulations to require nonpower reactor licensees to obtain fingerprint-based criminal history records checks before granting individuals unescorted access to their facilities. The final rule on enhancements to emergency preparedness at nuclear power plants was published. In conjunction with the Federal Emergency Management Agency (FEMA), five forums were held around the country to provide licensees, State, local, and Tribal emergency planning personnel with information on implementation of the emergency preparedness rule changes and associated NRC and FEMA emergency preparedness guidance changes.

The NRC research program addressed key areas that support the agency's safety mission. In FY 2012, the agency initiated a site PRA study to estimate consequences of severe accidents for all modes of operation and significant hazard categories and to consider multiunit operations. In addition, research focused on hazards from natural events, including seismic, flooding, and tsunami events. With support from the U.S. Army Corps of Engineers, the NRC directed its efforts toward updating guidance on the design and evaluation of flood protection features for nuclear power plants. Other important research in FY 2012 focused on fire protection and risk issues; materials degradation, particularly as related to license renewal periods; digital instrumentation and control systems; and reactor thermal-hydraulics.

In August 2012, the NRC participated in the Second Extraordinary Meeting of the Convention on Nuclear Safety (CNS), which was held at the International Atomic Energy Agency (IAEA) in Vienna, Austria. The objective was to review and discuss lessons learned from the accident at Fukushima Daiichi. Over 600 people participated in the meeting, representing 64 of the 75 contracting parties to the Convention. There were six topic areas pertaining to Fukushima discussed during working sessions. The importance of sharing lessons learned from the Fukushima Dai-ichi accident was stressed during the closing session of the meeting, which was open to the public and members of the media.

The NRC was actively involved in several exercises. The agency participated in the national level exercise series (NLE 12), the annual continuity of operations exercise (Eagle Horizon 12) for Federal Executive Branch departments and agencies, and several exercises with licensed facilities and affected States as a part of the NRC's ongoing response readiness program.

OUTPUT MEASURES

LICENSING

Completion of License Renewal Application Reviews						
	FY 2009	FY 2010	FY 2011	FY 2012	FY 2013	FY 2014
Target	Complete major milestones for 4 applications.	Complete major milestones for 3 applications.	Complete major milestones for 3 applications.	Make final decision on license renewal for 1 reactor unit.	TBD*	Make final decision on license renewal for 0 reactor units.*
Actual	Renewed 4 licenses.	Renewed 5 licenses. Completed safety evaluation reports for 3 applications and supplemental environmental impact statements for 2 applications.	Renewed 8 licenses.	Made final decision on license renewal on 2 units.		

- Final decisions for License Renewal applications are delayed throughout FY 2013 and FY 2014 due to Waste Confidence Decision.

Licensing Actions Completed per Year*						
	FY 2009	FY 2010	FY 2011	FY 2012	FY 2013	FY 2014
Target	Complete 1,150 licensing actions.	Complete 950 licensing actions.	Complete 950 licensing actions.	Complete950 licensing actions.	TBD***	Complete 900 licensing actions.*
Actual	1,002 completed	988 completed	849 completed	770 completed**		

*As limited by the number of licensing action requests submitted or accepted the previous fiscal year.

**660 license amendments requests were submitted in FY 2011.

***802 license amendments requests were submitted in FY 2012.

Age of the Other Licensing Task Inventory*

	FY 2009	FY 2010	FY 2011	FY 2012	FY 2013	FY 2014
Target	90% ≤ 1 year (yr) 100% ≤ 2 yr	90% ≤ 1 yr 100% ≤ 2 yr	90% ≤ 1 yr 100% ≤ 2 yr	90% ≤ 1 yr 100% ≤ 2 yr	TBD	90% ≤ 1 yr 100% ≤ 2 yr
Actual	90% ≤ 1 yr 100% ≤ 2 yr	94% ≤ 1 yr 100% ≤ 2 yr	94.2% ≤ 1 yr 99.6% ≤ 2 yr	94.6% ≤ 1 yr 100% ≤ 2yr		

Excludes multiplant actions and other unusually complex licensing tasks.

Age of Licensing Action Inventory*

	FY 2009	FY 2010	FY 2011	FY 2012	FY 2013	FY 2014
Target	93% ≤ 1 yr 100% ≤ 2 yr	90% ≤ 1 yr 100% ≤ 2 yr	95% ≤ 1 yr 100% ≤ 2 yr	95% ≤ 1 yr 100% ≤ 2 yr	TBD	95% ≤ 1 yr 100% ≤ 2 yr
Actual	94% ≤ 1 yr 100% ≤ 2 yr	93% ≤ 1 yr 100% ≤ 2 yr	90.3% ≤ 1 yr 99.9% ≤ 2 yr	95.8% < 1yr 100% < 2yr		

Excludes license renewal, improved standard technical specification conversions, and power uprates. Also excludes unusually complex LARs.

Other Licensing Tasks Completed per Year*

	FY 2009	FY 2010	FY 2011	FY 2012	FY 2013	FY 2014
Target	Complete 600 other licensing tasks.	Complete 600 other licensing tasks.	Complete 600 other licensing tasks.	Complete 600 other licensing tasks.	TBD**	Complete 500 other licensing tasks.*
Actual	541 other licensing tasks completed.	625 other licensing tasks completed.	465 other licensing tasks completed.	674 other licensing tasks completed.		

As limited by the number of other licensing task requests submitted or accepted the previous fiscal year.

**577 other licensing tasks submitted in FY 2012.*

Number of Operator Licensing Examinations Administered

	FY 2009	FY 2010	FY 2011	FY 2012	FY 2013	FY 2014
Target	Meet licensee demand estimated at 55 initial operator licensing examination sessions and 4 generic fundamentals examination sessions.	Meet licensee demand estimated at 55 initial operator licensing examination sessions and 4 generic fundamentals examination sessions.	Meet licensee demand estimated at 55 initial operator licensing examination sessions and 4 generic fundamentals examination sessions.	Meet licensee demand estimated at 55 initial operator licensing examination sessions and 4 generic fundamentals examination sessions.	TBD	Meet licensee demand estimated at 55 initial operator licensing examination sessions and 4 generic fundamentals examination sessions.
Actual	Met licensee demand estimated at 59 initial operator licensing examination sessions and 4 generic fundamentals examination sessions.	Met licensee demand estimated at 54 initial operator licensing examination sessions and 4 generic fundamentals examination sessions.	Met licensee demand estimated at 55 initial operator licensing examination sessions and 4 generic fundamentals examination sessions.	Met licensee demand estimated at 49 (with 55 originally estimated) initial operating licensing examination sessions and 4 generic fundamentals examination sessions.		

Minimize Necessary Communication Systems Devices for Senior Manager Use

	FY 2009	FY 2010	FY 2011	FY 2012	FY 2013	FY 2014
Target	New measure in FY 2011		Applicability still being checked.	$410,000 reduction	Measure discontinued.	
Actual						

OVERSIGHT

Number of Plants for Which the Baseline Inspection Program Was Completed during the Most Recently Ended Inspection Cycle*

	FY 2009	FY 2010	FY 2011	FY 2012	FY 2013	FY 2014
Target	All required baseline inspection procedures are completed at 104 operating reactors.	All required baseline inspection procedures are completed at 104 operating reactors.	All required baseline inspection procedures are completed at 104 operating reactors.	All required baseline inspection procedures are completed at 104 operating reactors.	TBD	All required baseline inspection procedures are completed at 104 operating reactors.
Actual	Completed all reactors.	Completed all reactors.	Completed all reactors.	Completed all reactors.		

*The baseline inspection program metric includes 104 operating reactors.

Percentage of Final Significance Determination Process Determinations Made within 90 Days for All Potentially Greater Than Green Findings

	FY 2009	FY 2010	FY 2011	FY 2012	FY 2013	FY 2014
Target	90%	90%	90%*	90%	TBD	90%
Actual	100%	93%	100%	100%		

*Target mistakenly reported to be 100% in the 2011 Congressional Budget Justification.

Time To Complete Reviews of Technical Allegations*						
	FY 2009	FY 2010	FY 2011	FY 2012	FY 2013	FY 2014
Target	90% ≤ 150 days 95% ≤ 180 days 100% ≤ 360 days	90% ≤ 150 days 95% ≤ 180 days 100% ≤ 360 days	90% ≤ 150 days 95% ≤ 180 days 100% ≤ 360 days	90% ≤ 150 days 95% ≤ 180 days 100% ≤ 360 days	TBD	90% ≤ 150 days 95% ≤ 180 days 100% ≤ 360 days
Actual	93% ≤ 150 days 98% ≤ 180 days 99% ≤ 360 days*	95% ≤ 150 days 98% ≤ 180 days 100% ≤ 360 days	98% ≤ 150 days 99% ≤ 180 days 100% ≤ 360 days	98% ≤ 150 days 99% ≤ 180 days 100 % ≤ 360 days		

*A few allegations exceeded the target because of complicated technical review or extended review at another Federal agency.

Timeliness in Completing Enforcement Actions*						
	FY 2009	FY 2010	FY 2011	FY 2012	FY 2013	FY 2014
Target	Investigation cases: 100% completed within 360 days of Office of Enforcement (OE) processing time. Noninvestigation cases: 100% completed within 180 days of OE processing time.	Investigation cases: 100% completed within 360 days of OE processing time. Noninvestigation cases: 100% completed within 180 days of OE processing time.	Investigation cases: 100% completed within 360 days of OE processing time. Noninvestigation cases: 100% completed within 180 days of OE processing time.	Investigation cases: 100% completed within 330 days of OE processing time. Noninvestigation cases: 100% completed within 160 days of OE processing time.	TBD	Investigation cases: 100% completed within 330 days of OE processing time. Noninvestigation cases: 100% completed within 160 days of OE processing time.
Actual	Investigation: None ≥ 360 days. Noninvestigation: None ≥ 180 days.	Investigation: None ≥ 360 days. Noninvestigation: None ≥ 180 days.	Investigation: None ≥ 360 days. Noninvestigation: None ≥ 180 days.	Investigation None ≥ 330 days. Noninvestigation: None ≥ 180 days.		

*(A) Cases involving investigations normally involve wrongdoing, including discrimination, and, by their nature, are more resource-intensive and less timely. Accordingly, the performance measure for cases involving investigations provides for more staff time.

(B) OE processing time is defined as that time from the date on which the case is opened or the licensee is briefed on the concern (exit) to the issuance of an enforcement action or other appropriate disposition less (1) any time the NRC could not act because the case resides with the U.S. Department of Labor, U.S. Department of Justice, other Government entity, or where the licensee or anyone outside the enforcement process causes a lengthy deferment and (2) any time the NRC could not act because of processing Freedom of Information Act requests.

Timeliness in Completing Investigations—Target 1

	FY 2009	FY 2010	FY 2011	FY 2012	FY 2013	FY 2014
Target	80% of investigations that developed sufficient information to reach a conclusion on wrongdoing will be completed in 10 months or less.	80% of investigations that developed sufficient information to reach a conclusion on wrongdoing will be completed in 10 months or less.	80% of investigations that developed sufficient information to reach a conclusion on wrongdoing will be completed in 10 months or less.	80% of investigations that developed sufficient information to reach a conclusion on wrongdoing will be completed in 10 months or less.	TBD	80% of investigations that developed sufficient information to reach a conclusion on wrongdoing will be completed in 9 months or less.
Actual	Completed 106 investigations; 98.1% (104) of those that developed sufficient information to reach a conclusion on wrongdoing were completed in 10 months or less.	Completed 40 investigations; 98% (39) of those that developed sufficient information to reach a conclusion on wrongdoing were completed in 9 months or less.	Completed 93 investigations; 84% (78) of those that developed sufficient information to reach a conclusion on wrongdoing were completed in 9 months or less.	Completed 114 investigations; 83% (95) of those that developed sufficient information to reach a conclusion on wrongdoing were completed in 9 months or less.		

Timeliness in Completing Investigations—Target 2

	FY 2009	FY 2010	FY 2011	FY 2012	FY 2013	FY 2014
Target	Close 100% of Office of Investigations (OI) investigations in time to initiate civil or criminal enforcement action.	Close 100% of OI investigations in time to initiate civil or criminal enforcement action.	Close 100% of OI investigations in time to initiate civil or criminal enforcement action.	Close 100% of OI investigations in time to initiate civil or criminal enforcement action.	TBD	Close 100% of OI investigations in time to initiate civil or criminal enforcement action.
Actual	Closed 100% of OI investigations in time to initiate civil or criminal enforcement action.	Closed 100% of OI investigations in time to initiate civil or criminal enforcement action.	Closed 100% of OI investigations in time to initiate civil or criminal enforcement action.	Closed 100% of OI Investigations in time to initiate civil or criminal enforcement action.		

RESEARCH

Timeliness of Completing Actions on Critical Research Programs*

	FY 2009	FY 2010	FY 2011	FY 2012	FY 2013	FY 2014
Target	90% of major milestones met on or before their due date.	90% of major milestones met on or before their due date.	90% of major milestones met on or before their due date.	90% of major milestones met on or before their due date.	TBD	90% of major milestones met on or before their due date.
Actual	100% across programs	100% across programs	100% across programs	100% across programs		

*Critical research programs typically respond to high-priority needs from the Commission and the NRC's licensing organizations. Critical research programs will be the highest priority needs identified at the beginning of each fiscal year.

Acceptable Technical Quality of Agency Research Technical Products*						
	FY 2009	FY 2010	FY 2011	FY 2012	FY 2013	FY 2014
Target	Combined score ≥ 3.5	Combined score ≥ 3.5	Combined score ≥ 3.5	Combined score ≥ 3.5	TBD	Combined score ≥ 3.75
Actual	4	4.6	4.8	4.5		

EVENT RESPONSE

Emergency Response Performance Index*						
	FY 2009	FY 2010	FY 2011	FY 2012	FY 2013	FY 2014
Target	100%	100%	100%	100%	TBD	100%
Actual	100%	100%	100%	100%		

*This performance index provides a single overall performance measure of the agency's readiness to respond to a nuclear or terrorist emergency situation or other events of national interest. The index measures several activities within the Incident Response Program that are critical to support the agency's preparedness and response ability.

NEW REACTORS

	New Reactors by Product Line (Dollars in Millions)					
	FY 2012 Enacted		FY 2014 Request		Delta FY 2014–FY 2012	
Product Line	**$M**	**FTE**	**$M**	**FTE**	**$M**	**FTE**
Licensing	131.9	483.1	104.8	439.9	(27.0)	(43.2)
Oversight	35.7	197.1	39.1	198.3	3.5	1.2
Rulemaking	1.8	9.0	2.6	14.1	0.7	5.0
International Activities	1.6	9.5	1.2	7.0	(0.3)	(2.5)
Research	9.6	37.0	9.1	27.3	(0.5)	(9.7)
Generic HLS	0.8	3.6	0.0	0.0	(0.8)	(3.6)
Subtotal	**$181.3**	**739.4**	**$156.9**	**686.6**	**($24.4)**	**(52.7)**
Corporate Support	84.1	185.2	83.6	178.9	(0.5)	(6.4)
Total	**$265.4**	**924.6**	**$240.5**	**865.5**	**($24.9)**	**(59.1)**

Numbers may not add due to rounding.

Locations of New Nuclear Power Reactors Applications

= A proposed new reactor at or near an existing nuclear plant

= A proposed reactor at a site that has not previously produced nuclear power

= Approved reactor

= 1 unit

= 2 units

* Review suspended ** COL application amended by applicant to ESP on March 25, 2010.
Note: Data is as of June 2012.

The work of the New Reactors Business Line responds to the industry's renewed interest in building new commercial nuclear power plants to meet the Nation's future electric power generation needs. All civilian nuclear power reactors must be licensed by the U.S. Nuclear Regulatory Commission (NRC) and adhere to the agency's regulations to operate in the United States. Renewed demand and national policy initiatives, such as the U.S. Department of Energy's Nuclear Power 2010 program and the Energy Policy Act of 2005, have stimulated a nuclear resurgence. The New Reactors Business Line is responsible for the regulatory activities associated with locating, licensing, and overseeing construction of new nuclear power reactors. The NRC reviews new nuclear power reactor design certification (DC), combined license (COL), and early site permit (ESP) applications consistent with Title 10 of the *Code of Federal Regulations* (10 CFR) Part 52, "Licenses, Certifications, and Approvals for Nuclear Power Plants," and industry's projected plans and schedules. The NRC also reviews new nuclear power reactor construction permit and operating license applications consistent with 10 CFR Part 50, "Domestic Licensing of Production and Utilization facilities." The new reactor activities ensure that the development of new civilian nuclear power reactor facilities is done in a way that protects the public health and safety, protects the environment, and provides high assurance of security.

The NRC has streamlined the application process for new reactors under 10 CFR Part 52, including publishing a major revision in fiscal year (FY) 2008. By issuing a COL, the NRC authorizes the licensee to construct and, with specified conditions, operate a nuclear power plant at a specific site. The application process prescribed under 10 CFR Part 50, which was implemented for all currently operating reactors, involves separate applications for the issuance of a construction permit and an operating license.

The NRC continues to interact with vendors and utilities on prospective new reactor applications and licensing activities.

The NRC continues to perform technical reviews of large light-water reactors and to provide oversight of construction activities. These activities include conducting inspections of plants under construction, conducting inspections of component suppliers, and supporting inspections of key international nuclear equipment. In addition, the NRC will begin to review multiple advanced reactor applications.

The NRC has organized New Reactors activities into product lines that best support Safety and Security strategies and that affect strategic outcomes as they relate to new civilian reactors. The resources requested support all direct aspects of new reactors within the following six product lines: Licensing, Oversight, Rulemaking, Research, International Activities, and Generic Homeland Security. The outputs of the product lines under this business line contribute to the scoring of the NRC Safety and Security Performance Measures and their contribution to the achievement of its Strategic Outcomes.

CHANGES FROM FY 2012 ENACTED BUDGET

Resources decreased to support the implementation of the Fukushima Near-Term Task Force (NTTF) recommendations that included a shift from New Reactors to Operating Reactors. Other changes include a decrease due an agencywide effort to reduce overhead resources through increased efficiency and effectiveness. The decreases are offset by an increase to support the anticipated receipt of two advanced reactor DC applications and associated advanced reactor license applications and by an increase to prepare guidance documents, such as design-specific review standards.

LICENSING

STRATEGIC GOAL STRATEGIES SUPPORTED BY LICENSING
Safety—develop, maintain, and implement licensing and regulatory programs for reactors.
Security—review security plans for consistency with security requirements.

For FY 2014, the NRC requests $104.8 million, including 439.9 FTE, for licensing activities. This funding level represents an overall decrease of $27.0 million, including 43.2 FTE, when compared with the FY 2012 enacted budget. Resources decreased to support implementation of the Fukushima NTTF recommendations that included a shift from New Reactors to Operating Reactors. Other changes include a decrease because of the completion of the Three White Flint North building, revised workload assumptions based on historical projected versus actual demand, and an agency wide effort to reduce overhead resources through increased efficiency and effectiveness.

The Licensing Product Line supports the licensing process—the NRC's determination that applicants' plans for the development, construction, and operation of new nuclear power plants provide an adequate margin of safety and security to ensure protection of the public health and safety and the environment, consistent with the NRC's rules and regulations.

Licensing includes reviewing and certifying new and advanced reactor designs and developing a regulatory framework, including the supporting technical basis to license advanced reactor designs.

The licensing workload includes the review of COL and operating license applications, including meetings before the Advisory Committee on Reactor Safeguards and hearing preparations before the Atomic Safety and Licensing Board Panel. A COL, issued by the NRC, authorizes the licensee to construct and, with specified conditions, operate a nuclear power plant at a specific site. As of June 2012, the NRC has received 18 COL applications from the nuclear power industry, and it is currently reviewing the 10 applications that remain active (2 applications were issued licenses, 5 applicants requested their reviews be suspended, and 1 application was amended to become an ESP). The NRC expects to complete the licensing process for one application in FY 2013 and to continue work on the balance during FY 2014. Resources will fund environmental reviews and safety reviews, which include emergency preparedness technical reviews, security plan technical reviews, security-related assessments, and financial analysis of COL applicants. Licensing also provides the resources to support licensing-related legal representation, independent advice, and adjudicatory reviews; IT for licensing activities; an operator licensing system; scheduler support; and the regulatory infrastructure for licensing activities.

The NRC issues a DC to certify a standard nuclear plant design that is independent of a specific site. This DC is valid for 15 years. Budgetary resources for licensing during FY 2014 will support the ongoing review of three DCs (U.S. Evolutionary Power Reactor (U.S.-EPR), U.S. Advanced Pressurized-Water Reactor (U.S.-APWR), and Korea Hydro Nuclear Power (formerly known as Korea Electric Power Corporation)); the continuing review of one DC renewal (advanced boiling-water reactor (ABWR)); startup reviews of a second DC renewal (ABWR); and two new DCs (Babcock & Wilcox mPower and NuScale).

Licensing resources support the review of two ESP applications received in FY 2010 and the initiation of a review of an advanced reactor ESP expected in FY 2014.

Resources also support license amendments for post-COL activities. The NRC projects that a significant percentage of amendments will be for important or significant design changes associated with resolving first-of-a-kind construction issues. Resources also will continue to support review and evidentiary hearing activities; license-related legal advice and representation, independent advice, and adjudicatory reviews; and the regulatory infrastructure for postlicensing.

Licensing resources support the expected reactivation of construction and licensing of Bellefonte, Unit 1.

New reactors licensing resources support incorporating interim staff guidance and lessons learned into regulatory guides and Standard Review Plans (SRPs), beginning the 5-year update of the SRP, developing and maintaining other staff guidance, and providing contract support for scheduling staff reviews. Resources continue to support the staff's effort to resolve identified policy and key technical issues facing advanced reactors. In addition, these resources support the implementation of issue resolutions through development of both new and revised rules and guidance documents. Resources also support the development and implementation of technical bases for anticipated advanced reactor applications.

OVERSIGHT

STRATEGIC GOAL STRATEGIES SUPPORTED BY OVERSIGHT
Safety—oversee the development and construction of new nuclear power reactors.
Security—evaluate license applicants' security plans.

For FY 2014, the NRC requests $39.1 million, including 198.3 FTE, for oversight activities. This funding level represents an increase of $3.5 million, including 1.2 FTE, when compared with the FY 2012 enacted budget. This increase is because of the inspection of six reactors under construction and an increase in vendor inspections from 15 to 30.

The Oversight Product Line provides resources to support construction inspection activities. During FY 2014, the NRC will develop and implement construction inspection activities to support inspection of six reactors under construction (Vogtle, Units 3 and 4; V.C. Summer, Units 2 and 3; Bellefonte, Unit 1; and Watts Bar, Unit 2). Oversight includes resources needed for an increase in enforcement-related casework, construction and vendor allegations, and investigations of wrongdoing. The NRC will continue inspection of construction and preoperational testing activities for Watts Bar, Unit 2, to support operation in FY 2014. For Bellefonte, Unit 1, the NRC will continue its inspections under the Deferred Plant Policy Statement on maintenance, preservation, and documentation activities and the program to assess the condition of the facility. Budgetary resources support an increase for up to 30 vendor inspections in FY 2014 to ensure integrity of the supply chain, consistent with the expected increase in the number of suppliers and sites under active construction. In addition, the NRC will support the continued implementation of a formal agency wide program to monitor and evaluate counterfeit, fraudulent, and suspect items, as developed in FY 2011.

Oversight seeks to verify that the new reactor construction process adequately protects public health and safety, protects the environment, and provides high assurance of the security of facilities through verification that plants are constructed to the requirements established during the licensing process.

In FY 2014, resources are needed to continue training, development, and construction of new reactor simulators at the Technical Training Center, the training development of new licensing examiners, and the Fitness-for-Duty (FFD) Program, including the operation and maintenance of the electronic reporting systems for FFD performance reports.

RULEMAKING

STRATEGIC GOAL STRATEGIES SUPPORTED BY RULEMAKING
Safety—use sound science and state-of-the--art methods to establish, where appropriate, risk-informed and performance-based regulations.
Security—use a framework of rules and regulations to guide the security activities of the agency.

For FY 2014, the NRC requests $2.6-million, including 14.1 FTE, for rulemaking activities. This funding level represents an increase of $0.7 million, including 5.0 FTE, when compared with the FY 2012 enacted budget, which represents a slight increase for high-priority rulemaking.

The Rulemaking Product Line supports activities to maintain the safety and security framework of rules, regulatory guidance, and SRPs. This framework promotes licensee compliance with underlying safety principles and security requirements. In FY 2014, resources support work on four high-priority rulemakings, two of which are directly related to DC activities, and the rulemaking under

10 CFR Part 21, "Reporting of Defects and Noncompliance," and associated guidance development to, in part, resolve commitments in response to Inspector General audits. These resources also support one medium-priority Commission-directed rulemaking related to amending Appendix I, "Numerical Guides for Design Objectives and Limiting Conditions for Operation To Meet the Criterion 'As Low As Is Reasonably Achievable' for Radioactive Material in Light-Water-Cooled Nuclear Power Reactor Effluents," to 10 CFR Part 50 to incorporate International Commission on Radiological Protection recommendations.

INTERNATIONAL ACTIVITIES

STRATEGIC GOAL STRATEGIES SUPPORTED BY INTERNATIONAL ACTIVITIES
Safety—use domestic and international operating experience to inform decisionmaking.
Security—work with international counterparts to exchange information.

For FY 2014, the NRC requests $1.2 million, including 7.0 FTE, for International Activities. This funding level represents an overall decrease of $0.3 million, including 2.5 FTE, when compared with the FY 2012 enacted budget, which does not represent a significant change in workload.

The International Product Line supports the NRC's interface with international counterparts to exchange information, expertise, operating experience, and research results. These activities help the NRC recognize and respond to emerging technical issues and to promote best safety and security practices. Resources support the continued participation in the Multinational Design Evaluation Program that will continue international exchanges of licensing and construction inspection activities to potentially increase safety at U.S. sites.

RESEARCH

STRATEGIC GOAL STRATEGIES SUPPORTED BY RESEARCH
Safety—improve the NRC's regulatory programs and apply safety-focused research to anticipate and resolve safety issues.
Security—use research to inform the security activities of the agency.

For FY 2014, the NRC requests $9.1 million, including 27.3 FTE, for research activities. This funding level represents an overall decrease of $0.5 million, including 9.7 FTE, when compared with the FY 2012 enacted budget, which does not represent a significant change in workload.

The NRC's research program mission is to evaluate and resolve safety issues for nuclear power plants and other facilities and materials that the agency regulates. This includes evaluating existing and potential safety issues; supplying independent expertise, information, and technical judgments to support timely and realistic regulatory decisions; reducing uncertainties in risk assessments; and developing technical regulations and standards.

New reactors research funding supports the resolution of technical issues in DC reviews; development of regulatory guidance for new reactor licensing; advancement of the NRC's knowledge of, and infrastructure for, earthquake engineering; and development of new reactor plant models. Research resources also support the advanced reactors program, including the development of expertise, tools, and data in thermal-hydraulics, severe accidents, probabilistic risk assessment, and seismic and structural analysis. Advanced reactor program research will support the review of integral pressurized-water reactors.

GENERIC HOMELAND SECURITY

STRATEGIC GOAL STRATEGIES SUPPORTED BY GENERIC HOMELAND SECURITY
Safety—effectively respond to events at NRC-licensed facilities and other events of national interest, including maintaining and enhancing the NRC's critical incident response and communication capabilities.
Security—support Federal response plans that use an approach to the security of nuclear facilities and radioactive material that integrates the efforts of licensees and Federal, State, local, and Tribal authorities.

THE NRC REVIEWED THE ACTIVITIES UNDER THE DEFINITIONS FOR THE GENERIC HLS PRODUCT AND SHIFTED SOME RESOURCES TO NON-GENERIC HLS PRODUCTS IN ORDER TO MORE ACCURATELY ALIGN RESOURCES TO THE PLANNED WORKLOAD.

SIGNIFICANT ACCOMPLISHMENTS IN FY 2012

The NRC continued the technical and safety reviews of 10 COLs, 2 ESPs, 2 DC amendments, and 2 DC renewals. The agency issued the first-ever COLs for Vogtle and V.C. Summer along with a limited work authorization for Vogtle. The NRC prepared two high-priority rulemakings for the Westinghouse AP1000 and ABWR final rule.

In addition, the staff completed the final supplemental environmental impact statement for Levy County COL. The NRC continued its safety and environmental reviews of two ESP applications: Victoria County and PSE&G. In August 2012, the ESP application for Victoria County Station was withdrawn by the applicant. The NRC initiated pre-licensing activities for the Blue Castle ESP application.

The agency provided Congress with a report describing the staff's overall strategy to prepare for reviewing advanced reactor designs. The NRC continued pre-application reviews for two small modular reactors. The NRC also began an extensive inspection and licensing effort associated with the reactivation of the Tennessee Valley Authority Watts Bar unit 2 Nuclear Power Plant.

OUTPUT MEASURES

LICENSING

Review ESP Applications on the Schedules Negotiated with the Applicants						
	FY 2009	FY 2010	FY 2011	FY 2012	FY 2013	FY 2014
Target	Complete one ESP review (Vogtle).	No ESPs planned for FY 2010.	No ESPs planned for FY 2011.	Review Victoria and PSE&G applications.*	TBD	Continue Victoria and PSE&G reviews.
Actual	Issued Vogtle ESP review on schedule.	Completed milestones for two ESP reviews (Vogtle and PSE&G).	No ESPs conducted during FY 2011.	Continued review of the PSEG ESP application. The Victoria County ESP application was withdrawn in August 2012.		

Change in previously reported FY 2012 because of resource planning changes.

Review DC Applications on the Schedules Negotiated with the Applicants						
	FY 2009	FY 2010	FY 2011	FY 2012	FY 2013	FY 2014
Target	Complete milestones necessary to support ESBWR, U.S.-EPR, and U.S.-APWR DC reviews. Complete review of AP1000 DC application.	Complete review of ESBWR DC application (rulemaking) and AP1000 amended application (rulemaking) and continue review of U.S.-EPR and U.S.-APWR DC applications.	Complete review of ESBWR DC application (rulemaking) and AP1000 amended application (rulemaking) and continue review of U.S.-EPR and APWR DC applications.	Complete rulemaking activities for AP1000 amendment and ESBWR and ABWR AIA amendment. Complete review of EPR design. Begin rulemaking activities for the EPR and the U.S.-APWR.*	TBD	Continue review of U.S.-APWR, KEPCO, and one ABWR DC renewal. Begin milestones necessary to support the second U.S.-ABWR DC renewal. Complete review of U.S.-EPR design and rulemaking. Continue rulemaking activities for U.S.-APWR.
Actual	Completed milestones necessary to support the ESBWR, U.S.-EPR, and U.S.-APWR DCs. Completed milestones associated with ABWR design certification amendment.	Completed milestones to support U.S.-ESBWR, U.S.-EPR, AP1000 amendment, U.S.-APWR design, and U.S.-ABWR amendment reviews.	Completed review of ESBWR DC application (rulemaking) and AP1000 amended application (rulemaking) and continued review of U.S.-EPR and U.S.-APWR.	Completed AP1000 DC amendment and the U.S.-ABWR amendment.		

Change to previously reported the FY 2012 and FY 2013 target is because the applicant inability to provide complete and timely submittals to allow the staff to complete safety reviews on the previously agreed upon schedules has led to the need to revise completion dates associated with the ESBWR, U.S.-EPR, and U.S.-APWR.

Review Small Modular Reactor DC Applications on the Schedules Negotiated with the Applicants

	FY 2009	FY 2010	FY 2011	FY 2012	FY 2013	FY 2014
Target	New measure in FY 2013				TBD	Complete milestones necessary to support the review of two SMR DC applications
Actual						

*Change to previously reported FY 2012 target because of resource planning changes. Excludes Watts Bar, Unit 2; Bellefonte, Unit 1; and Clinch-River.

**Five of the 17 COLs scheduled for review during FY 2011 remained in a suspended status (outside of the NRC's control).

***Excludes Watts Bar, Unit 2, and Bellefonte, Unit 1.

Identify and Resolve Policy and Key Technical Issues Facing the Review of SMR Applications Implement Resolutions through Rule Changes or Guidance Development

	FY 2009	FY 2010	FY 2011	FY 2012	FY 2013	FY 2014
Target	New measure for FY 2013				TBD	Complete milestones necessary to support the resolution of policy and key technical issues. In addition, complete milestones necessary to support implementation of resolutions.
Actual						

Review SMR Preapplication Submittals on the Schedules Negotiated with the Applicants

	FY 2009	FY 2010	FY 2011	FY 2012	FY 2013	FY 2014
Target	New measure in FY 2013				TBD	Complete milestones necessary to support preapplication activities for two DC applications.
Actual						

Review SMR COL and Construction Permit Applications on the Schedules Negotiated with the Applicants

	FY 2009	FY 2010	FY 2011	FY 2012	FY 2013	FY 2014
Target	New measure in FY 2013				TBD	Complete milestones necessary to support the review of the TVA construction permit.
Actual						

OVERSIGHT

	FY 2009	FY 2010	FY 2011	FY 2012	FY 2013	FY 2014
Complete All Vendor Inspections as Scheduled and Resourced						
Target	New measure in FY 2010	Complete 10 domestic and international vendor inspections.	Complete 15 domestic and international vendor inspections.	Complete 15 domestic and international vendor inspections.	TBD	Complete 30 domestic and international vendor inspections.
Actual		Completed 11 vendor inspections, 6 quality assurance implementation inspections, and 3 aircraft impact assessment inspections.	Completed 15 domestic and international vendor inspections.	Completed 27 vendor inspections.		

Nuclear Materials
and Waste Safety

NUCLEAR MATERIALS AND WASTE SAFETY

NUCLEAR MATERIALS AND WASTE SAFETY STRATEGIC GOALS
Safety—ensure adequate protection of public health and safety and the environment.
Security—ensure adequate protection in the secure use and management of radioactive materials.

The Nuclear Materials and Waste Safety Program encompasses the U.S. Nuclear Regulatory Commission (NRC) efforts to ensure that nuclear materials are used and that waste is managed in a manner that adequately protects the health and safety of the public, protects the environment, and promotes the common defense and security. Through this program, the NRC regulates uranium processing and fuel facilities; nuclear materials users (medical, industrial, research, and academic); spent fuel storage; transportation of radioactive materials; decontamination and decommissioning of facilities; and low-level and high-level radioactive waste. This program contributes to the NRC's Safety and Security goals through activities of the Fuel Facilities, Nuclear Materials Users, Spent Fuel Storage and Transportation, Decommissioning and Low-Level Waste Business Lines that license and regulate nuclear materials and waste to ensure their safe and secure handling. The Atomic Energy Act of 1954, as amended; the Energy Reorganization Act of 1974, as amended; the Nuclear Waste Policy Act of 1982; and the Energy Policy Act of 2005 are the foundations of the NRC's regulatory authority.

The nuclear fuel cycle process includes extraction of uranium from the ore, conversion of the uranium into a form suitable for enrichment, enrichment of the uranium to a level and type suitable for nuclear fuel, and use of the enriched uranium in fabricating fuel assemblies for use in nuclear reactors. The NRC licenses, oversees, and regulates the facilities involved in the process. Nuclear materials have many industrial, medical, and academic uses outside the nuclear fuel cycle. The NRC licenses, oversees, and regulates large and small users of nuclear materials, such as radiographers, hospitals, private physicians, nuclear gauge users, irradiators, and universities. Licensees with special nuclear material (SNM) verify and document their inventories in the Nuclear Materials Management and Safeguards System (NMMSS) database, which tracks material transfers and inventories. Both the NRC and the Agreement States carry out their respective radiation safety regulatory programs for nuclear materials users under the framework of the National Materials Program (NMP). This covers activities solely carried out by the NRC and 37 Agreement State programs, such as licensing, inspection, response to incidents, staffing and training, and enforcement and investigation.

About three million packages of radioactive materials are shipped each year in the United States by road, rail, air, or water. Regulating the safety of commercial radioactive material shipments is the joint responsibility of the NRC and the U.S. Department of Transportation. The NRC reviews and certifies shipping packages for the commercial transport of large quantities of radioactive materials to ensure transportation safety. In addition, the NRC reviews and certifies shipping package designs for the U.S. Department of Energy's noncommercial transuranic waste shipments.

The NRC ensures safety and security in the management and disposition of radioactive waste. Nuclear waste is categorized as either low-level radioactive waste (LLW) or high-level radioactive waste (HLW). The NRC and the Agreement States regulate the management and disposition of LLW. The NRC or Agreement States license, oversee, and regulate commercial LLW disposal facilities.

The majority of HLW is the irradiated fuel from commercial nuclear power reactors. The NRC licenses, oversees, and regulates the management and disposition of HLW from commercial nuclear power plants and other reactors. Irradiated fuel initially is stored in pools at reactor sites; after an appropriate time period, it is moved to dry storage. Dry storage is done in casks, or canisters, that the NRC has certified for such use. These casks are stored at independent spent fuel storage installations that the NRC licenses and regulates.

Decommissioning is the safe removal of a nuclear facility from service and reduction of residual radioactivity to a level that permits release of the property and termination of the NRC license. The NRC and Agreement States regulate the decontamination and decommissioning of uranium recovery facilities, materials and fuel cycle facilities, nuclear power plants, and research and test reactors.

Security efforts in this program include safeguards and security reviews and inspections, Force-on-Force (FOF) exercises for certain fuel cycle facilities, regulatory improvements, and implementation of a national registry (i.e., the National Source Tracking System (NSTS)) of radioactive sources of concern and the Integrated Source Management Portfolio (ISMP). The NRC will continue to maintain a high state of incident response readiness and coordination with other Federal, State, and local agencies.

Nuclear Materials and Waste Safety (Dollars in Millions)						
Business Line	FY 2012 Enacted $M	FTE	FY 2014 Request $M	FTE	Delta FY 2014–FY 2012 $M	FTE
Fuel Facilities	56.1	228.4	60.2	237.7	4.1	9.3
Nuclear Materials Users	93.0	344.7	86.9	318.7	(6.1)	(25.9)
Spent Fuel Storage and Transportation	40.8	155.1	45.4	160.7	4.6	5.6
Decommissioning and Low-Level Waste	37.3	142.1	39.0	142.1	1.8	(0.0)
Total	$227.1	870.4	$231.5	859.2	$4.4	(11.1)

Numbers may not add due to rounding.

PROGRAM RESOURCE SUMMARY

The FY 2014 proposed budget request for Nuclear Materials and Waste Safety is $231.5 million, which includes $94.1 million in contract support and travel, and $137.4 million in salaries and benefits to support 859.2 full-time equivalents (FTE). This would fund activities in Fuel Facilities, Nuclear Materials Users, Spent Fuel Storage and Transportation, and Decommissioning and LLW Business Lines. This funding level represents an increase of $4.4 million, including a decrease of 11.1 FTE when compared with the FY 2012 enacted budget, which is primarily because of support for a revised Waste Confidence decision.

FUEL FACILITIES

	Fuel Facilities by Product Line (Dollars in Millions)					
	FY 2012 Enacted		FY 2014 Request		Delta FY 2014–FY 2012	
Product Line	$M	FTE	$M	FTE	$M	FTE
Licensing	10.8	54.3	9.3	43.4	(1.5)	(10.8)
Oversight	17.8	103.0	20.3	112.6	2.5	9.6
Rulemaking	1.8	8.0	2.5	12.7	0.7	4.7
International Activities	1.1	5.1	2.0	11.4	0.9	6.3
Research	0.5	1.4	0.1	0.8	(0.3)	(0.6)
Generic HLS	3.1	8.4	2.8	5.2	(0.3)	(3.2)
Event Response	0.6	3.5	0.6	3.5	0.0	(0.0)
Subtotal	**$35.7**	**183.6**	**$37.7**	**189.5**	**$2.0**	**6.0**
Corporate Support	20.4	44.9	22.5	48.2	2.1	3.3
Total	**$56.1**	**228.4**	**$60.2**	**237.7**	**$4.1**	**9.3**

Numbers may not add due to rounding.

Locations of Fuel Cycle Facilities

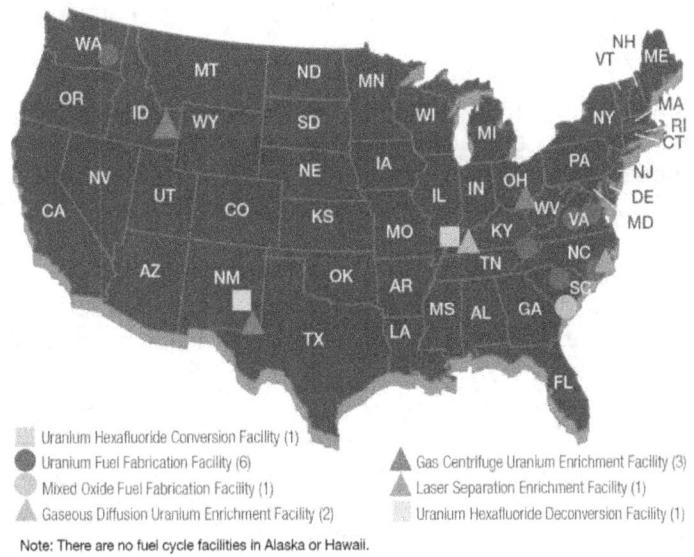

Uranium Hexafluoride Conversion Facility (1)
Uranium Fuel Fabrication Facility (6)
Mixed Oxide Fuel Fabrication Facility (1)
Gaseous Diffusion Uranium Enrichment Facility (2)

Gas Centrifuge Uranium Enrichment Facility (3)
Laser Separation Enrichment Facility (1)
Uranium Hexafluoride Deconversion Facility (1)

Note: There are no fuel cycle facilities in Alaska or Hawaii.

The Fuel Facilities Business Line activities ensure that fuel cycle facilities are licensed and operated in a manner that adequately protects the public health and safety, protects the environment, and promotes the common defense and security. Once uranium ore has been mined and milled (extraction of uranium from the ore), it moves on to conversion, enrichment, and fuel fabrication facilities. Conversion of the uranium changes it into a form suitable for enrichment. Enrichment processes the uranium to a level and type suitable for nuclear fuel, and fabrication uses the enriched uranium to make fuel assemblies for nuclear reactors. The NRC licenses, oversees, and regulates fuel cycle facilities, such as conversion, enrichment, and fuel fabrication facilities, as well as nuclear fuel research and pilot facilities. There are four uranium enrichment facilities and seven licensed major fuel fabrication and production facilities in the United States.

In fiscal year (FY) 2014, the NRC will oversee the construction of (1) the General Electric-Hitachi laser enrichment facility, (2) the AREVA centrifuge enrichment facility, and the (3) International Isotopes (INIS) depleted uranium deconversion facility and will continue conducting primary systems, structures, and components verifications for the Mixed-Oxide (MOX) Fuel Fabrication Facility. The NRC will continue to oversee operation of the other fuel cycle facilities.

The NRC will continue to evaluate routine license amendments to support changes in the plans for construction of approved facilities and in the operation of existing licensed facilities. Licensed fuel facilities possess special nuclear material (SNM), such as plutonium and enriched uranium. These SNM licensees verify and document their inventories and material transfers in the Nuclear Materials Management and Safeguard System (NMMSS) database.

Fuel Facilities Business Line activities also include the Nuclear Materials Information Program and the interagency agreement with the U.S. Department of Energy (DOE) for certification and accreditation of classified computer systems at enrichment facilities. Other activities include environmental, emergency preparedness, and licensee performance reviews; legal advice and representation; adjudicatory hearing-related activities; independent review and advice; security support for licensing activities; inspection oversight; allegations and enforcement activities; rulemaking; international cooperation and assistance; International Atomic Energy Agency (IAEA) missions; export and import licensing; and treaties, agreements, and conventions.

The NRC has organized the activities of the Fuel Facilities Business Line into product lines that best support Safety and Security strategies and accomplish strategic outcomes as they relate to fuel cycle facilities. The resources requested support all direct aspects of planned activities within the following seven product lines: Licensing, Oversight, Rulemaking, Research, International Activities, Generic Homeland Security, and Event Response.

The outputs of the product lines under this business line contribute to the scoring of the NRC Safety and Security Performance Measures and their contribution to the achievement of the agency's Strategic Outcomes.

CHANGES FROM FY 2012 ENACTED BUDGET

Resources increase to support construction oversight at the MOX, AREVA, General Electric-Hitachi and INIS facilities; continued enhancements to the fuel cycle oversight process (FCOP) and the oversight infrastructure; and activities related to applications of International Safeguards at enrichment facilities, such as Louisiana Energy Services (LES), General Electric-Hitachi, and AREVA Eagle Rock. These increases were partially offset by decreases to reflect the transfer of funding to support the medical isotope application review under Title 10 of the *Code of Federal Regulations* (10 CFR)

Part 50, "Domestic Licensing of Production and Utilization Facilities," that the Operating Reactor Business Line is funding and by a decrease in security support for licensing activities.

LICENSING

STRATEGIC GOAL STRATEGIES SUPPORTED BY LICENSING
Safety—develop, maintain, and implement licensing and regulatory programs for fuel facilities' material, spent fuel management, waste management, uranium recovery, and decommissioning.
Security—review security plans and changes for consistency with security requirements.

For FY 2014, the NRC requests $9.3 million, including 43.4 FTE, for licensing activities. This funding level represents a decrease of $1.5 million, including 10.8 FTE, when compared with the FY 2012 enacted budget. This decrease is because of the completion of existing license applications and the issuance of licenses.

Activities under the Licensing Product Line confirm that requests for new facilities and license renewals and amendments are consistent with the NRC's rules and regulations to ensure the adequate protection of the public health and safety, to protect the environment, and to promote the common defense and security.

Licensing provides resources for the following:

- Licensing actions for conversion and deconversion, enrichment, fuel fabrication and greater than critical mass (GTCM) facilities, including new facilities at MOX, AREVA, General Electric-Hitachi, and INIS. Resources allow for project management, technical reviews, and financial assurance and decommissioning plan reviews of all new applications, amendments, and renewals. In addition, resources support interagency agreements for classified computer networks. Resources also allow the Advisory Committee for Reactor Safeguards members and staff to provide timely and independent advice to the Commission on fuel-cycle-related matters. Further, resources support adjudicatory hearing-related activities and legal advice and representation on issues associated with licensing.

- Licensing support and reviews, including support to assist in the review of new reactor environmental reports and preparation of environmental impact statements, material control and accounting (MC&A), safeguards and criticality safety support to reactors, new reactors, and decommissioned sites.

- Emergency preparedness licensing reviews for operating fuel cycle facilities. Resources provide continued support for annual reviews of emergency plans for fuel fabrication facilities and review and analysis of licensee amendment requests.

- Environmental reviews for fuel cycle facility license applications, license renewals, amendments and preapplication activities. Additionally, resources support reviews for license transfer applications, provide hearing support for license applications, and provide support during license renewal. Examples include one complex amendment (Westinghouse Electric Corporation's potential change to a dry conversion process); INIS Phase 2; a license application for a source detection experiment and testing facility under 10 CFR Part 70, "Domestic Licensing of Special Nuclear Material"; and an MOX facility expansion.

- Regulatory activities related to agency followup to the Fukushima event, including actions from the Fukushima Near-Term Task Force, and inspections conducted under Temporary Instruction 2600/015, "Evaluation of Licensee Strategies for the Prevention and/or Mitigation of Emergencies at Fuel Facilities."

- Security support for licensing activities (includes fuel manufacturing facilities, new enrichment technologies, and enrichment and conversion facilities), including interoffice coordination and support for the increased number of operating facilities (LES and U.S. Enrichment Corp (USEC)).

OVERSIGHT

STRATEGIC GOAL STRATEGIES SUPPORTED BY OVERSIGHT
Safety—oversee licensee safety performance through inspections, investigations, enforcement, and performance assessment activities.
Security—oversee licensee security performance through inspections and Force-on-Force exercises.

For FY 2014, the NRC requests $20.3 million, including 112.6 FTE, for oversight activities. This funding level represents an increase of $2.5 million, including 9.6 FTE, when compared with the FY 2012 enacted budget. This increase is because of increased oversight to support significant construction activities.

The oversight process ensures that licensees take appropriate actions to maintain acceptable operating performance to ensure the adequate protection of the public health and safety, to protect the environment, and to promote the common defense and security. The oversight process also ensures that facilities under construction are built in accordance with NRC requirements.

The Oversight Product Line supports the following:

- Overall management of the oversight program for fuel facilities, including development and maintenance of policies, programs, and procedures for inspections of operating facilities and facilities under construction; assessment of the implementation of the inspection program; development a fuel cycle operating experience program; and development of a risk-informed FCOP. Resources also support coordination of inspection procedures, event coordination, and the MOX primary systems, structures, and components verification inspections. Resources support regional baseline and reactive inspections of operating fuel facilities and facilities under construction. This includes inspections of the Lead Cascade, Babcock & Wilcox, Nuclear Fuel Services, Paducah, Honeywell, Westinghouse, Global Nuclear Fuels, AREVA-Richland, URENCO USA, Global Laser Enrichment, MOX Fabrication, and INIS facilities. Resources also support the increase in construction and operational readiness for the MOX Fuel Fabrication Facility, AREVA-Eagle Rock, General Electric-Hitachi, and the INIS. Resources allow for regional support to FCOP and infrastructure enhancements and for regional inspections at General Electric-Vallecitos.

- Review of investigation reports, processing of enforcement actions, and oversight of project and contract management on the external safety culture and Alternative Dispute Resolution (ADR) Programs.

- Maintenance of baseline inspections for safety, security, physical projection, Force-on-Force, and reactive inspections of operating facilities. Inspection oversight will increase as LES, USEC/American Centrifuge Plant (ACP), AREVA, General Electric-Hitachi, MOX, and INIS begin or continue to construct their facilities. Inspection frequency has increased for these facilities based on concerns about control of access to sensitive information. In addition, the NRC is committed to enhancing FCOP to be more effective and efficient.

RULEMAKING

STRATEGIC GOAL STRATEGIES SUPPORTED BY RULEMAKING
Safety—maintain a framework of rules, regulatory guidance, and standard review plans that promote licensee compliance with underlying safety principles.
Security—use a risk-informed approach to implement appropriate regulatory controls for the possession, handling, import, export, and transshipment of radioactive materials.

For FY 2014, the NRC requests $2.5 million, including 12.7 FTE, for rulemaking activities. This funding level represents an increase of $0.7 million, including 4.7 FTE, when compared with the FY 2012 enacted budget. This increase is to support cyber security, chemical security, and fitness for duty. The Rulemaking Product Line supports developing cyber security regulations for fuel cycle facilities.

In addition, resources provide support for rulemaking in security-related areas, including enhanced security at fuel cycle facilities (Category I, II, and III and gaseous diffusion plants). This supports guidance development, outreach, and work with the interagency on material attractiveness. Further, resources will support proposed rule development and the updating of regulatory guidance for the enhancements to fuel cycle and special nuclear material (SNM) security.

INTERNATIONAL ACTIVITIES

STRATEGIC GOAL STRATEGIES SUPPORTED BY INTERNATIONAL ACTIVITIES
Safety—use international collaboration and coordination to inform decisionmaking.
Security—promote U.S. national security interests and nuclear proliferation policy objectives for NRC-licensed imports and exports of source and SNM and nuclear equipment.

For FY 2014, the NRC requests $2.0 million, including 11.4 FTE, for international activities. This funding level represents an increase of $0.9 million, including 6.3 FTE, when compared with the FY 2012 enacted budget. Resources primarily increase to reflect the reallocation of activities from the Material Users business line to more accurately align resources by business line. Resources also increase to strengthen IAEA safeguards approach to enrichment facilities being licensed and to support an increase in bi-lateral meetings to discuss safeguards approach at enrichment facilities and other fuel cycle facilities.

The NRC works with international counterparts to exchange information, expertise, operating experiences, and ongoing research to recognize and respond to emerging technical issues and to promote best safety and security practices. The International Activities Product Line supports the application of IAEA safeguards to fuel cycle facilities, international coordination, and assistance on next-generation safeguards designs.

The International Activities Product Line supports the following:

- Activities that include obligation tracking reviews, approvals, and treaty compliance activities that support the nonproliferation treaty, and Additional Protocol treaty for all NRC licensees (including Agreement States licensees).
- Activities involved in import and export license applications reviews, DOE Part 0810, and import and export of technology and equipment.
- Training and assistance to other countries through existing multilateral and bilateral agreements and through bilateral and multilateral discussions with, and support for, other countries and international organizations on physical protection matters.
- Bilateral visits involving physical protection conducted with other countries possessing or obtaining U.S.-origin SNM to conduct import or export licensing reviews.

RESEARCH

STRATEGIC GOAL STRATEGIES SUPPORTED BY RESEARCH
Safety—improve the NRC's regulatory programs and apply safety-focused research to anticipate and resolve safety issues.
Security—use research to inform the security activities of the agency.

For FY 2014, the NRC requests $0.1 million, including 0.8 FTE, for research activities, which is a decrease of $0.3 million, including 0.6 FTE, when compared to the FY 2012 enacted budget. Resources decrease to reflect the completion of reviews of fuel cycle facility applications and a long-term research project on advanced reprocessing. This decrease is partially offset by an increase to support the revised Fuel Cycle Oversight Program and cable fire testing for fuel facilities.

The Research Product Line supports the NRC's regulatory mission by providing technical advice, tools, and information to identify and resolve safety issues and to make regulatory decisions. This includes conducting confirmatory experiments and analyzing and preparing the agency for the future by evaluating the safety aspects of new technologies. Resources support user needs related to the FCOP and cable fire testing for fuel facilities.

GENERIC HOMELAND SECURITY

STRATEGIC GOAL STRATEGIES SUPPORTED BY GENERIC HOMELAND SECURITY
Safety—conduct NRC safety, security, and emergency preparedness programs in an integrated manner.
Security—support Federal response plans that use an approach to the security of nuclear facilities and radioactive material that integrates the efforts of licensees and Federal, State, local, and Tribal authorities.

In FY 2014, the NRC requests $2.8 million, including 5.2 FTE for generic homeland security activities. This funding level represents a decrease of $0.3 million and 3.2 FTE when compared with the FY 2012 enacted budget, which does not represent a significant change in workload.

The Generic Homeland Security Product Line supports security activities related to intergovernmental coordination and communication. It also supports security activities that are not plant-specific nor associated with a rulemaking, licensing, inspection, or oversight.

Resources support the NMMSS database, NMIP, and a contract with U.S. Department of Army to monitor domestic travel of classified technology. Resources also support activities related to intergovernmental coordination and cooperation and communication on homeland security matters.

EVENT RESPONSE

STRATEGIC GOAL STRATEGIES SUPPORTED BY EVENT RESPONSE
Safety—effectively respond to events at NRC-licensed facilities and other events of national interest, including maintaining and enhancing the NRC's critical incident response and communication capabilities.
Security—support Federal response plans that use an approach to the security of nuclear facilities and radioactive material that integrates the efforts of licensees and Federal, State, local, and Tribal authorities.

In FY 2014, the NRC requests $0.6 million, including 3.5 FTE, for event response activities, which does not represent a significant change in resources or workload when compared with the FY 2012 enacted budget.

The Event Response product line supports efforts to develop and enhance the fuel facilities event response program, plans, and procedures. Resources provide for one full-participation emergency preparedness exercise with an operating fuel facility. Resources also support the development and maintenance of the response capability associated with fuel facility-related incidents (i.e., emergency response coordinators, a training and qualification program, procedures, intra- and interagency coordination and outreach, and incident response actions for fuel facility licensees). Additional resources have been added to maintain 24 hour mobile response program, which will be used to predict chemical effects in drills and in real events at fuel facilities.

SIGNIFICANT ACCOMPLISHMENTS IN FY 2012

The agency completed review of the General Electric-Hitachi license application for the Wilmington laser enrichment facility and issued the safety evaluation report (SER) and FEIS in February 2012. The NRC staff concluded that the license application provides an adequate basis for safety and safeguards and that the operations from the proposed activities will not pose an undue risk to worker or public health and safety. The staff conducted a public meeting on May 10, 2012, in Wilmington to discuss its FEIS and SER findings. The mandatory hearing was held in July 2012 in Rockville, MD. The Atomic Safety and Licensing Board (ASLB) issued its determination decision in September 2012.

In December 2010, the agency issued the final SER for the license application by Shaw AREVA MOX Services, LLC, to possess and use radioactive material at the MOX fuel fabrication facility at the DOE's Savannah River Site near Aiken, SC. The SER was reviewed and approved. The licensing hearing was held on March 7–9, 2012. The ASLB made a ruling on June 29, 2012. In that ruling, the ASLB determined that additional information is needed from the applicant before disposition of the contentions can be made.

In May 2012, the agency issued the SER for the license application by International Isotopes Fluorine Products (IIFP) to construct and operate a facility to convert depleted uranium hexafluoride into an oxide form for ultimate disposal and to recover the fluorine for other commercial applications. The SER for IIFP was completed in May 2012 and published as NUREG-2116, "Safety Evaluation Report for the International Isotopes Fluorine Products, Inc., Fluorine Extraction Process and Depleted Uranium Deconversion Plant in Lea County, New Mexico." In August 2012, the FEIS was completed and published as NUREG-2113, "Final Environmental Impact Statement for the Proposed Fluorine

Extraction Process and Depleted Uranium Deconversion Plant." The license was issued in October 2012. Construction is scheduled to begin in mid-2013.

During FY 2012, the agency continued to define the technical basis needed to support the development of possible future regulations related to reprocessing facility licensing to resolve gaps and support an effective and efficient regulatory framework.

In FY 2009, the agency began an initiative to revise and consolidate the regulations for MC&A of SNM. During FY 2010, staff began developing the draft rule text, and this work continued into early FY 2013. The draft rule text is expected to be released for public comment in early FY 2014.

A proposed rule and draft guidance to require an integrated safety analysis for certain 10 CFR Part 40 facilities was published in the *Federal Register* on May 17, 2011. The public comment period ended in September 2011, and the staff considered public comments for the proposed Draft Final Rule. The Draft Final Rule is currently with the Commission for consideration.

OUTPUT MEASURES

LICENSING

Timeliness of Completing "Complex" Fuel Cycle Licensing Actions, from the Date of Acceptance, Excluding Requests for Additional Information (RAIs) with an Assumption of 30-Day Response to a Request for Additional Information						
	FY 2009	FY 2010	FY 2011	FY 2012	FY 2013	FY 2014
Target	New measure in FY 2012	100% ≤ 1.5 years (yr)	100% ≤ 1.5 yr	100% ≤ 1.5 yr	TBD	100% ≤ 1.5 yr
Actual		100% ≤ 1.5 yr	98% ≤ 1.5 yr*	96% ≤ 1.5 yr**		

The late licensing action was a complex review that included four separate actions. The licensee did not provide the final version in response to RAIs until late in the process (500 days). A field verification was required following receipt of the final documents, and the action was closed in 599 days.

**The late licensing action was due to the management decision to focus on higher priority licensing working, challenging and contentious nature of the safety and environmental reviews, extensive stakeholder interactions, and changing expectations in the depth and detail of the SER. The staff is developing and implementing lessons learned to improve the license renewal process and other significant licensing actions.*

Timeliness of Completing "Noncomplex" Fuel Cycle Licensing Actions (e.g., Amendments and Reviews) from the Date of Acceptance, including a 30-Day Response for an RAI						
	FY 2009	FY 2010	FY 2011	FY 2012	FY 2013	FY 2014
Target	New measure in FY 2010	85% ≤ 150 days 100% < 1 yr	85% ≤ 150 days 100% < 1 yr	85% ≤ 150 days 100% < 1 yr	TBD	85% ≤ 150 days 100% < 1 yr
Actual		92% ≤ 150 days 100% < 1 yr	92% ≤ 150 days 100% < 1 yr	93% ≤150 days 100% ≤ 1 yr		

New Fuel Facilities Hearing Support*						
	FY 2009	FY 2010	FY 2011	FY 2012	FY 2013	FY 2014
Target	New efficiency measure to begin in FY 2011		Actual hours expended on major tasks in support of licensing board hearings, as documented in the Fuel Cycle Safety and Safeguards Division Operating Plan, will not exceed the projected hours by more than 10%.*	Actual hours expended on major tasks in support of licensing board hearings, as documented in the Fuel Cycle Safety and Safeguards Division Operating Plan, will not exceed the projected hours by more than 10%.*	TBD	Actual hours expended on major tasks in support of licensing board hearings, as documented in the Fuel Cycle Safety and Safeguards Division Operating Plan, will not exceed the projected hours by more than 10%.*
Actual			Target was met.	Target was met.		

Targets, baselines, and calculation methods are under development, and the measure may be revised.

OVERSIGHT

Timeliness in Completing Reviews for Technical Allegations						
	FY 2009	FY 2010	FY 2011	FY 2012	FY 2013	FY 2014
Target	90% ≤ 150 days 95% ≤ 180 days 100% ≤ 360 days	90% ≤ 150 days 95% ≤ 180 days 100% ≤ 360 days	90% ≤ 150 days 95% ≤ 180 days 100% ≤ 360 days	90% ≤ 150 days 95% ≤ 180 days 100% ≤ 360 days	TBD	90% ≤ 150 days 95% ≤ 180 days 100% ≤ 360 days
Actual	100% ≤ 150 days 100% ≤ 180 days 100% ≤ 360 days	81% ≤ 150 days* 96% ≤ 180 days 100% ≤ 360 days	97% ≤ 150 days 98% ≤ 180 days 100% ≤ 360 days	94% ≤ 150 days 97% ≤ 180 days **97% ≤ 360 days		

*This metric was not met because allegations in the first quarter were not being closed in ≤ 150 days. Three of the four were affected by regional staff reassignments and case complexities requiring substantial staff and management review. The fourth case involved issues of dual regulation between the NRC and the U.S. Environmental Protection Agency (EPA) and required extensive research of EPA requirements and communications with State representatives. The region focused attention in this area throughout the remainder of FY 2010 (closed all but one fuel facility allegation in the second and third quarters in ≤ 150 days), but it was ultimately unable to meet the metric primarily because of the considerable staff and management effort required to evaluate three new fuel facility allegations in the fourth quarter of FY 2010 that each involved unusually large numbers of concerns, causing the time needed for closure to be greater than 150 (but less than 180) days.

**Allegations referred to the Office of Enforcement (OE) by the Office of the Inspector General (OIG) were misplaced by OE in mid October 2010, resulting in extensive delay (13 months or more) in allegation processing. The package from OIG was relocated in February 2012. The allegations involved Region II fuel cycle facilities and, once identified, were promptly forwarded to OE in Region II. One of the two allegations was subsequently closed in the second quarter of FY 2012, and the other remains open pending the results of an OI investigation. After discovery, the OE Allegation Program staff discussed the occurrence with OIG, Region II, and the agency's office allegation coordinators (OACs). OE discussed the event internally, and the Director of OE prepared a memorandum to all OE staff, reminding them of the event, staff responsibilities, and actions to prevent reoccurrence.

Safety and Safeguards Inspection Modules Complete All Core and Reactive Inspection Modules as Scheduled in Fuel Cycle Master Inspection Plan						
	FY 2009	FY 2010	FY 2011	FY 2012	FY 2013	FY 2014
Target	Complete 286 inspection modules.	Complete 286 inspection modules.	Complete 328 inspection modules.*	Complete 307 inspection modules.*	Measure discontinued in FY 2013.	
Actual	Completed 286 inspection modules.	Completed 289 inspection modules.	Completed 320 inspection modules.**	Completed 318 inspection modules		

*USEC/ACP began enrichment operations during FY 2010. LES is not expected to begin operations until after FY 2012.

**An MC&A inspection scheduled for LES in February was postponed to coincide with upcoming readiness review inspections; a low-enriched NFS inspection scheduled for July was moved to October to coincide with the high-enriched inspection; and an LES inspection report that was not issued in this fiscal year to resolve a nonconcurrence. Since the inspection program is conducted by calendar year (CY), postponement of the MC&A LES and NFS inspections to the first quarter of FY 2012 (while still in CY 2011 inspection year) will support completion of the core program.

Timeliness of Safety and Safeguards Inspection Modules Complete Core Inspection Modules As Scheduled in Fuel Cycle Master Inspection Plan						
	FY 2009	FY 2010	FY 2011	FY 2012	FY 2013	FY 2014
Target	> 97% completed on time	> 97% completed on time	> 99% completed on time	> 99% completed on time	Measure discontinued in FY 2013.	
Actual	100% completed on time	100% completed on time	100% completed on time	100% completed on time		

	FY 2009	FY 2010	FY 2011	FY 2012	FY 2013	FY 2014
Percentage of Operating Fuel Facilities for Which the Core Inspection Program Was Completed as Planned during the Most Recently Ended Inspection Cycle *						
Target	New measure in FY 2013				TBD	100%
Actual						

*Replaces former output measures on core and reactive inspection modules and timeliness of safety and safeguards inspection modules.

NUCLEAR MATERIALS USERS

	Nuclear Materials Users by Product Line (Dollars in Millions)					
	FY 2012 Enacted		FY 2014 Request		Delta FY 2014–FY 2012	
Product Line	$M	FTE	$M	FTE	$M	FTE
Licensing	13.4	67.1	13.0	67.7	(0.4)	0.6
Oversight	19.4	99.2	18.2	91.1	(1.2)	(8.1)
Rulemaking	3.7	20.3	2.4	12.6	(1.4)	(7.7)
International Activities	2.1	12.0	2.5	13.6	0.3	1.7
Research	1.0	4.1	1.4	3.8	0.4	(0.3)
Generic HLS	15.5	33.8	12.6	25.6	(2.8)	(8.2)
Event Response	0.9	5.1	0.9	5.1	0.0	(0.0)
State, Tribal, and Federal Programs	7.2	37.3	7.3	37.7	0.1	0.4
Subtotal	**$63.2**	**278.9**	**$58.1**	**257.1**	**($5.0)**	**(21.8)**
Corporate Support	29.8	65.7	28.8	61.6	(1.1)	(4.1)
Total	**$93.0**	**344.7**	**$86.9**	**318.7**	**($6.1)**	**(25.9)**

Numbers may not add due to rounding.

Nuclear materials have many industrial, medical, and academic uses. The U.S. Nuclear Regulatory Commission (NRC) licenses, oversees, and regulates large and small users of nuclear materials, such as radiographers, hospitals, private physicians, nuclear gauge users, irradiators, and universities.

Nuclear Materials Users' activities support the licensing, inspection, event evaluation, research, incident response, allegation, enforcement, and rulemaking to maintain the regulatory safety and security infrastructure needed to process and handle nuclear materials. The agency's safety activities include completion of approximately 2,300 materials licensing actions and 1,000 routine health and safety inspections. Work also will be conducted on approximately 4 to 6 active materials rulemakings.

The Agreement State program has been in existence since 1959 with the adoption of Section 274 of the Atomic Energy Act (AEA). At present, there are 37 Agreement States. Under Section 274 of the AEA, the NRC has programmatic oversight responsibility to periodically review the actions of the Agreement States to ensure compliance with the requirements in the AEA to maintain adequate and compatible programs. The current review process under the Integrated Materials Performance Evaluation Program (IMPEP) is conducted with State staff participation.

Nuclear Materials Users' activities include reviews and issuance of NRC import and export authorizations, materials-related wrongdoing investigations, adjudicatory hearings for materials licensing and enforcement proceedings, technical training, and continuous improvements and centralized oversight of information technology (IT) and information management.

Nuclear Materials Users' security activities include implementation and operation of a national registry to improve control of radioactive sources of concern and to prevent their malevolent use. The

Integrated Source Management Portfolio (ISMP) contract has integrated the three core systems that comprise the National Source Tracking System (NSTS), Web-Based Licensing (WBL), and the License Verification System (LVS). Together these systems will license and track sources and other radioactive materials under one management mechanism. Further, security activities include conducting inspections of security activities at materials facilities with radioactive materials in quantities of concern and prelicensing inspections of new materials license applicants. All of these activities strengthen controls for the possession, handling, import, and export of nuclear materials. In addition, resources will be used to conduct the NRC's Agreement State liaison activities on enhanced control and security actions for materials licensees and on cooperative efforts and liaison with all State and local Governments and Native American Tribal Governments in matters related to homeland security for nuclear waste and materials.

The NRC has organized Nuclear Materials Users' activities into product lines that best support Safety and Security strategies and affect Strategic Outcomes as they relate to materials licensing, inspection, and Agreement State activities. The resources requested support all direct aspects of Nuclear Materials Users within the following eight product lines: Licensing; Oversight; Rulemaking; Research; International Activities; Generic Homeland Security; Event Response; and State, Tribal, and Federal programs. The efforts under Nuclear Materials Users are designed to ensure that nuclear materials are licensed and used in a manner that adequately protects the public health and safety, protects the environment, and promotes the common defense and security.

The outputs of the product lines under this business line contribute to the scoring of the NRC Safety and Security Performance Measures and their contribution to the achievement of its Strategic Outcomes.

CHANGES FROM FY 2012 ENACTED BUDGET

Resources decreased in the Oversight, Rulemaking, and Generic Homeland Security Product Lines because of reductions in agency overhead, realignment of rulemaking resources, and reductions to IT and reclassification of generic homeland security resources within the budget structure.

LICENSING

STRATEGIC GOAL STRATEGIES SUPPORTED BY LICENSING
Safety—develop, maintain, and implement licensing and regulatory programs for fuel facilities, materials, spent fuel management, waste management, uranium recovery, and decommissioning activities.
Security—support Federal response plans that use an approach to the security of nuclear facilities and radioactive material that integrates the efforts of licensees, Federal, State, local, and Tribal authorities.

For fiscal year (FY) 2014, the NRC requests $13.0 million, including 67.7 FTE, for licensing activities. This funding level represents a decrease of $0.4 million when compared with the FY 2012 enacted budget, which does not represent a significant change in workload.

The Licensing Product Line supports completion of approximately 2,300 materials licensing actions (new applications, amendments, renewals, and terminations) in FY 2014. The NRC anticipates that materials licensing receipts will remain level and that the agency will be able to continue implementing the recommendations for enhanced security for licensing. Licensing confirms that requests to use nuclear materials or modify existing uses provide an adequate margin of safety and security consistent with the NRC's rules and regulations to ensure the adequate protection of the public health and safety, to protect the environment, and to promote the common defense and security. Resources also are budgeted over the planning period for legal assistance supporting materials licensing. In FY 2014, the agency supports adjudicatory hearing-related activities and limited appearance sessions for materials licensing proceedings. Legal advice and counsel will support materials licensing and enforcement actions based on new security requirements affecting materials licensees.

OVERSIGHT

STRATEGIC GOAL STRATEGIES SUPPORTED BY OVERSIGHT
Safety—oversee licensee safety performance through inspections, investigations, enforcement, and performance assessment activities.
Security—enhance programs to control the security of radioactive sources and strategic special nuclear materials commensurate with their risk, including enhancement required by the Energy Policy Act of 2005.

For FY 2014, the NRC requests $18.2 million, including 91.1 FTE, for oversight activities. This funding level represents a decrease of $1.2 million, including 8.1 FTE, when compared with the FY 2012 enacted budget. This decrease is because of an agencywide effort to reduce overhead resources through increased efficiency and effectiveness.

The Oversight Product Line activities ensure the continued safe and secure use of nuclear materials. These activities identify significant issues and ensure that licensees take appropriate actions to maintain acceptable levels of safety and security in their operating procedures, performance, and the use of nuclear materials. Oversight includes resources for inspections, event evaluations, allegations, investigations, enforcement, and related activities associated with the management and oversight of nuclear materials.

The workload includes completion of approximately 1,000 routine health and safety inspections in FY 2014, reciprocity and reactive inspections, and a registration and followup inspection program for certain general licensees. Resources will support implementation of the recommendation from the materials working group and the external independent review working group to revise the licensing and inspection infrastructure. The agency will support investigations of wrongdoing, materials-related enforcement actions, oversight of the Alternative Dispute Resolution (ADR) and allegation programs, and external safety culture program activities.

The resources support event and incident evaluation activities, which include the protective measures team emergency response support function and the orphan source activity, and funding for the Nuclear Materials Events Database.

Continued coordination with States on agreements, as authorized by Section 274i of the AEA, and homeland security are planned. These activities include development and distribution of advisories, development and implementation of additional security measures (e.g., development of implementing guidance), and assurance that other homeland security information is provided to authorized State and local Government officials. The agency will continue to develop, coordinate, and assist in the maintenance of Section 274i agreements with States to conduct security inspections on behalf of the NRC for NRC-issued security orders.

RULEMAKING

STRATEGIC GOAL STRATEGIES SUPPORTED BY RULEMAKING
Safety—use sound science and state-of-the-art methods to establish, where appropriate, risk-informed and performance-based regulations.
Security—use a risk-informed approach to implement appropriate regulatory controls for the possession, handling, import, export, and transshipment of radioactive materials.

For FY 2014, the NRC requests $2.4 million, including 12.6 FTE, for rulemaking activities. This funding level represents a decrease of $1.4 million, including 7.7 FTE, when compared with the FY 2012 enacted budget. This decrease is because of a realignment of rulemaking resources to reflect more appropriately the business lines that these resources currently support.

The Rulemaking Product Line will support rulemaking activities, including legal support to maintain the regulatory infrastructure needed to process and handle nuclear materials. Rules, guidance, and regulations promote licensee compliance with underlying safety principles and requirements.

In FY 2014, the NRC will work on approximately 4–6 active materials waste safety rulemakings and on continued interactive liaison with industry and professional societies to develop new codes and consensus standards and to address petitions for rulemaking submitted to the agency. An example of rulemakings determined as high priority are the amendments under Title 10 of the *Code of Federal Regulations* (10 CFR) Part 35, "Medical Use of Byproduct Material." Rulemaking resources systematically improve the NRC's regulatory program to ensure the safe use and management of nuclear materials and resolve safety issues. They also improve the NRC's regulations by adding needed requirements, eliminating unnecessary requirements, and minimizing jurisdictional overlaps. The NRC will continue to work on the highest priority rulemakings.

INTERNATIONAL ACTIVITIES

STRATEGIC GOAL STRATEGIES SUPPORTED BY INTERNATIONAL ACTIVITIES
Safety—use domestic and international collaboration and cooperation to inform decisionmaking.
Security—promote U.S. national security interests and nuclear proliferation policy objectives for NRC-licensed imports and exports of source and special nuclear materials and nuclear equipment.

For FY 2014, the NRC requests $2.5 million, including 13.6 FTE, for international activities. This funding level represents an increase of $0.3 million, including 1.7 FTE, when compared with the FY 2012 enacted budget, which does not represent a significant change in workload.

The International Activities Product Line increases slightly to support NRC reviews and decisions on import and export authorizations of nuclear components and radiological materials, Subsequent Arrangements and Proposed 810 Licenses, control and tracking of imports and exports of sources, and bilateral and multilateral activities initiated for the exchange of technical information for the safe handling, storage, transport, and disposal of nuclear waste. Resources also provide for assistance activities related to the safety and security of medical and industrial sources, support to IAEA missions for training and regulation of nuclear materials, and assistance to foreign regulatory bodies through the assignee program.

The International Activities Product Line provides the way to work with international counterparts to exchange information, expertise, operating experience, and ongoing research to recognize and respond to emerging technical issues and to promote best safety and security practices. The NRC also participates in the development of international standards to ensure that they are soundly based and to determine whether substantial safety and security improvements can be identified and incorporated domestically.

RESEARCH

STRATEGIC GOAL STRATEGIES SUPPORTED BY RESEARCH
Safety—improve the NRC's regulatory programs and apply safety-focused research to anticipate and resolve safety issues.
Security—use research to inform the security activities of the agency.

For FY 2014, the NRC requests $1.4 million, including 3.8 FTE, for research activities. This funding level represents an increase of $0.4 million, including a decrease of 0.3 FTE, when compared with the FY 2012 enacted budget, which does not represent a significant change in workload.

The Research Product Line supports activities to identify, lead, or sponsor reviews that support the resolution of ongoing and future safety issues, including providing tools and expertise to support the NRC's independent decisionmaking process.

The Research Product Line supports research on patient release experience to inform future policy actions. Research will continue on gemstone irradiation and consumer products. In addition, research activities for the medical and industrial sectors will support development and alignment of radiation protection regulations and guidance with the 2007 International Commission on Radiological Protection recommendations.

GENERIC HOMELAND SECURITY

STRATEGIC GOAL STRATEGIES SUPPORTED BY GENERIC HOMELAND SECURITY
Safety—use domestic and international collaboration and cooperation to inform decisionmaking.
Security—promote U.S. national security interests and nuclear proliferation policy objectives for NRC-licensed imports and exports of source and special nuclear materials and nuclear equipment.

For FY 2014, the NRC requests $12.6 million, including 25.6 FTE, for generic homeland security activities. This funding level represents a decrease of $2.8 million, including 8.2 FTE, when compared with the FY 2012 enacted budget. The NRC reviewed the activities under the definitions for the Generic HLS product and shifted some resources to non-Generic HLS products in order to more accurately align resources to the planned workload.

The Generic Homeland Security Product Line supports security coordination and liaison; security rulemaking activities, including legal support for the homeland security regulatory improvements initiatives; control and tracking of imports and exports of sources; homeland security travel funds; and the development and implementation of the ISMP.

The resources are for liaison activities related to security activities that support NRC policy interactions at IAEA and the Nuclear Energy Agency on security and safety issues, consultations on security standards, rulemakings, and intergovernmental coordination. Resources also support high-priority security rulemakings. The resources are also budgeted for the ISMP development that will integrate the three systems (NSTS, WBL, and LVS) that license and track sources and radioactive materials under one management mechanism. This development effort is vital to forming a comprehensive national materials license repository.

The near-term results in FY 2014 will be the first full year of operation of WBL and LVS, and the overall results will be enhanced control and accountability of radioactive materials.

EVENT RESPONSE

STRATEGIC GOAL STRATEGIES SUPPORTED BY EVENT RESPONSE
Safety—effectively respond to events at NRC-licensed facilities and other events of national interest, including maintaining and enhancing the NRC's critical incident response and communication capabilities.
Security—support Federal response plans that use an approach to the security of nuclear facilities and radioactive material that integrates the efforts of licensees and Federal, State, local, and Tribal authorities.

For FY 2014, the NRC requests $0.9 million, including 5.1 FTE, for event response activities. This funding level represents no change in resources or workload when compared with the FY 2012 enacted budget.

The Event Response Product Line provides the means to respond effectively to events that involve nuclear materials, including maintaining and enhancing the NRC's critical event response and communication capabilities. In FY 2014, the budget for the Event Response Product Line remains essentially flat to support event response actions for materials licensees, including the maintenance of a 24/7 response capability for materials-related incidents.

STATE, TRIBAL, AND FEDERAL PROGRAMS

SUPPORTED STRATEGIC GOAL STRATEGIES FOR STATE, TRIBAL, AND FEDERAL PROGRAMS
Safety—continue to support Agreement States in developing, maintaining, and implementing licensing and regulatory programs for materials users.
Security—share security information with appropriate stakeholders and international partners.

For FY 2014, the NRC requests $7.3 million, including 37.7 FTE, for State, Tribal, and Federal programs. This funding level represents an increase of $0.1 million, including 0.4 FTE, when compared with the FY 2012 enacted budget, which does not represent a significant change in workload.

The State, Tribal, and Federal Programs Product Line conducts materials activities related to Agreement States, including oversight, technical assistance, cooperative efforts, and coordination and liaison with States and local Governments, Federal agencies, Native American Tribal Governments, and interstate organizations on policy and notifications of interest for nuclear waste and materials. Together, the NRC and Agreement States regulate more than 22,000 specific and 150,000 general licenses.

Budgetary resources in FY 2014 will support continued implementation of the Agreement State program. Resources provide for conducting materials activities related to Agreement States and liaison, including oversight, technical assistance, cooperative efforts, and enhanced control and security actions for materials licensees. The resources provide support to conduct IMPEP reviews (10–12) to ensure they are adequate to protect public health and safety and are compatible with NRC programs; outreach to potential new Agreement States and process new agreements (1); process Agreement State incidents and events (50); participate in and coordinate State participation in regulatory development; coordinate and fund State participation in NRC training courses, including Agreement State training and travel funds; respond to State technical assistance requests; respond to and coordinate responses to allegations about Agreement State licensees or regulatory programs; interact with the Conference of Radiation Control Program Directors, Inc., and the Organization of Agreement States, Inc.; and develop and maintain policies and procedures for the program. This activity includes the statutory requirement for the NRC to make a determination that all applicable standards and requirements have been met before an Agreement State terminates a uranium milling license, and that alternate 11e.(2) standards are adequate before the Agreement State implements them (1 or 2 cases per year).

The NRC also coordinates with Agreement States on low-level waste (LLW) and decommissioning since all currently operating LLW sites are located in Agreement States. These activities provide public confidence and assurance that the Agreement States are conducting adequate and compatible programs.

This product line provides for the Materials State, Federal, and Tribal Liaison Program that informs, notifies, and coordinates with Governor-appointed representatives, other Federal agencies, and Native American Tribal Governments on matters involving the NRC. This outreach enhances public confidence in the national program and collects input from NRC stakeholders. Consistent with Executive Order 13175, "Consultation and Coordination with Indian Tribal Governments, dated November 6, 2000," the NRC has adopted agency practices that ensure consultation and cooperation with Tribal Governments. For example, the NRC interacts with Native American Tribal Governments on nuclear-related regulatory issues that include uranium recovery licensing and long-term strategies for remediation, reactor licensing and inspection activities, reactor license renewal, and nuclear waste transportation and disposal. The NRC is currently implementing an internal protocol for Government-to-Government interaction with Tribal Governments in response to Commission direction.

SIGNIFICANT ACCOMPLISHMENTS IN FY 2012

The NRC completed 2,104 materials licensing actions and 1,010 routine health and safety inspections. The agency maintained its high standards with timely reviews of nuclear material license renewals and sealed-source and device designs. The agency completed 96 percent of new application and license amendment reviews within 90 days of receipt and 97 percent of license renewal and sealed-source and device design reviews within 180 days of receipt.

The NRC amended its regulations governing the licensing and distribution of byproduct materials to make the regulations clearer, more risk-informed, and up to date. An agency working group continued development of a proposed rule on 10 CFR Part 35. The rule will address the following actions: modifying preceptor attestation requirements; extending grandfathering to certified individuals named in 10 CFR Part 35 before October 25, 2005; naming associate or assistant radiation safety officers on an NRC medical-use license; and likely changing the definition of a medical event, including revised reporting and notifications of medical events for permanent implant brachytherapy. The NRC expects to publish the proposed rule in FY 2013 for public comment.

The NRC continued public outreach on possible changes to the radiation protection regulations in 10 CFR Part 20, "Standards for Protection Against Radiation," which would increase alignment with international radiation protection recommendations. The staff provided the Commission with staff recommendations on the direction to pursue on a series of technical issues. The staff recommended that the Commission approve the staff continuing to expend resources to develop a detailed regulatory basis for proposed rulemaking.

The NRC issued final rules updating 10 CFR Part 110, "Export and Import of Nuclear Equipment and Material," to reflect the nuclear nonproliferation policy of the Executive Branch on U.S. Government obligations to the IAEA and to remove Oman from the list of restricted destinations.

The NRC engaged domestically and internationally in efforts to enhance nuclear safety and security through the regulatory oversight of radioactive sources. The staff participated in numerous meetings of technical and legal experts on the IAEA's Code of Conduct for the Safety and Security of Radioactive Sources, both to ensure that its implementing guidance is clear and accurate and to encourage Member States that have not yet made a political commitment to implement the Code to do so. The agency also worked with other U.S. Government agencies, such as the U.S. Department of State, U.S. Department of Energy, U.S. Department of Commerce, the National Security Council staff, and IAEA to develop international security guidance documents for radioactive sources.

The NSTS, WBL, and the future LVS are key components of a comprehensive program for the security and control of radioactive material (ISMP). The ISMP will provide a link to the Exhibit 300 and will include information on all U.S. licensees and more than 70,000 risk-significant radioactive sources that approximately 1,400 licenses possess. The ISMP will provide licensees, regulators, and Federal agencies with an additional round-the-clock way of determining the legitimacy of individuals possessing or seeking to obtain radioactive material.

OUTPUT MEASURES

LICENSING

Timeliness of Licensing Actions—Review of Application for New Materials Licenses and License Amendments						
	FY 2009	FY 2010	FY 2011	FY 2012	FY 2013	FY 2014
Target	85% ≤ 90 days 100% ≤ 2 years (yr)	90% ≤ 90 days 100% ≤ 2 yr	90% ≤ 90 days 100% ≤ 2 yr	92%<90 days 100%<2 yr	TBD	92% ≤ 90 days 100% ≤ 2 yr
Actual	97% ≤ 90 days 100% ≤ 2 yr	95% ≤ 90 days 100% ≤ 2 yr	97% ≤ 90 days 100% ≤ 2 yr	97% within 90 days; 100% within 2 yr		

Timeliness of Licensing Actions—Review of Applications for Materials License Renewals and Sealed Source and Device Designs						
	FY 2009	FY 2010	FY 2011	FY 2012	FY 2013	FY 2014
Target	80% ≤ 180 days 100% ≤ 2 yr	90% ≤ 180 days 100% ≤ 2 yr	92% ≤ 180 days 100% ≤ 2 yr	92% ≤ 180 days 100% ≤ 2 yr	TBD	92% ≤ 180 days 100% ≤ 2 yr
Actual	91% ≤ 180 days 100% ≤ 2 yr	95% ≤ 180 days 100% ≤ 2 yr	97% ≤ 180 days 100% ≤ 2 yr	98% within 180 days; 100% within 2 yr		

OVERSIGHT

Timeliness of Safety Inspections of Materials Licensees						
	FY 2009	FY 2010	FY 2011	FY 2012	FY 2013	FY 2014
Target	> 98% completed on time	> 98% completed on time	> 98% completed on time	> 98% completed on time	TBD	> 98% completed on time
Actual	99% completed on time	99% completed on time	99% completed on time	99% completed on time		

Timeliness in Completing Reviews For Technical Allegations						
	FY 2009	FY 2010	FY 2011	FY 2012	FY 2013	FY 2014
Target	90% ≤ 150 days 95% ≤ 180 days 100% ≤ 360 days	90% ≤ 150 days 95% ≤ 180 days 100% ≤ 360 days	90% ≤ 150 days 95% ≤ 180 days 100% ≤ 360 days	90% ≤ 150 days 95% ≤ 180 days 100% ≤ 360 days	TBD	90% ≤ 150 days 95% ≤ 180 days 100% ≤ 360 days
Actual	98% ≤ 150 days 100% ≤ 180 days 100% ≤ 360 days	94% ≤ 150 days 98% ≤ 180 days 100% ≤ 360 days	95% ≤ 150 days 100% ≤ 180 days 100% ≤ 360 days	93% ≤ 150 days 98% ≤ 180 days 100% ≤ 360 days		

Timeliness in Completing Enforcement Actions

	FY 2009	FY 2010	FY 2011	FY 2012	FY 2013	FY 2014
Target	Investigation cases: 100% completed within 360 days of OE processing time	Investigation cases: 100% completed within 360 days of OE processing time	Investigation cases: 100% completed within 360 days of OE processing time	Investigation cases: 100% completed within 330 days of OE processing time	TBD	Investigation cases: 100% completed within 330 days of OE processing time
	Noninvestigation cases: 100% completed within 180 days of OE processing time	Noninvestigation cases: 100% completed within 180 days of OE processing time	Noninvestigation cases: 100% completed within 180 days of OE processing time	Noninvestigation cases: 100% completed within 160 days of OE processing time		Noninvestigation cases: 100% completed within 160 days of OE processing time
Actual	Investigation: None ≥ 360 days	Investigation: None ≥ 360 days	Investigation: None ≥ 360 days	Investigation: None ≥ 330days		
	Noninvestigation: None ≥ 180 days	Noninvestigation: None ≥ 180 days	Noninvestigation: None ≥ 180 days	Noninvestigation: None ≥ 180 days		

Timeliness in Completing Investigations—Target 1

	FY 2009	FY 2010	FY 2011	FY 2012	FY 2013	FY 2014
Target	85% of investigations that developed sufficient information to reach a conclusion on wrongdoing will be completed in 10 months or less.	85% of investigations that developed sufficient information to reach a conclusion on wrongdoing will be completed in 9 months or less.	85% of investigations that developed sufficient information to reach a conclusion on wrongdoing will be completed in 9 months or less.	85% of investigations that developed sufficient information to reach a conclusion on wrongdoing will be completed in 9 months or less.	TBD	85% of investigations that developed sufficient information to reach a conclusion on wrongdoing will be completed in 9 months or less.
Actual	Completed 33 investigations; 100% (33) of those that developed sufficient information to reach a conclusion on wrongdoing were completed in 10 months or less.	Completed 18 investigations; 100% (18) of those that developed sufficient information to reach a conclusion on wrongdoing were completed in 9 months or less.	Completed 25 investigations; 88% (22) of those that developed sufficient information to reach a conclusion on wrongdoing were completed in 9 months or less.	Completed 19 investigations; 89% (17) of those that developed sufficient information to reach a conclusion on wrongdoing were completed in 9 months or less.		

Timeliness in Completing Investigations—Target 2

	FY 2009	FY 2010	FY 2011	FY 2012	FY 2013	FY 2014
Target	Close 100% of OI investigations in time to initiate civil or criminal enforcement action.	Close 100% of OI investigations in time to initiate civil or criminal enforcement action.	Close 100% of OI investigations in time to initiate civil or criminal enforcement action.	Close 100% of OI investigations in time to initiate civil or criminal enforcement action.	TBD	Close 100% of OI investigations in time to initiate civil or criminal enforcement action.
Actual	100%	100%	100%	100%		

RULEMAKING

Percentage of Materials and Waste Rulemaking Activities Completed On Schedule						
	FY 2009	FY 2010	FY 2011	FY 2012	FY 2013	FY 2014
Target	90%	90%	90%	90%	TBD	Discontinuing in 2014
Actual	100%	93%	80%*	100 %		

Four out of five rulemaking activities were completed on schedule in FY 2011. The single delayed rule was Requirements for Distribution of Byproduct Material, Parts 30, 31, 32, 40, and 70. Cumulatively, there was not a significant number of rulemaking activities completed to recover from one late submission. In FY 2012, the staff will continue to maintain focus on establishing early alignment among offices on schedule and content.

RESEARCH

Acceptable Technical Quality of Agency Research Technical Products*						
	FY 2009	FY 2010	FY 2011	FY 2012	FY 2013	FY 2014
Target	Combined score ≥3.5	Combined score ≥3.5	Combined score ≥3.5	Combined score ≥3.5	TBD	Combined score ≥ 3.75
Actual	4	4.6	4.4	4.5		

The NRC has developed a process to measure the quality of research products using surveys of endusers to determine the usability and value-added of the products. As appropriate, other mechanisms will be developed and added to this process to measure the quality of research products.

Timeliness of Completing Actions on Critical Research Programs*						
	FY 2009	FY 2010	FY 2011	FY 2012	FY 2013	FY 2014
Target	90% of major milestones met on or before their due date.	90% of major milestones met on or before their due date.	90% of major milestones met on or before their due date.	90% of major milestones met on or before their due date.	TBD	90% of major milestones met on or before their due date.
Actual	100% across programs	100% across programs	100% across programs	NA**		

Critical research programs typically respond to high-priority needs from the Commission and NRC's licensing organizations. Critical research programs on the highest priority needs are identified at the beginning of the fiscal year.

**No critical milestones were associated with the research activities conducted in this business line in FY 2012; therefore, there is no performance data to report.*

SPENT FUEL STORAGE AND TRANSPORTATION

Spent Fuel Storage and Transportation by Product Line (Dollars in Millions)						
	FY 2012 Enacted		FY 2014 Request		Delta FY 2014–FY 2012	
Product Line	$M	FTE	$M	FTE	$M	FTE
Licensing	12.5	59.1	11.5	54.5	(1.0)	(4.6)
Oversight	4.2	25.7	3.7	21.9	(0.6)	(3.8)
Rulemaking	3.9	12.6	8.4	31.4	4.5	18.8
International Activities	0.9	3.8	0.9	4.2	(0.0)	0.4
Research	4.5	20.7	4.5	12.1	(0.1)	(8.7)
Generic HLS	0.2	1.0	0.3	1.9	0.1	0.9
Subtotal	**$26.2**	**122.9**	**$29.2**	**125.9**	**$3.0**	**3.0**
Corporate Support	14.6	32.2	16.2	34.7	1.6	2.6
Total	**$40.8**	**155.1**	**$45.4**	**160.7**	**$4.6**	**5.6**

Numbers may not add due to rounding.

The Spent Fuel Storage and Transportation Business Line activities are conducted to ensure the safe and secure storage of spent fuel to support continued operations and the safe and secure transport of radioactive materials to support domestic and international commerce. Activities in this business line include Licensing, Oversight, Rulemaking, Research, International Activities, and Generic Homeland Security efforts associated with radioactive material transportation and the storage of spent nuclear fuel (SNF).

Resources in this business line support the following:

- Safety, security, and environmental reviews of SNF storage casks and transportation packages, including development and update of regulations and guidance.
- Safety inspections of transportation packages, storage cask vendors and fabricators, independent spent fuel storage installation (ISFSI) operations, and security inspections of SNF ISFSIs, and transportation and route surveys.
- Evaluation of storage and transport of high-burnup fuels (> 45 gigawatt-days/metric ton uranium (GWd/MTU)), computational fluid dynamic methods applied to storage and transport cask design, development of a technical basis to support the allowance of full (fission product and actinides) burnup credit for SNF transportation and storage casks, and benchmarking of structural computer codes using German and Japanese cask testing results.
- Assessment of the regulatory framework for extended storage and transportation (EST) through continued research on technical issues associated with extended dry spent fuel storage and transportation to support a technical basis for decisions on regulatory revisions.

- Security assessment scoping study to identify additional regulatory and technical needs for an EST security framework. Technical areas include concrete degradation; weld corrosion; impacts of high-burnup and mixed-oxide fuels; transportability of fuel after long-term storage; and the need for an improved hazards assessment, including the potential effects of long-term storage on eventual disposal.
- Analysis, data collection, and modeling for future alternate strategies for disposal of SNF and high-level waste to include laboratory studies and field investigations to understand key technical issues and risk insights, technical inputs to resolution of regulatory gaps, exercise of performance assessment scoping tool for risk insights, and continued coordination of alternative disposal strategies with other aspects of the back end of the fuel cycle.
- Development of a proposed security rulemaking supporting the regulatory guidance documents that will apply consistent security standards across a range of waste storage facilities.
- Monitoring national-level developments stemming from the January 2012 report of the Blue Ribbon Commission on America's Nuclear Future.
- Development of an environmental impact statement (EIS) to support a revised Waste Confidence decision. This EIS will address the Court decision to vacate the Waste Confidence decision and rule.
- Assessment of the regulatory framework for extended storage and transportation (EST) through continued research on technical issues associated with extended dry spent fuel storage and transportation to support a technical basis for decisions on regulatory revisions.

CHANGES FROM FY 2012 ENACTED BUDGET

Resources increase within the business line to develop a Waste Confidence generic environmental impact statement and rule. Waste Confidence will address the environmental impacts of spent fuel storage after the operating period of a reactor and prior to ultimate disposal in a permanent repository. The EST work concerns identifying and addressing the technical issues associated with continued, extended storage to ensure that NRC has the regulatory framework to address those issues. The EST work will support the regulations, guidance, and inspection programs needed to ensure the safety and security of EST.

LICENSING

STRATEGIC GOAL STRATEGIES SUPPORTED BY LICENSING

Safety—develop, maintain, and implement licensing and regulatory programs for fuel facilities, materials, spent fuel management, waste management, uranium recovery, and decommissioning activities.
Security—use a risk-informed approach to implement appropriate regulatory controls for the possession, handling, import, export, and transshipment of radioactive materials.

For fiscal year (FY) 2014, the NRC requests $11.5 million, including 54.5 FTE, for licensing activities. This funding request represents a decrease of $1.0 million, including 4.6 FTE, when compared with the FY 2012 enacted budget. This decrease is because of fewer license applications and amendments anticipated and because of the transition of the Storage Transportation Information Management System (STIMS) from development to operations and maintenance. The Licensing Product Line supports safety, security, and environmental licensing activities to confirm licensee requests for radioactive material transportation and interim SNF storage that provides an adequate margin of safety and security consistent with the NRC's rules and regulations. The NRC conducts safety and security reviews of radioactive material transportation package designs; safety and security reviews of SNF storage cask designs and ISFSIs; environmental reviews of ISFSIs; plant-specific security-related licensing reviews; updates to Standard Review Plans; and regulatory infrastructure to ensure that licensed activities are conducted in a manner that adequately protects the public health and safety, protects the environment, and promotes the common defense and security.

Licensing resources provide for the following:

- The review of approximately 72 radioactive material transportation package design applications and approximately 18 SNF storage applications to ensure the safe and secure storage of SNF.
- Technical/regulatory advice regarding proposed changes in the national strategy for the ultimate disposal of SNF.
- The renewal of the Prairie Island ISFSI license and related environmental assessment support and legal advice and representation on SNF and radioactive material transportation matters.
- Transportation certification security reviews, security reviews for onsite storage (licensees under Title 10 of the *Code of Federal Regulations* (10 CFR) Part 70, "Domestic Licensing of Special Nuclear Material"), issuance of ISFSI security orders, and ISFSI security licensing reviews.
- Information technology management and continued maintenance of STIMS and maintenance for the Transportation and Storage Computational Analysis Platform System.

OVERSIGHT

STRATEGIC GOAL STRATEGIES SUPPORTED BY OVERSIGHT
Safety—oversee licensee safety performance through inspections, investigations, enforcement, and performance assessment activities.
Security—use a risk-informed approach to implement appropriate regulatory controls for the possession, handling, import, export, and transshipment of radioactive materials.

For FY 2014, the NRC requests $3.7 million, including 21.9 FTE, for oversight activities. This funding level represents a decrease of $0.6 million, including 3.8 FTE, when compared with the FY 2012 enacted budget. The decrease is due to completion of the inspection improvement initiative and reduced workload projections.

The Oversight Product Line supports NRC activities to continually oversee the safe and secure licensee use of radioactive material transportation packages, SNF storage casks, and ISFSIs; identify significant performance issues; develop generic communications; and ensure that licensees take appropriate actions to maintain acceptable operating performance to ensure the adequate protection of the public health and safety and the environment.

Oversight resources provide for completion of 16 regional and headquarters safety inspections of storage and transportation cask vendors, fabricators, and designers; and ISFSI pad construction, dry-run operations, initial loading operations, and routine operations. Resources provide for the identification and implementation of near-term improvements to the storage and transportation inspection and enforcement programs. Resources also provide for regional security inspection oversight of SNF and wet and dry ISFSI operations. In addition, resources provide for SNF inspection program development, maintenance, update, and route surveys.

RULEMAKING

STRATEGIC GOAL STRATEGIES SUPPORTED BY RULEMAKING
Safety—use sound science and state-of-the-art methods to establish, where appropriate, risk-informed and performance-based regulations.
Security—use a risk-informed approach to implement appropriate regulatory controls for the possession, handling, import, export, and transshipment of radioactive materials.

For FY 2014, the NRC requests $8.4 million, including 31.4 FTE, for Rulemaking activities. This funding level represents an increase of $4.5 million, including an increase of 18.8 FTE, when compared with the FY 2012 enacted budget. This increase reflects the shift of resources from the Research Product Line to support the Waste Confidence Rule. In addition, resources the NRC reviewed the activities under the definitions for the Generic HLS product and shifted some resources to non-Generic HLS products in order to more accurately align resources to the planned workload.

The Rulemaking Product Line supports the development and update of rules and regulatory guidance that promote licensee compliance with underlying safety and security principles and requirements. This regulatory framework guides the safety and security activities of the agency and its licensees. Resources provide for the development of an EIS to support a revised Waste Confidence decision. This EIS will address the Court decision to vacate the Waste Confidence decision and rule.

Resources provide for identification and implementation of near-term improvements to the storage and transportation licensing program, including a comprehensive review of licensing guidance and regulations; an evaluation and integration of dual-purpose cask reviews; an improvement to cask certification rulemaking processes; and the implementation of enhancements to the rules for storage and transportation under 10 CFR Part 71, "Packaging and Transportation of Radioactive Material," and 10 CFR Part 72, "Licensing Requirements for the Independent Storage of Spent Nuclear Fuel, High-Level Radioactive Waste, and Reactor-Related Greater Than Class C Waste."

Resources also support high-priority rulemakings (five certificate of compliance rulemakings and ISFSI security requirements for radiological sabotage).

Further, resources support the proposed security rulemaking and development of supporting regulatory guidance documents. In addition, resources would be used to assess the need for digital and security systems to defend against a cyber attack at standalone ISFSIs and to make necessary changes to the existing regulations through rulemaking or orders.

INTERNATIONAL ACTIVITIES

STRATEGIC GOAL STRATEGIES SUPPORTED BY INTERNATIONAL ACTIVITIES
Safety—use domestic and international collaboration and cooperation to inform decisionmaking.
Security—use a risk-informed approach to implement appropriate regulatory controls for the possession, handling, import, export, and transshipment of radioactive materials.

For FY 2014, the NRC requests $0.9 million, including 4.2 FTE, for international activities. This request represents an increase of 0.4 FTE when compared with the FY 2012 enacted budget, which does not represent a significant change in workload.

The International Activities Product Line supports the NRC's international work, which assists decisionmaking; awareness of, and responses to, emerging technical issues; and promotion of best practices in realizing the Safety and Security goals and related strategic measures and outcomes. Additionally, the NRC participates in the development and evaluation of international standards to ensure that they are soundly based and to determine whether they should be implemented domestically.

Resources provide for international coordination with the International Atomic Energy Agency to compare regulatory frameworks, share research on storage and transport matters, and harmonize the certification of SNF transport packages and the licensing of storage cask designs with international standards. Resources are also provided for investigation and participation in select international activities, experiments, and collaboration in dealing with regulatory, technical, and legal aspects of waste disposal.

RESEARCH

STRATEGIC GOAL STRATEGIES SUPPORTED BY RESEARCH
Safety—improve the NRC's regulatory programs and apply safety-focused research to anticipate and resolve safety issues.
Security—use research to inform the security activities of the agency.

For FY 2014, the NRC requests $4.5 million, including 12.2 FTE, for research activities. This funding level represents a funding decrease of $0.1 million, including 8.7 FTE, when compared with the FY 2012 enacted budget. This decrease is the result of the completion of research related to high-burnup fuel cladding integrity performance. This was offset by new work in security assessments. Further, resources decrease to reflect the shift of resources to the Rulemaking Product Line to support the Waste Confidence Rule while maintaining the technical basis for EST.

The Research Product Line supports the NRC's regulatory mission by providing technical advice, tools, and information to identify and resolve safety issues and to make regulatory decisions. This includes the conduct of confirmatory experiments and analyses and preparation of the agency for the future through evaluation of the safety aspects of new technologies and designs for radioactive material transportation packages and spent fuel storage casks and ISFSIs; research on technical issues associated with extended and long-term storage; and analysis and modeling for future waste management strategies.

Further, resources provide for participation in a U.S. cask demonstration and monitoring program of extended dry cask storage with high-burnup fuel and performance of a security assessment scoping study to identify additional regulatory and technical needs for a EST security framework. Technical areas include concrete degradation; weld and canister corrosion; impacts of high-burnup and mixed-oxide fuels; transportability of fuel after long-term storage; and the need for an improved hazards assessment, including the potential impacts of long-term storage on eventual disposal.

GENERIC HOMELAND SECURITY

STRATEGIC GOAL STRATEGIES SUPPORTED BY GENERIC HOMELAND SECURITY
Safety—conduct NRC safety, security, and emergency preparedness programs in an integrated manner.
Security—support Federal response plans that use an approach to the security of nuclear facilities and
radioactive material that integrates the efforts of licensees and Federal, State, local, and Tribal authorities.

For FY 2014, the NRC requests $0.3 million, including 1.9 FTE, for generic homeland security activities. This funding level represents an increase of $0.1 million, including 0.9 FTE, when compared with the FY 2012 enacted budget. The NRC reviewed the activities under the definitions for the Generic HLS product and shifted some resources to non-Generic HLS products in order to more accurately align resources to the planned workload.

The Generic Homeland Security (HLS) Product Line supports security activities related to intergovernmental coordination and communication. It also supports security activities that are not plant-specific, or associated with a class of licensees, which contribute to the common defense and security of the Nation's critical infrastructure.

Resources provide for ongoing security activities in response to the events of September 11, 2001. This encompasses Generic HLS improvements to address new threats and also includes developing interagency agreements and working arrangements with other Federal agencies on issues related to safety, security, and emergency response.

SIGNIFICANT ACCOMPLISHMENTS IN FY 2012

The NRC completed 52 transport package designs and 17 storage cask and facility license reviews. The review of transportation and interim storage licensing requests ensures that shipments are made in NRC-approved packages that meet rigorous performance requirements and verifies that spent fuel is safely stored, thereby enabling continued reactor and decommissioning operations. The agency also conducted 19 inspections of activities related to radioactive material package certificate holders, spent fuel storage cask certificate holders, and inspections at ISFSI to ensure that casks are being designed, fabricated, and used according to approved safety requirements.

The agency developed a plan for integrating SNF regulatory activities to address more effectively the regulatory and licensing aspects of extended storage and transportation (i.e., greater than 120 years), reprocessing, and disposal of SNF and high-level waste. The purpose of the plan is to ensure that the regulation of the back end of the fuel cycle accomplishes safety, security, and environmental protection in an efficient and effective manner and that decisions made about one component or area of this system adequately consider other components or areas (i.e., treating spent fuel and high-level waste regulation as a system of interrelated activities). By coordinating the approach for regulation of SNF or high-level waste storage, potential reprocessing, transportation, and disposal, the agency can improve the efficiency and effectiveness of NRC regulatory processes and provide stability and predictability to stakeholders in a dynamic environment.

The Commission approved a final rule amending the security requirements for irradiated fuel in transit in 10 CFR Part 73, "Physical Protection of Plants and Materials." This rule establishes generically applicable security requirements similar to the requirements that NRC Order EA-02-109, "Issuance of Order for Interim Safeguards and Security Compensatory Measures for the Transportation of Spent Nuclear Fuel Greater than 100 Grams," currently imposes. This rule also establishes acceptable performance standards and objectives for the protection of SNF shipments from theft, diversion, or radiological sabotage. Additionally, this rule addresses, in part, a 1999 petition for rulemaking from the State of Nevada (PRM-73-10) that asked the NRC to strengthen its regulations governing the security of SNF shipments against malevolent acts.

The NRC also began a comprehensive review of the spent fuel storage and transportation regulatory programs to evaluate their adequacy for ensuring safe and secure storage of spent fuel for extended periods beyond 120 years, including research to enhance the regulatory framework in support of extended periods.

The NRC provided resources to continue research on technical issues associated with very long-term dry spent fuel storage, such as concrete degradation, weld corrosion; impacts of high-burnup and mixed-oxide fuels; climate change effects on cask performance; transportability of fuel after long-term storage; and the need for an improved hazards assessment, including the potential impact of long-term storage on eventual disposal.

The NRC staff continued research efforts to address the safe long-term storage of SNF. The technical bases for extended storage and transportation are being strengthened to ensure that environmental effects and material property changes do not affect the safety of licensed dry cask storage systems. In May 2012, the NRC was on the U.S. Government delegation to the Review Meeting of Contracting Parties to the Joint Convention on the Safety of Spent Fuel Management and the Safety of Radioactive Waste Management. In May 2012, the NRC also supported the U.S. Government delegation to the Preparatory Committee for the Nuclear Non-Proliferation Treaty.

In September 2012, in response to a court decision vacating the NRC's 2010 Waste Confidence Decision, the Commission directed the staff to proceed with the development of a generic EIS to support an updated Waste Confidence Decision and temporary storage rule. Because of the high priority of the issue, the Commission directed the staff to publish a final rule and EIS within 24 months.

OUTPUT MEASURES

LICENSING

Complete Storage Container and Installation Design Reviews within Timeliness Goals						
	FY 2009	FY 2010	FY 2011	FY 2012	FY 2013	FY 2014
Target	80% ≤ 12.6 months (mo) 100% ≤ 2 years (yr)*	80% ≤ 12.6 mo 100% ≤ 2 yr	80% ≤ 12.6 mo 100% ≤ 2 yr	80% < 12.6 mo 100% < 2 yr	TBD	80% < 12.6 mo 100% < 2 yr
Actual	82% ≤ 12.6 mo 100% ≤ 2 yr	92% ≤ 12.6 mo 100% ≤ 2 yr	100% ≤ 12.6 mo 100% ≤ 2 yr	71% ≤ 12.6 mo 100% ≤ 2 yr**		

*Output targets for FY 2009 and beyond are being held at the FY 2007 metric to reflect the changing profile of the casework, based on the increased technical complexity and applicants "bundling" of multiple requests in a single application, and updated labor rates for the current mix of casework.

**There were four requests for security exemptions at decommissioned ISFSI sites to address security requirements meant for operating reactors under 10 CFR 73.55, "Requirements for Physical Protection of Licensed Activities in Nuclear Power Reactors against Radiological Sabotage." The multipart exemption requests were large and very complex, requiring consensus among multiple offices. The final two were completed in the fourth quarter with timeliness at approximately 20 months.

Complete Transportation Container Design Reviews within Timeliness Goals						
	FY 2009	FY 2010	FY 2011	FY 2012	FY 2013	FY 2014
Target	80% ≤ 7.4 mo 100% ≤ 2 yr*	80% ≤ 7.4 mo 100% ≤ 2 yr	80% ≤ 7.4 mo 100% ≤ 2 yr	80% < 7.4 mo 100% < 2 yr	TBD	80% <7.4 mo 100% < 2 yr
Actual	86% ≤ 7.4 mo 100% ≤ 2 yr	87% ≤ 7.4 mo 100% ≤ 2 yr	100% ≤ 7.4 mo 100% ≤ 2 yr	96% ≤ 7.4 mo 100% ≤ 2yr		

*Output targets for FY 2009 and beyond are being held at the FY 2007 metric to reflect the changing profile of the casework, based on the increased technical complexity and applicants "bundling" of multiple requests in a single application, and updated labor rates for the current mix of casework. The labor rates were updated based on historical expenditures during FY 2006 and FY 2007.

Using Intraagency Contracting						
	FY 2009	FY 2010	FY 2011	FY 2012	FY 2013	FY 2014
Target	New measure in FY 2013				TBD	Projected savings of $40,000 (50% savings)
Actual						

Waste Confidence and Extended Long-Term Storage Activities—Percent of Planned Products Completed within a Fiscal Year						
	FY 2009	FY 2010	FY 2011	FY 2012	FY 2013	FY 2014
Target	New measure in FY 2013				TBD	Discontinued in FY 2014
Actual						

OVERSIGHT

Number of Spent Fuel Storage and Transportation Inspections Completed						
	FY 2009	FY 2010	FY 2011	FY 2012	FY 2013	FY 2014
Target	16 inspections	16 inspections	16 inspections	16 inspections	TBD	16 inspections
Actual	17 inspections	20 inspections	19 inspections	19 Inspections		

RESEARCH

Timeliness of Completing Actions on Critical Research Programs*						
	FY 2009	FY 2010	FY 2011	FY 2012	FY 2013	FY 2014
Target	90% of major milestones met on or before their due date.	90% of major milestones met on or before their due date.	90% of major milestones met on or before their due date.	90% of major milestones met on or before their due date.	TBD	90% of major milestones met on or before their due date.
Actual	100% across programs	100% across programs	100% across programs	NA**		

*Critical research programs typically respond to high-priority needs from the Commission and the NRC's licensing organizations. Critical research programs on the highest priority needs are identified at the beginning of the fiscal year.

**No critical milestones were associated with the research activities conducted in this business line in FY 2012; therefore, there are no performance data to report.

Acceptable Technical Quality of Agency Research Technical Products*						
	FY 2009	FY 2010	FY 2011	FY 2012	FY 2013	FY 2014
Target	Combined score ≥ 3.5	Combined score ≥ 3.5	Combined score ≥ 3.5	Combined score ≥ 3.5	TBD	Combined score ≥ 3.75
Actual	4	4.6	4.75	4.5		

*The NRC has developed a process to measure the quality of research products using surveys of endusers to determine the usability and value-added of the products. As appropriate, other mechanisms will be developed and added to this process to measure the quality of research products.

DECOMMISSIONING AND LOW-LEVEL WASTE

	FY 2012 Enacted		FY 2014 Request		Delta FY 2014–FY 2012	
Decommissioning and Low-Level Waste by Product Line (Dollars in Millions)						
Product Line	$M	FTE	$M	FTE	$M	FTE
Licensing	16.4	72.3	17.0	72.0	0.6	(0.3)
Oversight	4.6	26.3	5.2	26.8	0.6	0.5
Rulemaking	1.2	4.0	1.4	5.8	0.2	1.9
International Activities	1.0	5.1	0.9	5.0	(0.0)	(0.2)
Research	0.8	5.2	0.4	2.5	(0.4)	(2.7)
Subtotal	**$24.0**	**112.9**	**$25.0**	**112.1**	**$1.0**	**(0.8)**
Corporate Support	13.3	29.3	14.0	30.0	0.7	0.8
Total	**$37.3**	**142.1**	**$39.0**	**142.1**	**$1.8**	**(0.0)**

Numbers may not add due to rounding.

Decommissioning and Low-Level Waste (LLW) activities include licensing and oversight of licensed and unlicensed facilities undergoing decommissioning, licensing and oversight of new and operating uranium recovery facilities, oversight of the national LLW management program, and consultation and monitoring related to the U.S. Department of Energy (DOE) waste management activities at the Savannah River and Idaho Waste Incidental to Reprocessing (WIR) facilities consistent with the U.S. Nuclear Regulatory Commission's (NRC's) responsibilities in the Ronald W. Reagan National Defense Authorization Act for Fiscal Year 2005. This Act requires DOE to consult with the NRC on its WIR determinations for facilities in South Carolina and Idaho. It also requires the NRC to monitor those sites after DOE has completed waste determinations. Activities include interfacing with licensees, applicants, Federal and State agencies, the public, other stakeholders, and Native American Tribal Governments.

Decommissioning is the safe removal of a nuclear facility from service and the reduction of residual radioactivity to a level that permits release of the property and termination of the NRC license. NRC rules for decommissioning establish site-release criteria and unrestricted and—under certain conditions—restricted release of a site. The NRC regulates the decommissioning of complex materials and fuel cycle facilities, power and early test reactors, research and test reactors (RTRs), and uranium recovery facilities, with the ultimate goal of license termination.

The NRC performs project management, financial, policy, technical, safety, security, and environmental reviews for decommissioning power and early demonstration reactors, RTRs, complex materials facilities, and uranium recovery facilities and reviews for licensing new and operational uranium recovery facilities. In addition, the NRC develops guidance and import and export reviews of nuclear waste and performs research activities that include the development and improvement of data, models, and other analytical tools for assessing the environmental effects of releases from NRC-licensed facilities.

The NRC has organized Decommissioning and LLW activities into product lines that best support Safety and Security strategies and that affect strategic outcomes as they relate to decommissioning and LLW activities, uranium recovery licensing, inspection, and related environmental activities. The resources requested support the following five product lines: Licensing, Oversight, Rulemaking, Research, and International Activities.

The outputs of the product lines under this business line contribute to the scoring of the NRC Safety and Security Performance Measures and their contribution to the achievement of its Strategic Outcomes.

CHANGES FROM FY 2012 ENACTED BUDGET

Resources increase slightly to support licensing casework related to decommissioning activities and to address environmental reviews, as well as the associated legal advice and representation and Atomic Safety and Licensing Board activities.

LICENSING

STRATEGIC GOAL STRATEGIES SUPPORTED BY LICENSING
Safety—oversee the decontamination and decommissioning of nuclear facilities in license termination and license new facilities as applications are submitted.
Security—review security plans for decommissioning for consistency with security requirements.

For fiscal year (FY) 2014, the NRC requests $17.0 million, including 72.0 FTE, to support licensing activities. This funding level represents an increase of $0.6 million, including a decrease 0.3 FTE, when compared with the FY 2012 enacted budget, which does not represent a significant change in workload.

The Licensing Product Line supports reviews of requests to terminate a license through a decommissioning process, licensing of operational and new uranium recovery and LLW disposal sites, and supporting Agreement State licensing. Licensing supports project management, financial, policy, technical, safety, security, environmental reviews, and other licensing activities that support operational uranium recovery facilities. It also supports the decommissioning power and early demonstration reactors, RTRs, complex materials sites, and inactive uranium recovery facilities. Resources support interfaces with NRC licensees, applicants, Federal and State agencies, the public, other stakeholders, and Tribal Governments, in addition to legal advice and representation and Licensing Board activities.

The resources for decommissioning support reviews for 14 power and early demonstration reactors, 7 research and test reactors, 23 decommissioning complex materials facilities, 38 decommissioning uranium recovery facilities, and military sites with possession-only licenses. These activities include reviews of license applications and termination plans, decommissioning plans, reclamation plans, long-term surveillance plans, and license amendments. Complex environmental reviews for decommissioning cases and for licensing actions also will be performed.

The agency will perform safety reviews, environmental reviews, and project management for uranium recovery licensing. FY 2014 resources will support eight environmental and eight safety reviews (hearings included) of applications and licensing activities associated with 11 operating uranium recovery facilities. The resources also support legal advice and representation and Licensing Board activities for activities related to decommissioning power reactors and complex materials sites, uranium recovery licensing, adjudications, LLW, and WIR activities.

OVERSIGHT

STRATEGIC GOAL STRATEGIES SUPPORTED BY OVERSIGHT
Safety—develop, maintain, and implement licensing and regulatory programs for fuel facilities material, spent fuel management, waste management, uranium recovery, and decommissioning.
Security—review security plans and changes for consistency with security requirements.

For FY 2014, the NRC requests $5.2 million, including 26.8 FTE, for oversight activities. This funding level represents an increase of $0.6 million, including 0.5 FTE, when compared with the FY 2012 enacted budget, which does not represent a significant change in workload.

The Oversight Product Line supports the NRC in continuously overseeing decommissioning and LLW activities to ensure that licensees continue to maintain acceptable safe and secure practices. In FY 2014, resources provide for decommissioning and uranium recovery inspections, LLW program activities, and WIR activities at two DOE sites.

Budgetary resources remain level to perform decommissioning and uranium recovery inspections to ensure that these operations are conducted safely and in accordance with NRC regulations; and to oversee LLW program activities, which include updating storage inspection procedures, support of Greater than Class C activities, and support to Agreement States.

RULEMAKING

STRATEGIC GOAL STRATEGIES SUPPORTED BY RULEMAKING
Safety—use sound science and state-of-the-art methods to establish, where appropriate, risk-informed and performance-based regulations.
Security—use a risk-informed approach to implement appropriate regulatory controls.

For FY 2014, the NRC requests $1.4 million, including 5.8 FTE, for rulemaking activities. This funding level represents an increase of $0.2 million, including 1.9 FTE, when compared with the FY 2012 enacted budget, which does not represent a significant change in workload.

The Rulemaking Product Line supports the NRC goal of maintaining a safety and security framework of rules, regulatory guidance, and Standard Review Plans that promote licensee compliance with underlying safety principles and security requirements.

INTERNATIONAL ACTIVITIES

STRATEGIC GOAL STRATEGIES SUPPORTED BY INTERNATIONAL ACTIVITIES
Safety—use domestic and international operating experience to inform decisionmaking.
Security—use a risk-informed approach to implement appropriate regulatory controls for the possession, handling, import, export, and transshipment of radioactive materials.

For FY 2014, the NRC requests $0.9 million, including 5.0 FTE, for international activities. This funding level represents a decrease of 0.2 FTE, when compared with the FY 2012 enacted budget, which does not represent a significant change in workload.

The International Activities Product Line supports activities with international counterparts to exchange information, expertise, operating experiences, and ongoing research to recognize and respond to emerging technical issues and to promote best safety and security practices. The NRC also participates in developing international standards to ensure that they are soundly based and to determine whether substantial safety improvements can be identified and incorporated domestically. Resources provide support for international activities and bilateral assistance to foreign counterparts on decommissioning issues, licensing of uranium recovery facilities, and development of regulations for the handling and disposal of LLW and decommissioning of power reactors and other nuclear facilities.

Resources provide assistance to the International Atomic Energy Agency (IAEA), the Nuclear Energy Agency, IAEA's Waste Safety Standards Committee, the Joint Convention on the Safety of Spent Fuel Management and on the Safety of Radioactive Waste Management, and many other working groups and committees for preparing and updating of safety guides and standards. In addition, resources provide for staff assistance to the foreign assignee program and for bilateral and multilateral exchanges of technical information.

RESEARCH

STRATEGIC GOAL STRATEGIES SUPPORTED BY RESEARCH
Safety—improve the NRC's regulatory programs and apply safety-focused research to anticipate and resolve safety issues.
Security—use research to inform the security activities of the agency.

For FY 2014, the NRC requests $0.4 million, including 2.5 FTE, for research activities. This funding level represents a decrease of $0.4 million, including 2.7 FTE, when compared with the FY 2012 enacted budget, which does not represent a significant change in workload.

The Research Product Line supports activities to identify, lead, and sponsor reviews that support the resolution of ongoing and future safety issues, including providing tools and expertise needed to support the NRC's independent decision-making process. The FY 2014 budget allocates resources to provide analytical assistance on complex licensing cases, such as application of codes for decommissioning reviews and site cleanup at sites with uranium contamination and in situ uranium recovery facilities.

SIGNIFICANT ACCOMPLISHMENTS IN FY 2012

The NRC has completed decommissioning at 21 materials sites and 9 power or research reactors for a total of 30 sites since 2006. The agency oversaw decommissioning activities at approximately 85 power and early demonstration reactors, RTRs, uranium recovery sites, complex materials sites, and fuel cycle facilities. Additionally, the NRC published a final rule amending its regulations to improve decommissioning planning, thereby reducing the likelihood that a current operating facility will become a legacy site. The agency continued its activities at military sites with radium-226 and Army sites with depleted uranium contamination from military munitions. The agency continued its emphasis on the oversight decommissioning of legacy uranium recovery sites and began several initiatives to improve the program, including updating guidance and enhancing communication with DOE, States, Native American Tribes, and stakeholders.

The NRC conducted regulatory oversight at eight operational uranium recovery sites and reviewed and approved, if regulations were met, the applications for new, restarting, or expanding uranium recovery facilities. The agency had seven applications for new, restarting, or expanding uranium recovery facilities and had two license renewal applications in-house. The agency worked on seven of those applications because two of the applications were withdrawn. These reviews included both safety and environmental reviews.

The NRC conducted regulatory activities to help ensure the safe management and disposal of low-level radioactive waste generated by radioactive material users, nuclear power plants, and other NRC licensees. The agency performed monitoring visits and issued reports for the DOE's Savannah River Site (SRS) Saltstone facility and the Idaho National Laboratory. The agency completed consultation on the waste determination for the F Tank Farm at the SRS. In addition, the agency also conducted outreach with stakeholders and licensees on issues related to issuing guidance on how to classify waste for disposal and potential draft rule language for a proposed change to Title 10 of the *Code of Federal Regulations* (10 CFR) Part 61, "Licensing Requirements for Land Disposal of Radioactive Waste," for site evaluation before receiving long-lived or blended wastes.

The NRC held the third in a series of uranium recovery workshops for international counterparts through its international assistance program activities in Tanzania. Regulatory bodies from 16 African countries were represented. The focus of the workshop was to assist countries that are initiating or restarting uranium recovery regulatory programs. The overall goal of the workshop was to provide information on regulatory development, licensing, regulatory oversight, and prevention of legacy sites when uranium production ceases.

OUTPUT MEASURES

LICENSING

Support Program Licensing Activities by Reviewing Environmental Reports and Preparing Environmental Review Documents						
	FY 2009	FY 2010	FY 2011	FY 2012	FY 2013	FY 2014
Target	Complete 1 final EIS or draft EIS.* Complete 3 complex EAs.	Complete 2 draft EIS.* Complete 2 complex EAs.	Complete environmental reviews consistent with the Environmental Protection and Performance Assessment Operating Plan.	Complete environmental reviews consistent with the Environmental Protection and Performance Assessment Operating Plan.	TBD	Complete environmental reviews consistent with the Environmental Protection and Performance Assessment Operating Plan.
Actual	Completed GEIS for uranium recovery. Three complex EAs were completed for Areva, Global Nuclear Fuel-Americas, and Oconee.	Completed draft EISs for AREVA, Eagle Rock, and GE-Silex license applications. Completed the final supplemental EIS for the Moore Ranch ISR license application. Completed one complex EA for the Prairie Island ISFSI license amendment.	Completed final supplemental EISs for the Nichols Ranch and Lost Creek ISR license applications. Completed final EIS for AREVA, Eagle Rock Enrichment Facility license application. Issued draft complex EA for Nuclear Fuel Service license renewal application for public review and comment. Completed complex EA supplement for the Pa'ina Hawaii, LLC, Underwater irradiator license application.	Issued final EIS for proposed GE-Hitachi Global Laser Enrichment, LLC, Facility. Issued both draft and final EIS for proposed International Isotopes deconversion facility. Issued final complex EA for proposed Nuclear Fuel Service License Renewal and issued final EA for proposed Calvert Cliffs ISFSI license renewal.		

Within 45 days of acceptance of application and environmental report, publish notice of intent to prepare the environmental impact statement (EIS) and proposed schedule in the Federal Register.

Eliminate the Need for Some Site-Specific Environmental Impact Statements (i.e., by Reducing Resource Needs) by Developing a Generic Environmental Impact Statement (GEIS) for Uranium Recovery Environmental Reviews*						
	FY 2009	FY 2010	FY 2011	FY 2012	FY 2013	FY 2014
Target	Projected savings of $1,040 K and 1 FTE	Projected Savings of $1,100 K and 4 FTE	Projected savings of $450 K and 0.7 FTE	Projected savings of $450 K and 0.7 FTE	TBD	Being replaced by new efficiency measure.
Actual	$2.2 million and 0.6 FTE	$1.2 million and 0 FTE**	$773 K and 0 FTE**	$773 K and 0.7 FTE		

Between FY 2008 and FY 2013, the staff expects to receive 18 in situ recovery (ISR) uranium recovery license applications. The development of a GEIS is expected to eliminate the need to develop site-specific EISs for some of these applications. Instead of developing a site-specific EIS for each site, the staff will be able to "tier off" the GEIS and rely on a less resource-intensive supplemental EIS or a site-specific supplemental EIS to evaluate the environmental impacts of the site-specific ISR license request (total savings of at least $2.0 million and 7.0 FTE in FY 2008–FY 2011 and beyond.) The final GEIS was issued in June 2009 on schedule.

**The target was not met because of a decrease in the actual number of reviews and because of increasing stakeholder involvement.*

	FY 2009	FY 2010	FY 2011	FY 2012	FY 2013	FY 2014
	Clean Up Complex Material Sites, Fuel Cycle Sites, Power Reactors, and Research and Test Reactors and Complete Uranium Recovery License Reviews					
Target	Complete decommissioning and uranium recovery licensing actions as scheduled in the Decommissioning Operating Plan.	Complete licensing actions consistent with the Decommissioning Operating Plan.	Complete licensing actions consistent with the Decommissioning Operating Plan.	Complete licensing actions as scheduled in the Decommissioning Operating Plan.	TBD	Complete licensing actions as scheduled in the Decommissioning Operating Plan.
Actual	Completed decommissioning at 1site. Completed final rule for preventing future legacy sites.	Consistent with the Decommissioning Operating Plan, completed 15 financial assurance reviews. Completed 55 licensing actions related to decommissioning and operating facilities.	Completed 29 financial assurance reviews. Completed 25 licensing actions related to decommissioning and operating facilities.	Completed decommissioning at 4 sites (3 Research Reactors and 1 complex materials site). Completed 52 regulatory licensing actions, including 41 financial assurance reviews, and completed 2 uranium recovery presubmission reviews.		

OVERSIGHT

Provide Support to DOE for WIR Activities					
	FY 2009	FY 2010	FY 2011	FY 2012	FY 2013	FY 2014
Target	Complete WIR review or monitoring plan/activities as scheduled in the Environmental Protection and Performance Assessment Operating Plan.	Complete WIR review or monitoring plan/activities as scheduled in the Environmental Protection and Performance Assessment Operating Plan.	Complete WIR review and monitoring plan activities as scheduled in the Environmental Protection and Performance Assessment Operating Plan.	Complete WIR review and monitoring plan activities as scheduled in the Environmental Protection and Performance Assessment Operating Plan.	TBD	Complete WIR review or monitoring plan/activities as scheduled in the Environmental Protection and Performance Assessment Operating Plan.
Actual	Completed 3 WIR monitoring visits and reviewed 11 technical reports related to the Savannah River site's Saltstone Disposal Facility.	Completed 3 monitoring visits and issued a request for additional information on the revised performance assessment for the Savannah River site's Saltstone Disposal Facility. Completed 1 monitoring visit for Idaho National Laboratory.	Completed 2 monitoring visits and issued a second request for additional information for the Savannah River site's Saltstone Disposal Facility. Issued a request for additional information and technical evaluation report for the Savannah River site's F-Tank Farm. Issued a request for additional information, a waste determination, and technical evaluation report for the West Valley Melter Feed Tanks.	Completed 4 WIR monitoring visits at 3 sites, issued technical evaluation reports for both the Savannah River site's Saltstone Disposal Facility revised performance assessment and the F-Tank Farm draft waste determination, and issued the technical evaluation report on the West Valley Melter Feed Tanks draft waste determination.		

RESEARCH

Timeliness of Completing Actions on Critical Research Programs*					
	FY 2009	FY 2010	FY 2011	FY 2012	FY 2013	FY 2014
Target	90% of major milestones met on or before their due date.	90% of major milestones met on or before their due date.	90% of major milestones met on or before their due date.	90% of major milestones met on or before their due date.	TBD	90% of major milestones met on or before their due date.
Actual	100% across programs	100% across programs	NA**	100% across programs		

*Critical research programs typically respond to high-priority needs from the Commission and the NRC's licensing organizations. Critical research programs on the highest priority needs are identified at the beginning of the fiscal year.

**No critical milestones were associated with the research activities conducted in this business line in FY 2012; therefore, there are no performance data to report.

Acceptable Technical Quality of Agency Research Technical Products*						
	FY 2009	FY 2010	FY 2011	FY 2012	FY 2013	FY 2014
Target	Combined score ≥ 3.5	Combined score ≥ 3.5	Combined score ≥ 3.5	Combined score ≥ 3.5	TBD	Combined score ≥ 3.75
Actual	4	4.6	NA**	4.5		

*The NRC has developed a process to measure the quality of research products using surveys of endusers to determine the usability and value-added of the products. As appropriate, other mechanisms will be developed and added to this process to measure the quality of research products.

**No research products were produced for this business line during FY 2011.

INTERNATIONAL ACTIVITIES

Provide Support to IAEA Waste Safety Standards Committee Reviews, Consultancies/Expert Missions, Joint Convention, and Nuclear Energy Agency Support*						
	FY 2009	FY 2010	FY 2011	FY 2012	FY 2013	FY 2014
Target	New measure in FY 2012			Complete actions as scheduled in the Decommissioning and Environmental Protection and Performance Assessment Operating Plans.	TBD	Discontinued in FY 2014*
Actual				(a) Two Waste Safety Standards Committee meetings for 20 documents, (b) OEDO for two Commission on Safety Standards meetings for eight documents, (c) 10 IAEA consultancies/expert missions, (d) Led NRC effort on Joint Convention, including being a Group Chair, (e) One Plenary and 10 working group Nuclear Energy Agency/Working Party on Decommissioning and Dismantling meetings.		

*Staff is proposing to discontinue this measure in FY 2014. It only minimally meets the Office of the Chief Financial Officer threshold of 4 FTE or $500 K at the Product Line and is not supported by the Office of International Programs.

Performance Measurement

PERFORMANCE MEASUREMENT

The U.S. Nuclear Regulatory Commission's (NRC's) Updated Strategic Plan for fiscal years (FYs) 2008–2013 describes the agency's mission and establishes the Commission's direction by defining its goals, strategic outcomes, and implementation strategies and programs that support these implementation strategies. The plan's goal structure ensures a focus on outcomes. The FY 2014 Congressional Budget Justification uses the Strategic Plan structure to align resources and show a clear link between programs and the agency's goals.

Measuring and monitoring performance is one of the four components of the NRC's Planning, Budgeting, and Performance Management (PBPM) process. The other components are setting the strategic direction, determining planned activities and resources, measuring and monitoring performance, and assessing performance.

The components of the PBPM process are closely linked and complementary, reflecting a continuous cycle of performance management centered on outcomes. This document integrates the agency's PBPM functions by aligning resources with the agency's goals and by establishing performance measures to enable periodic measurement and monitoring of program execution. Annual performance assessments are used to analyze performance and seek improvements in effectiveness and efficiency.

RELATING GOALS TO RESOURCES

The NRC has implemented the PBPM process to accomplish performance budgeting, performance measuring and monitoring, and performance assessments within the agency. The performance budget integrates the agency's PBPM functions by aligning resources with the agency's goals and by establishing performance measures to enable measurement and monitoring of program execution. The business line descriptions in this document identify how each business line contributes to the strategic goals of Safety or Security.

The agency has aligned its budget and accounting structures. This enables the NRC to use cost and other financial data together to evaluate agency program performance. The integration of financial, budget, and performance data provides managers the kind of information that can be used to drive improved agency performance.

The NRC identifies which activities under the agency's two major program areas support the NRC's outcome-based performance measures and uses these as guides to formulate the budget. Specifically, the agency develops program considerations and priorities that identify key external factors and internal influences that would significantly affect the NRC's work activities and resource requirements. For each major activity, the NRC identifies the products needed to achieve the outcome-based performance measures, taking into consideration the program considerations and priorities. The NRC also identifies and prioritizes products needed based on their contribution to goals. Lastly, the NRC determines the resource requirements needed to achieve each product, forming the basis for developing the agency's budget for each program area. Each of the NRC's performance budget review levels takes into consideration those factors described above in relating outcome-based performance measures and output-based measures to resources in making budget recommendations and decisions.

GOALS

The table below shows the alignment of the NRC's fully costed Nuclear Reactor Safety Program and Nuclear Materials and Waste Safety Program with the Safety and Security goals. The full cost includes an allocation of the agency's infrastructure and support costs to specific programs.

	Alignment of Resources to NRC Goals (Dollars in Millions) (Excludes Office of the Inspector General)					
	FY 2012 Enacted			FY 2014 Request		
Major Programs	Safety	Security	Total	Safety	Security	Total
Nuclear Reactor Safety	755.2	45.0	800.1	770.0	42.3	812.4
Nuclear Materials and Waste Safety	193.6	19.6	227.1	200.7	18.2	231.5
Total	$948.8	$64.6	$1,027.2	$970.8	$60.5	$1,043.9

Numbers may not add due to rounding.

PERFORMANCE MEASURES

Goal: *Safety*

The Performance Measures presented here and the Output Measures presented previously for each business line section support the justification of the agency's budget request and measure the performance of the agency's business lines to gauge the productivity of the resources allocated to the agency's internal processes and activities. The output measures are productivity measures that show the quantity, quality, and/or the timeliness of activities that drive progress on these Performance Measures.

1	NRR	Number of New Conditions Evaluated as Red by the NRC's Reactor Oversight Process*					
	FY 2009	FY 2010	FY 2011	FY 2012	FY 2013	FY 2014	
Target	≤ 3	≤ 3	≤ 3	≤ 3	TBD	≤ 3	
Actual	0	0	1	1			

*This measure is the number of new red inspection findings and the number of new red performance indicators during the fiscal year. Programmatic issues at multiunit sites that result in red findings for each individual unit are considered separate conditions for purposes of reporting for this measure. A red performance indicator and a red inspection finding that are due to an issue with the same underlying causes also are considered separate conditions for purposes of reporting for this measure. Red inspection findings are included in the fiscal year in which the final significance determination was made. Red performance indicators are included in the fiscal year in which the Reactor Oversight Process (ROP) external Web page was updated to show the red indicator.

2	RES	Number of Significant Accident Sequence Precursors *(ASPs) of a Nuclear Reactor Accident					
		FY 2009	FY 2010	FY 2011	FY 2012	FY 2013	FY 2014
Target		≤ 0	≤ 0	≤ 0	≤ 0	TBD	≤ 0
Actual		0	0	0	0		

Significant ASP events have a conditional core damage probability (CCDP) or ΔCDP of greater than $1x10^{-3}$. Such events have a 1/1000 ($1x10^{-3}$) or greater probability of leading to a reactor accident involving core damage. An identical condition affecting more than one plant is counted as a single ASP event if a single accident initiator would have resulted in a single reactor accident.

3	NRR	Number of Operating Reactors with Integrated Performance That Entered the Multiple/Repetitive Degraded Cornerstone Column or the Unacceptable Performance Column of the Reactor Oversight Process Action Matrix, or the Inspection Manual Chapter 0350 Process is ≤ 3 with No Performance Leading to the Initiation of an Accident Review Group*					
		FY 2009	FY 2010	FY 2011	FY 2012	FY 2013	FY 2014
Target		≤ 3	≤ 3	≤ 3	≤ 3	TBD	≤ 3
Actual		0	0	2	1		

This measure is the number of plants that have entered the process in Manual Chapter 0350, "Oversight of Reactor Facilities in a Shutdown Condition due to Significant Performance and/or Operational Concerns," dated December 15, 2006; the multiple/repetitive degraded cornerstone column; or the unacceptable performance column during the fiscal year (i.e., were not in these columns or process the previous fiscal year). Data for this measure are obtained from the NRC's external Web Action Matrix Summary page, which provides a matrix of the five columns with the plants listed within their applicable column and notes the plants in the Manual Chapter 0350 process. For reporting purposes, plants that are the subject of an approved deviation from the Action Matrix are included in the column or process in which they appear on the Web page. The target value is set based on the expected addition of several indicators and a change in the long-term trending methodology (which will no longer be influenced by the earlier data and will be more sensitive to changes in current performance).

4	NRR	Number of Significant Adverse Trends in Industry Safety Performance is ≤ 1*					
		FY 2009	FY 20109	FY 2011	FY 2012	FY 2013	FY 2014
Target		≤ 1	≤ 1	≤ 1	≤ 1	TBD	≤ 1
Actual		0	0	0	0		

Considering all indicators qualified for use in reporting.

5		Number of Events with Radiation Exposures to the Public or Occupational Workers That Exceed Abnormal Occurrence (AO) Criterion I.A.3*						
		FY 2009	FY 2010	FY 2011	FY 2012	FY 2013	FY 2014
Reactors	Target	0	0	0	0	TBD	0
Reactors	Actual	0	0	0	0		
Materials	Target	≤ 2	≤ 2	≤ 2	≤ 2	TBD	≤ 2
Materials	Actual	0	0	0	0		
Waste	Target	0	0	0	0	TBD	0
Waste	Actual	0	0	0	0		

Releases for which a 30-day report is required under Title 10 of the Code of Federal Regulations (10 CFR) 20.2203(a)(3).

6				Number of Radiological Releases to the Environment That Exceed Applicable Regulatory Limits*			
		FY 2009	FY 20110	FY 2011	FY 2012	FY 2013	FY 2014
Reactors	Target**	0	0	0	0	TBD	0
Reactors	Actual	0	0	0	0		
Materials	Target	≤ 2	≤ 2	≤ 2	≤ 2	TBD	≤ 2
Materials	Actual	0	0	0	0		
Waste	Target	0	0	0	0	TBD	0
Waste	Actual	0	0	0	0		

*Releases for which a 30-day report is required under 10 CFR 20.2203(a)(3).

**With no event exceeding AO Criterion 1.B.1.

Goal: _Security_

The Performance Measures connect to the Output Measures by supporting the justification of the agency's budget request and to measure the performance of the agency's business lines to gauge the productivity of the resources allocated to the agency's internal processes and activities. Output measure is a productivity measure which shows the quantity, quality, and/or the timeliness of the agency and they support the Performance Measures.

1	NSIR		Unrecovered Losses of Risk-Significant* Radioactive Sources				
		FY 2009	FY 2010	FY 2011	FY 2012	FY 2013	FY 2014
Target		0	0	0	0	TBD	0
Actual		0	0	1**	0		

*"Risk-significant" is defined as any unrecovered, lost, or abandoned sources that exceed the values listed in Appendix P, "Category 1 and 2 Radioactive Material," to 10 CFR Part 110, "Export and Import of Nuclear Equipment and Material." Excluded from reporting under this criterion are those events involving sources that are lost or abandoned under the following conditions: (1) sources abandoned in accordance with the requirements in 10 CFR 39.77(c), (2) recovered sources with sufficient indication that doses in excess of the reporting thresholds specified in AO Criteria I.A.1 and I.A.2 did not occur during the time that the source was missing, (3) unrecoverable sources lost under such conditions that doses in excess of the reporting thresholds specified in AO Criteria I.A.1 and I.A.2 were not known to have occurred, (4) other sources that are lost or abandoned and declared unrecoverable , (5) a source for which the agency has made a determination that its risk significance is low based on its location (e.g., water depth) or its physical characteristics (e.g., half-life and housing) and its surroundings, (6) cases in which all reasonable efforts have been made to recover the source, and (7) the determination was made that the source is not recoverable and will not be considered a realistic safety or security risk under this measure. (This includes licenses under the Agreement States.)

**There were no losses and one theft of radioactive nuclear material that the NRC considered to be risk significant during FY 2011.

2	NSIR		Number of Substantiated* Cases of Actual Theft or Diversion of Licensed, Risk-Significant Radioactive Sources or Formula Quantities** of Special Nuclear Material or Attacks That Result in Radiological Sabotage***				
		FY 2009	FY 2010	FY 2011	FY 2012	FY 2013	FY 2014
Target		0	0	0	0	TBD	0
Actual		0	0	0	0		

3	NSIR	Number of Substantiated Losses of Formula Quantities of Special Nuclear Material or Substantiated Inventory Discrepancies of Formula Quantities of Special Nuclear Material That Are Judged To Be Caused by Theft or Diversion or by Substantial Breakdown of the Accountability System					
		FY 2009	FY 20010	FY 2011	FY 2012	FY 2013	FY 2014
Target		0	0	0	0	TBD	0
Actual		0	0	0	0		

4	NSIR	Number of Substantial Breakdowns* of Physical Security or Material Control (i.e., Access Control, Containment, or Accountability Systems) That Significantly Weakened the Protection against Theft, Diversion, or Sabotage					
		FY 2009	FY 2010	FY 2011	FY 2012	FY 2013	FY 2014
Target		≤ 1	≤ 1	≤ 1	≤ 1	TBD	≤ 1
Actual		0	0	0	0		

*A "substantial breakdown" is defined as a red finding in the security cornerstone of the ROP or any plant or facility that is determined to either have overall unacceptable performance or be in a shutdown condition (inimical to the effective functioning of the Nation's critical infrastructure) as a result of significant performance problems or operational events.

5	NSIR	Number of Significant Unauthorized Disclosures *of Classified and/or Safeguards Information					
		FY 2009	FY 2010	FY 2011	FY 2012	FY 2013	FY 2014
Target		0	0	0	0	TBD	0
Actual		0	0	0	0		

*"Significant unauthorized disclosure" is defined as a disclosure that harms national security or public health or safety.

Data Collection Procedures for Verification and Validation of Performance Measures

Most of the data used to measure the U.S. Nuclear Regulatory Commission's (NRC's) performance against its strategic goals related to Safety and Security are obtained or derived from the NRC's abnormal occurrence (AO) data and reports or preliminary notifications of events submitted by licensees. The AO criteria have been amended to ensure that they are consistent with the NRC's Updated Strategic Plan for fiscal year (FY) 2008–FY 2013 and the NRC rulemaking on Title 10 of the *Code of Federal Regulations* (10 CFR) Part 35, "Medical Use of Byproduct Materials."

The NRC developed its AO criteria to comply with the legislative intent of Section 208 of the Energy Reorganization Act of 1974, as amended. The Act requires the NRC to inform Congress of unscheduled incidents or events that the Commission determines to be significant from the standpoint of public health and safety. NUREG-0090, "Report to Congress on Abnormal Occurrences," issued annually, includes events that meet the AO criteria. In addition, in 1997, the Commission determined that events occurring at Agreement State licensed facilities that meet the AO criteria should be reported in the annual AO report to Congress. Therefore, the AO criteria that the NRC developed are uniformly applied to events that occur at facilities licensed or otherwise regulated by the NRC and the Agreement States.

Data for AOs originate from external sources, such as Agreement States and NRC licensees. The NRC believes these data are credible because (1) the information needed from external sources must be reported to the NRC by regulations, (2) the NRC maintains an aggressive inspection program that, among other activities, audits licensees and evaluates Agreement State programs to determine whether information is being reported as the regulations require, and (3) there are agency procedures for reviewing and evaluating licensees. The NRC database systems for safety that support this process include the Licensee Event Report (LER) Search System, the Accident Sequence Precursor (ASP) Database, the Nuclear Material Events Database (NMED), and the Radiation Exposure Information Report System. The NRC database systems for security that support this process include the Suspicious Incidents Data System (SIDS).

The NRC has established procedures for the systematic review and evaluation of events that NRC licensees and Agreement State licensees report. The objective of the review is to identify events that are significant from the standpoint of public health and safety based on criteria that include specific thresholds. The NRC uses a number of sources to determine the reliability and the technical accuracy of event information reported to the NRC. Such sources include (1) NRC licensee reports, (2) NRC inspection reports, (3) Agreement State reports, (4) periodic review of Agreement State regulatory programs, (5) NRC consultant and contractor reports, and (6) U.S. Department of Energy Operating Experience Weekly Summaries. In addition, there are daily interactions and exchanges of event information between headquarters (HQ) and the regional offices, as well as periodic conference calls among HQ, the regions, and Agreement States to discuss event information. Identified events that meet the AO criteria are validated and verified by all applicable NRC HQ program offices, regional offices, and agency management before submission to Congress.

The following performance measures have been identified for verification and validation.

GOAL 1—SAFETY: ENSURE ADEQUATE PROTECTION OF PUBLIC HEALTH AND SAFETY AND THE ENVIRONMENT.

NUCLEAR REACTOR SAFETY

Strategic Outcomes:

- Prevent the occurrence of any nuclear reactor accidents.
- Prevent the occurrence of any inadvertent criticality events.
- Prevent the occurrence of any acute radiation exposures resulting in fatalities.
- Prevent the occurrence of any releases of radioactive materials that result in significant radiation exposures.
- Prevent the occurrence of any releases of radioactive materials that cause significant adverse environmental impacts.

Performance Measures:

1–Number of new conditions evaluated as red by the NRC's Reactor Oversight Process.

Reactor Safety Target: Less than or equal to three

Verification: The data for this performance measure are collected in two ways as part of the NRC's Reactor Oversight Process (ROP). NRC inspectors collect inspection findings at least quarterly. Inspectors use formal detailed inspection procedures to review plant operations and maintenance. NRC managers review inspection findings to assess their significance as part of the ROP's significance determination process (SDP). Licensees collect the data for performance indicators and submit it to the NRC at least quarterly. The significance of the data is determined by thresholds for each indicator. The NRC conducts inspections of licensee processes for collecting and submitting the data to ensure completeness, accuracy, consistency, timeliness, and validity.

The NRC enhances the quality of its inspections through inspector feedback and periodic reviews of results. The inspectors are trained through a rigorous qualification program. The quality of performance indicators is improved through continuous feedback from licensees and inspectors that is incorporated into guidance documents. The NRC publishes the inspection findings and performance indicators on the agency's Web site and incorporates feedback received from all stakeholders as appropriate.

Validation: The inspection findings and performance indicators that the ROP uses cover a broad range of plant operations and maintenance. NRC managers review significant issues that are identified, and inspectors conduct supplemental inspections of selected aspects of plant operations as appropriate. Senior agency managers review plants annually that are identified as having performance issues and a self-assessment of the ROP and report the results to the Commission.

This measure is the number of new red inspection findings plus the number of new red performance indicators during the fiscal year. Programmatic issues at multiunit sites that result in red findings for each individual unit are considered separate conditions for purposes of reporting for this measure. A red performance indicator and a red inspection finding that are because of an issue with the same underlying causes are also considered separate conditions for the purposes of reporting for this measure. Red inspection findings are included in the fiscal year in which the final significance determination was made. Red performance indicators are included in the fiscal year in which the ROP external Web page was updated to show the red indicator.

2—Number of significant accident sequence precursors of a nuclear accident.

Reactor Safety Target: Zero

Verification: The NRC has an ASP Program to evaluate U.S. nuclear power plant operating experience to identify, document, and rank operating events that were most significant in terms of the potential for inadequate core cooling and core damage (i.e., precursors). The ASP Program evaluation process has five steps. First, the NRC screens operating experience data to identify events or conditions that may be potential precursors to a nuclear accident. The data that are evaluated include LERs, Augmented Inspection Team or special team reports, and other events that the NRC staff has identified as potential precursors. The second step is to conduct an engineering review of these screened events, using specific criteria, to identify those events requiring detailed analyses as candidate precursors. Third, the NRC staff calculates a conditional core damage probability (CCDP) or increase in core damage probability (ΔCDP) by mapping failures observed during the event or condition to accident sequences in risk models. Fourth, the preliminary potential precursor analyses are provided to the NRC staff and the licensee for independent peer review. However, for ASP analyses of noncontroversial, low-risk precursors, formal peer reviews by licensees may not be performed. The NRC staff will continue to perform an inhouse review process for all analyses. Lastly, findings from the analyses are provided to the licensee and the public. Note that there is a time lag in obtaining ASP analysis results because they are often based on LERs (submitted up to 60 days after an event) and completed inspection activities in which most take months to complete. Final data will be reported in the year in which the event occurred.

Validation: The ASP program identifies significant precursors as those events that have a 1/1000 (1×10^{-3}) or greater probability of leading to a nuclear reactor accident. Significant accident sequence precursor events have a CCDP or ΔCDP of $\geq 1\times10^{-3}$.

3—Number of operating reactors with integrated performance that entered the multiple/repetitive degraded cornerstone column or the unacceptable performance column of the Reactor Oversight Process Action Matrix, or the Inspection Manual Chapter 0350 process is ≤3, with no performance leading to the initiation of an Accident Review Group.

Reactor Safety Target: Less than or equal to 3

Verification: The NRC ROP collects the data for this performance measure on a continuous basis, and the information is published at least quarterly. NRC inspectors use detailed formal procedures to conduct inspections of licensee performance, and NRC managers review the results to ensure the completeness, accuracy, consistency, timeliness, and validity of the data.

The NRC enhances the quality of its inspections through inspector feedback and periodic reviews of results. The inspectors are trained through a rigorous qualification program. The quality is also improved through continuous feedback from licensees and inspectors that is incorporated into guidance documents. The NRC publishes the data on the agency's Web site and incorporates feedback received from all stakeholders as appropriate.

Validation: The information that the ROP collects covers a broad range of plant operations and maintenance. NRC managers review significant issues that are identified, and inspectors conduct supplemental inspections of selected aspects of plant operations as appropriate. Senior agency managers review plants annually that are identified as having performance issues and report the results to the Commission. The same is true of the agency's ROP self-assessment.

This measure is the number of plants that have entered the process in Inspection Manual Chapter 0350, "Oversight of Reactor Facilities in a Shutdown Condition due to Significant Performance and/or Operational Concerns," dated December 15, 2006; the multiple/repetitive degraded cornerstone column; or the unacceptable performance column during the fiscal year (i.e., were not in these columns or process the previous fiscal year). Data for this measure are obtained from the NRC external Web Action Matrix Summary page that provides a matrix of the five columns with the plants listed within their applicable column and notes the plants in the Manual Chapter 0350 process. For reporting purposes, plants that are the subject of an approved deviation from the Action Matrix are included in the column or process in which they appear on the Web page.

The Accident Review Group is described in the NRC's Management Directive 8.9, "Accident Investigation," dated August 26, 2005.

4—Number of significant adverse trends in industry safety performance is ≤ 1.

Reactor Safety Target: Less than or equal to 1

Verification: Data for this performance measure are derived from data supplied by all power plant licensees in LERs, monthly operating reports, and performance indicator data submitted for the ROP. These data are required by 10 CFR 50.73, "Licensee Event Report System," or plant-specific technical specifications, or they are submitted by all plants as part of the ROP. Detailed NRC guidelines and procedures are in place to control each of these reporting processes. The NRC reviews these procedures for appropriateness both periodically and in response to licensee feedback. The NRC also conducts periodic inspections of licensees' processes for collecting and submitting the data to ensure completeness, accuracy, consistency, timeliness, and validity.

All licensees report the data at least quarterly. The NRC staff reviews all of the data and conducts inspections to verify safety-significant information. The NRC also employs a contractor to review the data that licensees submit, input the data into a database, and compile the data into various indicators. Quality assurance processes for this work have been established and included in the contract statement of work. The experience and training of key personnel are controlled through administration of the contract. The contractor identifies discrepancies to licensees and the NRC for resolution. The NRC reviews the indicators and publishes them on the agency's Web site quarterly. The agency also incorporates feedback from licensees and the public, where appropriate. The target value is set based on the expected addition of several indicators and a change in the long-term trending methodology.

Validation: The data and indicators that support reporting against this performance measure provide a broad range of information on nuclear power plant performance. The NRC staff tracks indicators and applies statistical techniques to indicate whether industry performance is improving, steady, or degrading over time. If the staff identifies any adverse trends, the NRC addresses the problem through its processes for addressing generic safety issues and issuing generic communications to licensees. The NRC is developing additional, risk-informed indicators to enhance the current set of indicators. In doing so, the staff considers the costs and benefits of collecting the data through ongoing, extensive interactions with industry about the indicators. Senior agency managers review the Industry Trends Program annually and report the results to the Commission.

5–Number of events with radiation exposures to the public and occupational workers from nuclear reactors that exceed Abnormal Occurrence Criterion I.A.3

Reactor Safety Target: Zero

Verification: Licensees report overexposures through the LER process, which are then entered into a searchable database. The database is used to identify those LERs that report overexposures. NRC resident inspectors stationed at each nuclear power plant provide a high degree of assurance that all events meeting reporting criteria are reported to the NRC. In addition, the NRC conducts inspections if there is any indication that an exposure exceeded, or could have exceeded, a regulatory limit. Finally, areas of the facility that may be subject to radiation contamination have monitors that record radiation levels. These monitors would immediately reveal any instances in which high levels of radiation exposure occurred.

Validation: Given the nature of the process of using radioactive materials to generate power, overexposure to radiation is a potential danger from the operation of nuclear power plants. Such exposure to radiation in excess of the applicable regulatory limits may potentially occur through either a nuclear accident or other malfunctions at the plant. Consequently, tracking the number of overexposures that occur at nuclear reactors is an important indicator of the degree to which safety is being maintained.

6–Number of radiological releases to the environment from nuclear reactors that exceed applicable regulatory limits.

Reactor Safety Target: Zero

Verification: As with worker overexposures, licensees report environmental releases of radioactive materials that are in excess of regulations or license conditions through the LER process, which are then entered into a searchable database. The database is used to identify those LERs reporting releases, and the number of reported releases is then applied to this measure. The NRC also conducts periodic inspections of licensees to ensure that they properly monitor and control releases to the environment through effluent pathways. In addition, onsite monitors would record any instances in which the plant releases radiation into the environment. If the inspections or the monitors reveal any indication that an accident or inadvertent release has occurred, the NRC conducts followup inspections.

Validation: The generation of nuclear power creates radioactive materials that are released into the environment in a controlled manner. These radioactive discharges are subject to regulatory controls that limit the amount discharged and the resultant dose to members of the public. Consequently, the NRC tracks all releases of radioactive materials in excess of regulatory limits as a performance measure because large releases in excess of regulatory limits have the potential to endanger public safety or harm the environment. The NRC inspects every nuclear power plant for compliance with regulatory requirements and specific license conditions related to radiological effluent releases. The inspection program includes enforcement actions that must be taken for violations of the regulations or license conditions, based on the severity of the event. This performance measure includes dose values that are classified as being as low as is reasonably achievable (ALARA) in Appendix I, "Numerical Guides for Design Objectives and Limiting Conditions for Operation To Meet the Criterion 'As Low As Is Reasonably Achievable' for Radioactive Material in Light-Water-Cooled Nuclear Power

Reactor Effluents," to 10 CFR Part 50, "Domestic Licensing of Production and Utilization Facilities," and the public dose limits in 10 CFR Part 20, "Standards for Protection against Radiation." Because the performance measure includes ALARA values, which are not safety limits, and because Appendix I to 10 CFR Part 50 allows licensees to temporarily exceed the ALARA dose values, for good reason, the performance measure is set to 2.

NUCLEAR MATERIAL AND WASTE SAFETY

Strategic Outcomes:

- Prevent the occurrence of any inadvertent criticality events.
- Prevent the occurrence of any acute radiation exposures resulting in fatalities.
- Prevent the occurrence of any releases of radioactive materials that result in significant radiation exposures.
- Prevent the occurrence of any releases of radioactive materials that cause significant adverse environmental impacts.

Performance Measures:

1–Number of events with radiation exposures to the public and occupational workers from radioactive material that exceed Abnormal Occurrence Criteria I.A.3

Materials Safety Target: Less than or equal to 2

Waste Safety Target: Zero

Verification: This performance measure includes any event involving licensed radioactive materials that results in significant radiation exposures to members of the public or occupational workers that exceed the dose limits in the AO reporting criteria. Because of the extremely high doses used during medical applications of radioactive materials, it is also appropriate to use a radiation exposure that results in unintended permanent functional damage to an organ or a physiological system as determined by a physician as a criterion for this measure. AO Criterion I.A.3 is used as the basis for this measure.

Should an event meeting this threshold occur, it would be reported to the NRC or Agreement States, or both, through a number of sources but primarily through required licensee notifications. These events are summarized in event notifications and preliminary notifications, which are used to widely disseminate the information to internal and external stakeholders.

The fuel facilities, nuclear material users, spent fuel storage and transportation, decommissioning, and low-level waste programs contain elements that verify the completeness and accuracy of licensee reports. The Integrated Materials Performance Evaluation Program (IMPEP) also provides a mechanism to verify that Agreement States and NRC regions are consistently collecting and reporting such events as received from the licensees and entering them into NMED.

The NRC has taken a number of steps to improve the timeliness and completeness of materials event data. These steps include assessment of the NMED data during monthly staff reviews; emphasis and analysis during the IMPEP reviews; NMED training in HQ, the regions, and Agreement States; and discussions at all Agreement State and the Conference of Radiation Control Program Directors (CRCPD) meetings.

Validation: There is a logical basis for using events involving radiation exposures to the public and occupational workers from radioactive material that exceed AO Criterion I.A as a performance measure for ensuring the protection of public health and safety. An event is considered an AO if it is determined to be significant from the standpoint of public health or safety. The NRC's regulatory process, including licensing, inspection, guidance, regulations, and enforcement activities, is designed to mitigate the likelihood of an event that would exceed AO Criterion I.A.3.

Events of this magnitude are rare. In the unlikely event that an AO should occur, the NRC or Agreement State technical specialists will confirm whether the criteria were met, with input provided by expert consultants, as necessary.

The NRC does not use statistical sampling of data to determine results. Rather, all event data are reviewed to determine whether the performance measure has been met. There are two important data limitations in determining this performance measure. These include delay time for receiving information and failure of the NRC to become aware of an event that causes significant radiation exposures to the public or occupational workers. The NRC regulations associated with event reporting include specific requirements for timely notifications; there is a lag time separating the occurrence of an event and the known consequences of an event. The NRC believes the probability of not being aware of an event that causes significant radiation exposures to the public or occupational workers is very small. Periodic licensee inspections and regulatory reporting requirements are sufficient to ensure that an event of this magnitude would become known. If such an event occurred, it would result in a prompt and thorough investigation of the event, its consequences, its root causes, and the necessary actions by the licensee and the NRC to mitigate the situation and prevent recurrence. In addition to these immediate actions, the NRC holds periodic meetings, in which staff and management validate the occurrence of these events.

2–Number of radiological releases to the environment that exceed applicable regulatory limits.

Materials Safety Target: Less than or equal to 2

Waste Safety Target: Zero

Verification: This performance measure is defined as any release to the environment from the following activities: fuel facilities, nuclear material users, spent fuel storage and transportation, decommissioning, and low-level waste activities that exceed applicable regulations as defined in 10 CFR 20.2203(a)(3). A 30-day written report is required on such releases.

Should an event meeting this threshold occur, it would be reported to the NRC or Agreement States, or both, through a number of sources but primarily through required licensee notifications. These events are summarized in event notifications and preliminary notifications, which are used to widely disseminate the information to internal and external stakeholders.

The fuel facilities, nuclear material users, spent fuel storage and transportation, decommissioning, and low-level waste programs contain elements that verify the completeness and accuracy of licensee reports. The IMPEP also provides a mechanism to verify that Agreement States and NRC regions are consistently collecting and reporting such events, as received from the licensees, and entering them into NMED.

The NRC has taken a number of steps to improve the timeliness and completeness of materials event data. These steps include assessment of the NMED data during monthly staff reviews; emphasis and analysis during the IMPEP review; NMED training in HQ, the regions, and Agreement States; and discussions at all Agreement State and CRCPD meetings.

Validation: The regulations in 10 CFR Part 20 provide standards for protection against radiation. There is a logical basis for tracking releases subject to the 30-day reporting requirement in 10 CFR 20.2203(a)(3)(ii) as a performance measure for ensuring the protection of the environment. The NRC's regulatory process, including licensing, inspection, guidance, regulations, and enforcement activities, is sufficient to ensure that releases of radioactive materials that exceed regulatory limits are infrequent.

In the unlikely event that a release to the environment exceeds regulatory limits, the NRC, Agreement State technical specialists, or agency consultants will confirm whether the criteria were met, with input provided by expert consultants, as necessary.

The NRC does not look at statistical sampling of data to determine results; instead, all event data are reviewed to determine whether the performance measure has been met. There are two important data limitations in determining this performance measure. These include delay time for receiving information or the failure of the NRC to become aware of an event that causes environmental impacts. The NRC regulations associated with event reporting include specific requirements for timely notifications; there is a lag time separating the occurrence of an event and the known consequences of an event.

The NRC believes the probability of not being aware of an event that causes a radiological release to the environment that exceeds applicable regulations is very small. Periodic licensee inspections and regulatory reporting requirements are sufficient to ensure that an event of this magnitude would become known.

If such an event occurred, it would result in a prompt and thorough investigation of the event, its consequences, its root causes, and the necessary actions by the licensee and the NRC to mitigate the situation and prevent recurrence. In addition to these immediate actions, the NRC holds periodic meetings, in which staff and management validate the occurrence of these events.

Goal 2—Security: Ensure the secure use and management of radioactive materials.

NUCLEAR REACTOR AND NUCLEAR MATERIALS AND WASTE SECURITY

Strategic Outcome

Prevent any instances in which licensed radioactive materials are used domestically in a manner hostile to the security of the United States.

Prevent unauthorized public disclosures of classified or Safeguards Information through quality measures.

Performance Measures

1–Number of unrecovered losses or thefts of risk-significant radioactive sources.

Target: Zero

Under AO Criterion I.C.1, the agency counts any unrecovered lost, stolen, or abandoned sources that exceed the values listed in Appendix P, "Category 1 and 2 Radioactive Material," to 10 CFR Part 110, "Export and Import of Nuclear Equipment and Material." Excluded from reporting under this criterion are those events involving sources that are lost, stolen, or abandoned under certain conditions, specifically, (1) sources abandoned in accordance with the requirements of 10 CFR 39.77(c), (2) sealed sources contained in labeled, rugged source housings, (3) recovered sources with sufficient indication that doses in excess of the reporting thresholds specified in AO Criteria I.A.1 and I.A.2 did not occur during the time the source was missing, (4) unrecoverable sources lost under such conditions that doses in excess of the reporting thresholds specified in AO Criteria I.A.1 and I.A.2 were not known to have occurred, and (5) other sources that are lost or abandoned and declared unrecoverable for which the agency has determined that the risk significance of the source is low based on the location (e.g., water depth) or physical characteristics (e.g., half-life and housing) of the source and its surroundings where all reasonable efforts have been made to recover the source and where it has been determined that the source is not recoverable and would not be considered a realistic safety or security risk under this measure.

Verification: Losses or thefts of radioactive material greater than or equal to 1,000 times the quantity specified in Appendix C, "Quantities of Licensed Material Requiring Labeling," to 10 CFR Part 20 must be reported (in accordance with 10 CFR 20.2201(a)) by telephone to the NRC HQ Operations Center or Agreement State immediately (interpreted as within 4 hours) if the licensee believes that an exposure could result to persons in unrestricted areas. If an event meeting the thresholds described above occurs, it would be reported through a number of sources but primarily through this required licensee notification. Events that are publicly available are then entered and tracked in NMED, which is an essential system used to collect and store information on such events. Separate methods are used to track events that are not publicly available. Additionally, licensees must meet the reporting and accounting requirements in 10 CFR Part 73, "Physical Protection of Plants and Materials," and 10 CFR Part 74, "Material Control and Accounting of Special Nuclear Material."

The NRC's inspection programs are key elements in verifying the completeness and accuracy of licensee reports. The IMPEP also provides a mechanism to verify that Agreement States and the NRC regions are consistently collecting and reporting such events as received from the licensees and are entering these events in NMED. In some cases, upon receiving a report, the NRC or Agreement State initiates an independent investigation that verifies the reliability of the reported information. When performed, these investigations enable the NRC or Agreement State to verify the accuracy of the reported data.

The regulation at 10 CFR 20.2201(b) requires a 30-day written report for lost or stolen sources that are greater than or equal to 10 times the quantity specified in Appendix C to 10 CFR Part 20 if the source is still missing at that time. In addition, 10 CFR 20.2201(d) requires an additional written report within 30 days of a licensee learning any additional substantive information. The NRC interprets this requirement as including reporting recovery of sources.

The NRC issued guidance in Regulatory Issue Summary (RIS) 2005-21, "Clarification of the Reporting Requirements in 10 CFR 20.2201," dated November 14, 2005, to clarify the current requirement in

10 CFR 20.2201(d) for reporting recovery of a risk-significant source. The NRC asked the Agreement States to send copies of RIS 2005-21 (or an equivalent document) to its licensees. The NRC issued the National Source Tracking System (NSTS) final rule in November 2006. On January 31, 2009, NRC licensees and Agreement State licensees were required to begin reporting information on source transactions to the NSTS. Implementation of this system creates an inventory of risk-significant sources. This rulemaking established reporting requirements for risk-significant sources (including reporting timeframes) by adding specific requirements to 10 CFR 20.2201, "Reports of Theft or Loss of Licensed Material," for risk-significant sources, including a requirement for licensees to report the recovery of a risk-significant source within 30 days of recovery.

Validation: Events collected under this performance measure are actual losses, thefts, or diversions of materials described above. Such events could compromise public health and safety, the environment, and the common defense and security. Events of this magnitude are expected to be rare. The information reported under 10 CFR Part 73 and 10 CFR Part 74 is required so that the NRC is aware of events that could endanger public health and safety or national security. Any failures at the level of the strategic plan would result in immediate investigation and followup.

If an event subject to the reporting requirements described above occurs, it would result in a prompt and thorough investigation of the event, its consequences, its root causes, and the necessary actions by the licensee, the NRC, or an Agreement State to mitigate the situation and prevent recurrence.

2–Number of substantiated cases of theft or diversion of licensed risk-significant radioactive sources or formula quantities of special nuclear material or attacks that result in radiological sabotage.

Target: Zero

Verification: In AO Criterion I.C.2, "substantiated" means a situation that requires additional action by the agency or other proper authorities because of an indication of loss, theft, or unlawful diversion— such as an allegation of diversion, report of lost or stolen material, statistical processing difference, or other indication of loss of material control or accountability—that cannot be refuted following an investigation. A formula quantity of special nuclear material (SNM) is defined in 10 CFR 70.4, "Definitions." Radiological sabotage is defined in 10 CFR 73.2, "Definitions." Licensees subject to the requirements in 10 CFR Part 73 must call the NRC within 1 hour of an occurrence to report any breaches of security or other event that may potentially lead to theft or diversion of material or to sabotage at a nuclear facility. The NRC's safeguards requirements are described in 10 CFR 73.71, "Reporting of Safeguards Events"; Appendix G, "Reportable Safeguards Events," to 10 CFR Part 73; and 10 CFR 74.11, "Reports of Loss or Theft or Attempted Theft or Unauthorized Production of Special Nuclear Material." The information assessment team composed of NRC HQ and regional staff members would conduct an immediate assessment for any significant events to determine any further actions that are needed, including coordination with the intelligence community and law enforcement. In accordance with 10 CFR 73.71(d), the licensee must also file a written report within 60 days of the incident describing the event and the steps that the licensee took to protect the nuclear facility. This information will enable the NRC to adequately assess whether radiological sabotage has occurred.

Validation: Events subject to reporting requirements are those that endanger the public health and safety and the environment through deliberate acts of theft or diversion of material or through sabotage directed against the nuclear facilities that the agency licenses. Events of this type are extremely rare. If such an event occurs, it would result in a prompt and thorough investigation of the event, its consequences, its root causes, and the necessary actions by the licensee or the NRC to mitigate the situation and prevent recurrence. The investigation ensures the validity of the information and assesses the significance of the event.

3–Number of substantiated losses of formula quantities of special nuclear material or substantiated inventory discrepancies of a formula quantity of special nuclear material that are judged to be caused by theft, diversion, or substantial breakdown of the accountability system.

Target: Zero

Verification: Licensees must record events associated with AO Criterion I.C.3 within 24 hours of the identified event in a safeguards log that the licensee maintains. The licensee must retain the log as a record for 3 years after the last entry is made or until termination of the license. The NRC relies on its safeguards inspection program to ensure the reliability of recorded data. The NRC makes a determination of whether a substantiated breakdown has resulted in a vulnerability to radiological sabotage, theft, diversion, or unauthorized enrichment of SNM. When making substantiated breakdown determinations, the NRC evaluates the materials event data to ensure that licensees are reporting and collecting the proper event data.

Validation: "Substantiated" means a situation that requires additional action by the agency or other proper authorities because of an indication of loss, theft, or unlawful diversion—such as an allegation of diversion, report of lost or stolen material, statistical processing difference, other system breakdown closely related to the material control and accounting program (such as an item control system associated with the licensee's facility IT system), or other indication of loss of material control or accountability—that cannot be refuted following an investigation. A formula quantity of SNM is defined in 10 CFR 70.4. Events collected under this performance measure may indicate a vulnerability to radiological sabotage, theft, diversion, or loss of SNM. Such events could compromise public health and safety, the environment, and the common defense and security. The NRC relies on its safeguards inspection program to help validate the reliability of recorded data and to determine whether a breakdown of a physical protection or material control and accounting system has actually resulted in vulnerability.

4–Number of substantial breakdowns of physical security or material control (i.e., access control containment or accountability systems) that significantly weaken the protection against theft, diversion, or sabotage.

Target: Less than or equal to 1

Verification: In AO Criterion I.C.4, a "substantial breakdown" is defined as a red finding in the security cornerstone of the ROP or significant performance problems or operational events resulting in a determination of overall unacceptable performance or in a shutdown condition (inimical to the effective functioning of the Nation's critical infrastructure). Radiological sabotage is defined in 10 CFR 73.2. Licensees are required to report to the NRC, immediately after the occurrence becomes known, any known breakdowns of physical security, based on the requirements in 10 CFR 73.71 and Appendix G to 10 CFR Part 73. If a licensee reports such an event, the HQ operations officer prepares an official record of the initial event report. The NRC begins responding to such an event immediately upon notification with the activation of its information assessment team. A licensee must follow its initial telephone notification with a written report submitted to the NRC within 30 days.

The licensee records breakdowns of physical protection resulting in a vulnerability to radiological sabotage, theft, diversion, or loss of SNM or radioactive waste within 24 hours in a safeguards log that the licensee maintains. The licensee must retain the log as a record for 3 years after the last entry is made or until termination of the license. Licensees subject to 10 CFR Part 73 must also meet the reporting requirements detailed in 10 CFR 73.71. The NRC evaluates all of the reported events based on the criteria in 10 CFR 73.71 and Appendix G to 10 CFR Part 73. The NRC also maintains and relies on its safeguards inspection program to ensure the reliability of recorded and reported data.

Validation: Events assessed under this performance measure are those that threaten nuclear activities by deliberate acts, such as radiological sabotage, directed against facilities. If a licensee reports such an event, the information assessment team evaluates and validates the initial report and determines any further actions that may be necessary. Tracking breakdowns of physical security indicates whether the licensee is taking the necessary security precautions to protect the public, given the potential consequences of a nuclear accident attributable to sabotage or the inappropriate use of nuclear material either in this country or abroad.

Events collected under this performance measure may indicate a vulnerability to radiological sabotage, theft, diversion, or loss of SNM or radioactive waste. Such events could compromise public health and safety, the environment, and the common defense and security. The NRC relies on its safeguards inspection program to help validate the reliability of recorded data and to determine whether a breakdown of a physical protection or material control and accounting system has actually resulted in a vulnerability.

5–Number of significant unauthorized disclosures of classified or Safeguards Information.

Target: Zero

Verification: In regard to AO Criterion I.C.5, any alleged or suspected violations by NRC licensees of the Atomic Energy Act, Espionage Act, or other Federal statutes related to classified or Safeguards Information must be reported to the NRC under the requirements in 10 CFR 95.57(a) (for classified information), 10 CFR Part 73 (for Safeguards Information), and NRC orders (for Safeguards Information subject to modified handling requirements). However, for performance reporting, the NRC would only count those disclosures or compromises that actually cause damage to national security or to public health and safety. Such events would be reported to the cognizant security agency (i.e., the security agency with jurisdiction) and the regional administrator of the appropriate NRC regional office, as listed in Appendix A, "U.S. Nuclear Regulatory Commission Offices and Classified Mailing Addresses," to 10 CFR Part 73. The regional administrator would then contact the Division of Security Operations at NRC HQ, which would assess the violation and notify other NRC offices and Government agencies, as appropriate. A determination would be made as to whether the compromise damaged national security or public health and safety. Any unauthorized disclosures or compromises of classified or Safeguards Information that damaged national security or public health and safety would result in immediate investigation and followup by the NRC. In addition, NRC inspections will verify that licensees' routine handling of classified information and Safeguards Information (including Safeguards Information subject to modified handling requirements) conforms to established security information management requirements.

Any alleged or suspected violations of this performance measure by NRC employees, contractors, or other personnel would be reported in accordance with NRC procedures to the Director of Division of Facilities and Security at NRC HQ. The NRC maintains a strong system of controls over national security and Safeguards Information, including (1) annual required training for all employees, (2) safe and secure document storage, and (3) physical access control in the form of guards and badged access.

Validation: Events collected under this performance measure are unauthorized disclosures of classified information or Safeguards Information that damage the national security or public health and safety. Events of this magnitude are not expected and would be rare. If such an event occurs, it would result in a prompt and thorough investigation, including consequences, root causes, and necessary actions by the licensees and the NRC to mitigate the consequences and prevent recurrence. NRC investigation teams also validate the materials event data to ensure that licensees are reporting and collecting the proper event data.

The following table shows the relationship between the agency's goals, performance measures, and its seven program business lines. For example, the strategic outcome of "prevent the occurrence of any nuclear reactor accidents" relates to the New Reactors and Operating Reactors business lines. The strategic outcome of "prevent the occurrence of any inadvertent criticality events" relates to all of the agency's business lines. Each program evaluates event reports and other pertinent data[i] to report the results for each strategic outcome, performance measure, and output measure. For each output measure, the specific product line involved is identified in the table.

Goals, Performance Measure, and Program Crosswalk—Safety

Measures	NRC Business Lines					
	New Reactors	Operating Reactors	Fuel Facilities	Materials Users	Decomm & Low-Level Waste	Spent Fuel
Strategic Outcomes						
Prevent the occurrence of any nuclear reactor accidents.	x	x	x			
Prevent the occurrence of any inadvertent criticality events.	x	x	x	x	x	x
Prevent the occurrence of any acute radiation exposures resulting in fatalities.	x	x	x	x	x	x
Prevent the occurrence of any releases of radioactive materials that result in significant radiation exposures.	x	x	x	x	x	x
Prevent the occurrence of any releases of radioactive materials that cause significant adverse environmental impacts.	x	x	x	x	x	x
Performance Measures						
Number of new conditions evaluated as red by the NRC's reactor oversight process.		x				
Number of significant accident sequence precursors (ASPs) of a nuclear reactor accident.		x				
Number of operating reactors whose integrated performance entered the Manual Chapter 0350 process or the multiple/repetitive degraded or unacceptable cornerstone of the Reactor Oversight Program (ROP) Action Matrix with no performance exceeding Abnormal Occurrence (AO) criteria.		x				
Number of significant adverse trends in industry safety performance.		x				
Number of events with radiation exposures to the public or occupational workers that exceed AO Criterion I.A.3.	x	x	x	x	x	X
Number of radiological releases to the environment that exceed applicable regulatory limits.	x	x	x	x	x	x
Output Measures						
Completion of license renewal application reviews.		Licensing				
Licensing actions completed per year.		Licensing				
Age of other licensing task inventory.		Licensing				
Age of licensing action inventory.		Licensing				

Goals, Performance Measure, and Program
Crosswalk—Safety

Measures	NRC Business Lines					
	New Reactors	Operating Reactors	Fuel Facilities	Materials Users	Decomm & Low-Level Waste	Spent Fuel
Other licensing tasks completed per year.		Licensing				
Number of operator licensing examinations administered.		Licensing				
Efficiency measure: Minimize necessary communication systems devices for senior manager use.		Oversight				
Number of plants for which the baseline inspection program was completed during the most recently ended inspection cycle.		Oversight				
Timeliness of significance determination process (SDP) evaluations.		Oversight				
Time to complete reviews of technical allegations.		Oversight				
Timeliness in completing enforcement actions.		Oversight				
Timeliness in completing investigations—Target 1.		Oversight				
Timeliness in completing investigations—Target 2		Oversight				
Timeliness in completing actions on critical research programs.		Research				
Acceptable technical quality of agency research technical products.		Research				
Emergency Response Performance Index.		Event Response				
Review early site permit applications on the schedules negotiated with the applicants.	Licensing					
Review design certification (DC) applications on the schedules negotiated with the applicants.	Licensing					
Review combined operating license (COL) applications on the schedules negotiated with the applicants.	Licensing					
Review small modular reactor (SMR) DC applications on the schedules negotiated with the applicants.	Licensing					
Identify and resolve policy and key technical issues facing the review of SMR applications. Implement resolution through rule changes or guidance development.	Licensing					
Review SMR preapplication submittals on the schedules negotiated with the applicants.	Licensing					
Review SMR COL and construction permit applications on the schedules negotiated with the applicants.	Licensing					
Complete all vendor inspections as scheduled and resourced.	Oversight					
Timeliness of completing "complex" fuel cycle			Licensing			

Goals, Performance Measure, and Program Crosswalk—Safety

Measures	NRC Business Lines					
	New Reactors	Operating Reactors	Fuel Facilities	Materials Users	Decomm & Low-Level Waste	Spent Fuel
licensing actions from the date of acceptance, excluding request for additional information with an assumption of 30-day response to a request for additional information.						
Timeliness of completing "noncomplex" fuel cycle licensing actions (e.g., amendments and reviews) from the date of acceptance, including a 30-day response for a request for additional information.			Licensing			
Efficiency measure: New fuel facilities hearing support.			Licensing			
Timeliness in completing reviews for technical allegations.			Oversight			
Safety and safeguards inspection modules. Complete all core and reactive inspect ion modules as scheduled in Fuel Cycle Master Inspection Plan.			Oversight			
Timeliness of safety and safeguards inspection modules. Complete core inspection modules as scheduled in Fuel Cycle Master Inspection Plan.			Oversight			
Percentage of operating facilities for which the core inspection program was completed during the most recently ended inspection cycle.			Oversight			
Timeliness of licensing actions—reviews of application for new materials licenses and license amendments.				Licensing		
Timeliness of licensing actions—reviews of application for materials license renewals and sealed source and device designs.				Licensing		
Timeliness of safety inspections of materials licensees.				Oversight		
Timeliness in completing reviews for technical allegations.				Oversight		
Timeliness in completing enforcement actions.				Oversight		
Timeliness in completing investigations—Target 1.				Oversight		
Timeliness in completing investigations—Target 2.				Oversight		
Percentage of materials and waste rulemakings completed on schedule.				Rulemaking		
Timeliness of completing actions on critical research programs.				Research		
Acceptable technical quality of agency research technical products.				Research		
Complete storage container and installation design reviews within timeliness goals.						Licensing

Goals, Performance Measure, and Program Crosswalk—Safety

Measures	NRC Business Lines					
	New Reactors	Operating Reactors	Fuel Facilities	Materials Users	Decomm & Low-Level Waste	Spent Fuel
Complete transportation container design reviews within timeliness goals.						Licensing
Using intraagency contracting.						Licensing
Waste Confidence and Extended Long-Term Storage Activities – Percent of Planned Products Completed within a Fiscal Year.						Licensing
Number of spent fuel storage and transportation inspections completed.						Oversight
Timeliness of completing actions on critical research programs.						Research
Acceptable technical quality of agency research technical products.						Research
Support program licensing activities by preparing or reviewing environmental reports and preparing environmental review documents.					Licensing	
Eliminate the need for some site-specific environmental impact statements (i.e., by reducing resource needs) by developing a generic environmental impact statement for uranium recovery environmental reviews.					Licensing	
Cleanup complex materials, fuel cycle sites, and power reactors; complete uranium recovery licensing reviews.					Oversight	
Provide support to U.S. Department of Energy for waste incidental to reprocessing (WIR) activities.					Oversight	
Timeliness of completing actions on critical research programs.					Research	
Acceptable technical quality of agency research technical products.					Research	
Provide support to International Atomic Energy Agency Waste Safety Standards Committee reviews, consultancies and expert missions, Joint Convention, and Nuclear Energy Agency.					International Activities	

Goals, Performance Measure, and Program Crosswalk—Security

Measures	NRC Business Lines					
	New Reactors	Operating Reactors	Fuel Facilities	Materials Users	Decomm & Low-Level Waste	Spent Fuel
Strategic Outcome						
No instances where licensed radioactive materials are used domestically in a manner hostile to the security of the United States.	X	X	X	X	X	X
Performance Measures						
Unrecovered losses of risk-significant radioactive sources.	X	X	X	X	X	X
Number of substantiated cases of actual theft or diversion of licensed, risk-significant radioactive sources or formula quantities of special nuclear material (SNM), or attacks that result in radiological sabotage.	X	X	X	X	X	X
Number of substantiated losses of formula quantities of SNM or substantiated inventory discrepancies of formula quantities of SNM judged to be caused by theft or diversion or substantial breakdown of the accountability system.	X	X	X	X	X	X
Number of substantial breakdowns of physical security or material control (i.e., access control, containment, or accountability systems) that significantly weakened the protection against theft, diversion, or sabotage.	X	X	X	X	X	X
Number of significant unauthorized disclosures of classified information or Safeguards Information.	X	X	X	X	X	X

Office of the
Inspector General

Office of the Inspector General

The U.S. Nuclear Regulatory Commission's (NRC's) Office of the Inspector General (OIG) was established as a statutory entity on April 15, 1989, in accordance with the 1988 amendments to the Inspector General Act. The OIG mission is to (1) independently and objectively conduct and supervise audits and investigations relating to NRC programs and operations, (2) prevent and detect fraud, waste, and abuse, and (3) promote economy, efficiency, and effectiveness in the NRC's programs and operations.

In addition, OIG reviews existing and proposed regulations, legislation, and directives and provides comments, as appropriate, and makes recommendations to the agency concerning their impact on the economy and efficiency of agency programs and operations. The Inspector General keeps the NRC Chairman and members of Congress informed about problems, recommends corrective actions, and monitors NRC's progress in implementing these actions.

Budget Overview Budget Authority by Program (Dollars in Millions)						
Summary	FY 2012 Enacted $M	FTE	FY 2014 Request $M	FTE	Delta FY 2014–FY 2012 $M	FTE
Program Support	1.276		1.245		-0.031	
Program Salaries and Benefits	9.584	58	9.860	58	0.276	0
Total	$10.860	58	$11.105	58	$0.245	0

Numbers may not add due to rounding.

PROGRAM RESOURCE SUMMARY

The fiscal year (FY) 2014 proposed budget request for OIG is $11.105 million, which includes $9.860 million in salaries and benefits to support 58 full-time equivalents (FTE) and $1.245 million in program support. These resources will fund the activities of the Audits and Investigations Programs.

	Budget Authority and FTE by Program Budget Authority by Program (Dollars in Millions)					
	FY 2012 Enacted		FY 2014 Request		Delta FY 2014–FY 2012	
Summary	$M	FTE	$M	FTE	$M	FTE
Audits	7.171	37	7.314	37	0.143	0
Investigations	3.689	21	3.791	21	0.102	0
Total	**$10.860**	**58**	**$11.105**	**58**	**$0.245**	**0**

Numbers may not add due to rounding.

In accordance with Office of Management and Budget (OMB) requirements, OIG is showing the full cost associated with its programs for the FY 2014 budget with the following caveat. As a result of an October 1989 memorandum of understanding between the NRC's Chief Financial Officer and the Inspector General and a subsequent amendment in March 1991, OIG no longer requests that funding for some OIG management and support services be included in the OIG appropriation. It was agreed that funds for OIG infrastructure requirements and other agency support services would instead be included in the NRC's main appropriation. For the most part, these costs are not readily severable. Thus, this funding continues to be included in the NRC's main appropriation.

AUDITS PROGRAM

	Audits Budget Authority by Program (Dollars in Millions)					
	FY 2012 Enacted		FY 2014 Request		Delta FY 2014–FY 2012	
Summary	$M	FTE	$M	FTE	$M	FTE
Program Support	7.171	37	7.314	37	0.143	0
Total	**$7.171**	**37**	**$7.314**	**37**	**$0.143**	**0**

Numbers may not add due to rounding.

HIGHLIGHTS

The OIG Audits Program focuses on the agency's management and financial operations; economy and efficiency with which an organization, program, or function is managed; and whether the programs achieve intended results. OIG auditors assess the degree to which an organization complies with laws, regulations, and internal policies in carrying out programs, and they test program effectiveness and the accuracy and reliability of financial statements. The overall objective of an audit is to identify ways to enhance agency operations and to promote greater economy and efficiency.

For FY 2014, OIG requests $7.314 million and 37 FTE to carry out its Audits Program activities. With these resources, the Audits Program will conduct approximately 22 audits and evaluations. This will enable the OIG to provide coverage of the NRC's Reactor Safety, Materials and Waste Safety, Security, and Corporate Support Programs. OIG's assessment of these mission critical programs will support the agency in accomplishing its goals to ensure adequate protection of public health and safety and the environment and in the secure use and management of radioactive materials.

CHANGES FROM FY 2012 ENACTED

Resources increase in the Audits Program to fund the January 2014 pay raise, within-grade and benefits costs increases in FY 2013 and FY 2014.

FY 2013–FY 2014 AUDITS PROGRAM PERFORMANCE GOALS

- Safety Area: 85 percent of audit products and activities undertaken will identify critical risk areas or management challenges relating to the improvement of the NRC's safety programs.
- Security Area: 90 percent of audit products and activities undertaken will identify critical risk areas or management challenges relating to the improvement of the NRC's security programs.
- Corporate Management Area: 80 percent of audit products and activities undertaken will identify critical risk areas or management challenges relating to the improvement of the NRC's corporate management programs.
- Eighty-five percent of completed audit products or activities will have a high impact on strengthening the NRC's safety, security, and corporate management programs.
- Obtain agency agreement on at least 92 percent of OIG audit recommendations.
- Obtain final agency action on an aggregate of 70 percent of OIG audit recommendations within 2 years.

SELECTED FY 2012 AUDITS PROGRAM ACCOMPLISHMENTS

In FY 2012, OIG issued 22 reports pertaining to NRC programs and operations. These reports either evaluate high-risk agency programs or comply with mandatory financial and computer security-related legislation.

EXAMPLES OF RECENTLY COMPLETED WORK ARE AS FOLLOWS:

Audit of NRC's Oversight of Industrial Radiography:

The NRC regulates the use of ionizing radiation for nondestructive examination of the structure of materials in its jurisdiction. This process is known as industrial radiography. Radiographers use radiography devices, or cameras, to produce images used in the examination of structures, such as pipelines. The cameras contain radioactive sealed sources. When the source is exposed, radiation penetrates the material and produces a shadow image on film or some other detection medium. The NRC's regulatory requirements for industrial radiography are provided in Title 10 of the *Code of Federal Regulations* (10 CFR) Part 34, "Licenses for Industrial Radiography and Radiation Safety Requirements for Industrial Radiographic Operations." These regulations require radiographers to perform radiography in a safe manner. The audit objective was to determine the adequacy of NRC's processes for overseeing licensee activities addressing the safety and control of radiography sources.

Audit Results:

Generally, the NRC's oversight of industrial radiography is effective, and the agency has taken steps to improve its oversight by updating some guidance for radiography and stressing the importance of safety culture during radiography inspections. However, OIG identified the following areas that could be improved: (1) clarity and consistency of what activities licensees are authorized to conduct or when licensees may conduct them, (2) routine inspection program for licensees, (3) temporary jobsite inspections, and (4) approach to inspecting NRC licensees located in Agreement States. Addressing these concerns will improve the NRC's oversight of industrial radiography by ensuring that inspections are conducted where needed and at the proper frequency.

Audit of NRC's Management of Import/Export Authorizations:

One of the NRC's statutorily mandated responsibilities under the Atomic Energy Act of 1954, as amended (AEA), is to license the import and export of nuclear materials and equipment into and from the United States. The NRC's Office of International Programs (OIP) is assigned to process specific nuclear import and export licensing actions under 10 CFR Part 110, "Export and Import of Nuclear Equipment and Material," after receiving any necessary guidance from the Commission.

From FY 2008 through FY 2010, OIP completed between 123 and 139 licensing actions per year. The audit objectives were to determine whether the NRC (1) properly reviews and approves import/export authorizations in a timely manner, (2) effectively coordinates this activity with other Federal agencies, and (3) efficiently and effectively coordinates import/export authorizations internally.

Audit Results:

In general, OIP is properly reviewing and approving import/export license authorizations (applications) in a timely fashion and coordinates effectively with external stakeholders. However, OIG identified opportunities for improvement for more efficient and effective internal coordination on import and export authorizations. Specifically, (1) OIP does not have a systematic approach to biennial fee reviews and adjustments, (2) OIP does not reconcile import and export license application revenue, and (3) OIP does not employ an adequate quality control review process over application files. Addressing these concerns will strengthen the NRC's internal control over import and export licensing and result in excess of $357,000 in funds being put to better use.

Audit of NRC's Protection of Safeguards Information:

Safeguards Information (SGI) is a category of sensitive unclassified information that is unique to NRC. SGI is detailed security-related information that identifies security measures for the physical protection of special nuclear material or security measures for the physical protection and location of certain plant equipment vital to the safety of production or utilization facilities. Unauthorized disclosure of SGI could have a significant adverse effect on public health and safety and the common defense and security by significantly increasing the likelihood of theft, diversion, or sabotage of materials or facilities subject to NRC jurisdiction. The audit objective was to determine whether the NRC adequately ensures the protection of SGI. This audit was conducted to followup on an audit issued in January 2004, OIG-04-A-04, "Audit of NRC's Protection of Safeguards Information." The 2004 audit found that the benefit of having an SGI program was unclear and that the NRC lacked a central authority for controlling, coordinating, and communicating SGI program requirements. The audit also found examples in which NRC and licensee representatives inappropriately released SGI to unauthorized individuals.

Audit Results:

Since the 2004 audit, the NRC has made improvements to the SGI program, including the development of a Management Directive specifically for SGI and identification of a lead program office for developing SGI policies and procedures. However, OIG identified the following areas for further improvement of the SGI program: The NRC (1) lacks a structured process for tracking SGI releases, (2) lacks guidance on granting "outsiders" access to SGI, and (3) has inadequate business processes over the SGI designator role. Addressing these areas will strengthen the agency's ability to protect SGI from unauthorized disclosure and enhance its SGI program.

Audit of NRC's Use of Confirmatory Action Letters:

The NRC regulates commercial nuclear power plants and other civilian uses of nuclear materials, such as in nuclear medicine, through licensing, inspection, and enforcement of its requirements. In exercise of its regulatory responsibilities, the NRC uses administrative actions, such as confirmatory action letters (CALs), to supplement the agency's enforcement program. CALs are "letters confirming a licensee's agreement to take certain actions to remove significant concerns about health and safety, safeguards, or the environment." The audit objective was to determine the effectiveness of NRC's use of CALs as a regulatory tool. To meet this objective, OIG auditors focused on the agency's administration of the CAL process.

Audit Results:

The NRC's administration of the CAL process is not as effective as it could be. Specifically, CAL guidance is inconsistent because the CAL guidance does not include some offices' roles nor clearly identify all CAL recipients. Further, NRC program and regional offices do not fully comply with CAL guidance. Despite requirements in the "NRC Enforcement Manual" for the concurrence, tracking, and numbering of CALs, (1) some required office concurrences on CALs are missing, (2) CAL tracking practices vary among offices, and (3) CAL numbering conventions vary among offices. Weaknesses in the NRC's CAL guidance and compliance with the guidance exists because the agency does not have a centralized control point for agencywide oversight and implementation of a fully effective CAL process, including consistent CAL guidance, compliance with the guidance, and the tracking of CALs. Consequently, the NRC may be missing opportunities to effectively use CALs for potential CAL recipients not identified in current guidance and to efficiently track and trend CALs.

EXAMPLES OF ONGOING AUDIT WORK ARE AS FOLLOWS:

Audit of NRC's Travel Charge Card Program:

The NRC's Travel Charge Card Program is part of the Governmentwide Commercial Charge Card Program established to pay the official travel expenses of employees while on temporary duty or other official business travel. The intent of the program is to improve convenience for the traveler and to reduce the Government's costs of administering travel. OMB has issued guidance that establishes requirements (including internal controls designed to minimize the risk of travel card misuse) and has suggested best practices for Government travel card programs. During FY 2011, 2,613 NRC employees charged approximately $9 million on travel charge cards, primarily issued to employees as individually billed accounts. Travel cardholders are directly responsible for all charges incurred on their account. The Office of the Chief Financial Officer administers the NRC's travel charge card program and controls the use of agency funds to ensure that they are expended in accordance with applicable laws and standards. The audit objective is to assess whether the NRC's policies and procedures are effective in preventing and detecting travel charge card misuse and delinquencies.

2012 NRC Safety Culture and Climate Survey

In 1998, 2002, 2006, and 2009, OIG contracted with an international survey firm to conduct surveys that evaluated the organizational safety culture and climate of the NRC's workforce and identified agency strengths and opportunities for improvements. Comparisons were made to the previous surveys and to national and Government norms. In response to the survey results, the agency evaluated the key areas for improvement and developed strategies for addressing them. A clear understanding of the NRC's current safety culture and climate will facilitate identification of agency strengths and opportunities as it continues to experience significant challenges. These challenges include the licensing of new nuclear facilities, disposal of high-level waste, the loss of valuable experience from retirements, operating under continuing resolutions, smaller budgets, and legislation that froze Federal civilian employee pay rates. The survey results are also useful to OIG in programming future work. The survey objectives are to (1) measure the NRC's safety culture and climate to identify areas of strength and opportunities for improvement, (2) compare the results of this survey against the survey results that OIG reported previously, and (3) provide, where practical, benchmarks for the qualitative and quantitative findings against other organizations.

Audit of NRC's Implementation of Its NEPA Responsibilities

The National Environmental Policy Act (NEPA) of 1969 requires Federal agencies, as part of their decisionmaking process, to consider the environmental impacts of actions under their jurisdiction. NEPA requires that an environmental impact statement of the proposed action be prepared for "major Federal actions significantly affecting the quality of the human environment." Consultations to ensure compliance with other statutory mandates, such as with Section 7 of the Endangered Species Act of 1973 and Section 106 of the National Historic Preservation Act of 1966, are also part of the NEPA review process. Environmental reviews occur at three levels, ranging from categorical exclusion to an environmental assessment or to the detailed environmental impact statement. NRC has issued regulations to implement NEPA requirements in 10 CFR Part 51, "Environmental Protection Regulations for Domestic Licensing and Related Regulatory Functions." The audit objective is to determine whether the NRC implements its environmental review and consultation responsibilities, as prescribed by NEPA.

OIG Evaluation of the NRC's Use and Security of Social Media

Social media technologies, commonly referred to as Web 2.0, allow individuals and organizations to create, edit, organize, and share content in user-generated virtual communities. Web 2.0 technologies include (1) Web logs (blogs)—a Web site containing the writer's or group of writers' opinions on a topic, including photographs and links to other Web sites, (2) social media sites, such as Twitter and Facebook, and (3) video sharing sites such as YouTube. The evaluation objective is to determine how the NRC uses social media, the effectiveness and efficiency of the NRC's use of social media, and whether the NRC staff are using social media in a secure manner. The evaluation will also assess the extent to which the NRC has developed and implemented policies and procedures for protecting information associated with the use of social media and regulatory or budgetary constraints impeding the agency's use of social media.

INVESTIGATIONS PROGRAM

	Investigations Budget Authority by Program (Dollars in Millions)					
	FY 2012 Enacted		FY 2014 Request		Delta FY 2014–FY 2012	
Summary	$M	FTE	$M	FTE	$M	FTE
Program Support	$3.689	21	$3.791	21	$0.102	0
Total	$3.689	21	$3.791	21	$0.102	0

Numbers may not add due to rounding.

HIGHLIGHTS

OIG's responsibility for detecting and preventing fraud, waste, and abuse within the NRC includes investigating possible violations of criminal statutes relating to the agency's programs and activities;

investigating misconduct by NRC employees; interfacing with the U.S. Department of Justice on OIG-related criminal matters; and coordinating investigations and other OIG initiatives with Federal, State, and local investigative agencies and other OIGs. Investigations may be initiated as a result of allegations or referrals from private citizens; licensee employees; NRC employees; Congress; other Federal, State, and local law enforcement agencies; OIG audits; the OIG hotline; and Inspector General initiatives directed at bearing a high potential for fraud, waste, and abuse.

For FY 2014, OIG requests $3.791 million and 21 FTE to carry out its Investigations Program activities. Reactive investigations into allegations of criminal and other wrongdoing will continue to claim priority on OIG's use of available resources. Because the NRC's mission is to protect the public health and safety, the Investigations Program's main concentration of effort and resources will involve investigations of alleged NRC staff misconduct that could adversely affect matters related to health and safety. OIG has also implemented a series of proactive initiatives designed to identify specific high-risk areas that are most vulnerable to fraud, waste, and abuse. With these resources, OIG will conduct approximately 60 investigations and Event Inquiries covering a broad range of allegations concerning misconduct and mismanagement affecting various NRC programs.

CHANGES FROM FY 2012 ENACTED

Resources increase in the Audits Program to fund the January 2014 pay raise, within-grade and benefits costs increases.

FY 2013–FY 2014 INVESTIGATIONS PROGRAM PERFORMANCE GOALS

- Safety Area: 85 percent of investigation products and activities undertaken will identify critical risk areas or management challenges relating to the improvement of the NRC's safety programs.
- Security Area: 90 percent of investigation products and activities undertaken will identify critical risk areas or management challenges relating to the improvement of the NRC's security programs.
- Corporate Management Area: 80 percent of investigation products and activities undertaken will identify critical risk areas or management challenges relating to improvement of the NRC's corporate management programs.
- Eighty-five percent of investigations or activities completed will have a high impact on strengthening the NRC's safety, security, and corporate management programs.
- Obtain 90 percent agency action in response to OIG investigative reports.
- Complete 90 percent of active cases in less than 18 months on average.

SELECTED FY 2012 INVESTIGATIONS PROGRAM ACCOMPLISHMENTS

In FY 2012, OIG completed 55 investigations. These investigative efforts focused on violations of law or misconduct by NRC employees and contractors and allegations of irregularities or inadequacies in NRC programs and operations.

EXAMPLES OF RECENTLY COMPLETED WORK ARE AS FOLLOWS:

Release of Predecisional Information on Commission Notation Vote

OIG conducted an investigation into an allegation that sensitive information concerning the outcome of a nonpublic Commission vote was leaked to a congressional member. The vote pertained to a "Statement of Interest" (i.e., Federal preemption) by the U.S. Department of Justice in a lawsuit filed by Entergy Nuclear against the State of Vermont.

Investigative Results:

OIG found that numerous NRC employees received e-mails from each Commission member stating how he or she voted on the "Statement of Interest" matter. In addition, these same employees received an e-mail from the Office of the Chairman providing the final 3 to 2 vote tally, including a breakout of how each Commission member voted. OIG found that a congressional members' office was aware of the overall 3 to 2 vote before its official release. OIG was unable to determine how the congressional members learned about the vote tally.

Potential Ethics Violation Involving Outside Employment by an Office of Nuclear Regulatory Research Employee

OIG conducted an investigation into an allegation that an NRC employee was serving on a peer review panel in South Africa but did not obtain management approval to work on the panel.

Investigative Results:

OIG found that the NRC employee was a paid consultant for a panel; however, the NRC employee sought guidance from the agency's Office of the General Counsel on employment with the panel. There were no costs incurred to the NRC and no indications that the NRC employee used NRC resources to conduct work on behalf of the panel. OIG determined that the South African peer review panel was a foreign government entity and that, by accepting compensated employment, the employee violated the Emoluments Clause of the U.S. Constitution. OIG also determined that the NRC employee failed to report his or her association with the South African peer review panel to the Division of Facilities and Security (DFS) in violation of an NRC Management Directive. As a result of this investigation, the employee returned the compensation received from the South African peer review panel.

Failure to Inspect North Anna Nuclear Plant, Unit 1, after Earthquake and Inspection of Unit 2

The OIG conducted an investigation into an allegation that an NRC senior official failed to protect public health and safety by not inspecting North Anna Nuclear Power Plant (North Anna), Unit 1, internals after it was shut down because of an August 2011 earthquake centered in Mineral, VA.

Investigative Results:

The OIG determined that NRC headquarters dispatched an augmented inspection team (AIT) to the facility following the earthquake. OIG reviewed the NRC's technical evaluation of the event that documented the agency's inspection activities and conclusions supporting its decision to allow North Anna to restart to include a conclusion on the functionality of the reactor vessel internals. The technical evaluation explained in detail the inspection activities of both Units 1 and 2. The technical evaluation also explained why certain inspection results of Unit 2 would be representative of the findings for Unit 1. Further, the decision to restart North Anna was not the Regional Administrator's responsibility. NRC headquarters personnel declared the facility safe and was ultimately authorized to restart after confirming that regulatory requirements were met.

Mishandling of Personally Identifiable Information by an iLearn Contractor

OIG conducted an investigation into an allegation of a possible leak of NRC employees' personally identifiable information (PII) in an e-mail sent from an Office of Personnel Management's (OPM) training provider, which manages the agency's learning management system known as *iLearn*. The NRC uses the OPM training provider to manage *iLearn* as part of an OMB requirement that all agencies use one of five authorized certified training providers to track Federal employee training. The e-mail in question was sent to three NRC employees located in the Office of the Chief Human Capital Officer and one training provider contractor employee.

Investigative Results:

OIG found that the training provider mishandled NRC employee PII by sending it in clear text as an attachment to a regular e-mail. Upon notification of the PII transmittal by an NRC employee, the training provider coordinated with OPM to remove all remnants of the e-mail, the attachment, and all documents used to create the attachment. The training provider also implemented steps to prevent this from happening in the future and committed to re-educating its employees on the future handling and transporting of PII through secure transfer methods.

OIG also found that the NRC's task order with OPM did not adequately address the retention and destruction of NRC employee PII the training provider used to update the training database. This shortcoming put the agency at risk of having outdated sets of PII in the possession of OPM's contractor for inadvertent misuse. This investigation identified a shortcoming in the NRC's contractual arrangement that required the training provider to provide NRC employee PII to OPM to meet the training documentation requirement in OPM's e-Government initiative, Enterprise Human Resources Integration.

Possible Violations of the NRC's Internal Commission Procedures and the Reorganization Plan No. 1 of 1980 by Former Chairman

OIG conducted an investigation into four allegations concerning a former NRC Chairman's exercise of his authority under the Reorganization Plan No. 1 of 1980 (Reorganization Plan) and the Energy Reorganization Act of 1974. The investigation also addressed allegations concerning the former Chairman's interactions with NRC officials and the Chairman's testimony during U.S. House of Representatives and Senate committee hearings in December 2011.

Investigative Results:

OIG found the former Chairman did not exceed his authorities under the Reorganization Plan in leading NRC's response to events in Japan following the March 2011 earthquake and tsunami that caused a crisis at the six-unit Fukushima Dai-ichi Nuclear Power station in Japan. The Chairman is authorized to direct the NRC's response to emergencies under Sections 2 and 3 of the Reorganization Plan. Section 2 allows the Chairman to direct the agency's response as the NRC's principal executive officer and to communicate to the public about the response as the official Commission spokesman. Section 3 provides special authority for the Chairman to respond to an emergency concerning an NRC licensee without consulting with the Commission on matters that would otherwise require a collegial approach. OIG found that the Reorganization Plan gives the Chairman sole authority to declare the existence of a Section 3 emergency but does not specifically require the Chairman to declare use of the Section 3 authority. Moreover, OIG did not identify any NRC procedure requiring the Chairman to make a Section 3 declaration, and the Chairman did not make such a declaration. OIG found that the former Chairman made reasonable efforts to keep Commissioners informed of actions taken during the emergency period.

OIG found the Chairman's actions concerning the withdrawal and resubmission of a revised SECY paper[1] did not violate the Internal Commission Procedures in regard to "withdrawal of papers submitted to the Commission." However, OIG found that the Chairman's direction not to include the Executive Director for Operations' perspective on the SECY paper was inconsistent with the Commissioners' expectations to receive the staff's written views, analysis, and recommendations as part of SECY papers. OIG found the Reorganization Plan assigns the Chairman responsibility for "developing policy planning and guidance for consideration by the Commission," but it does not define these terms or articulate the limits on the Chairman's authority in this area. Moreover, the legislative history provides conflicting interpretations as to whether the Chairman can direct the staff not to submit written policy proposals to the Commission or alter the information that the staff provides in its written policy proposals.

OIG found that the former Chairman initially instructed the Secretary of the Commission not to follow the consensus approach of the four Commissioners concerning moving forward to finalize the revised Internal Commission Procedures. OIG found conflicting direction in the Reorganization Plan and an NRC Management Directive concerning the Chairman's supervisory authority over the Secretary and noted that, although the Chairman is authorized to provide administrative supervision and oversight of the Secretary, the Secretary must also be responsive to Commission direction concerning matters under its purview.

OIG identified more than 15 examples of interactions between the Chairman and NRC senior executives and Commissioners in which the Chairman's behavior was not supportive of an open and collaborative work environment. In addition, OIG found the Chairman's testimony of December 2011 before the House and Senate committees was inconsistent, in five areas, with testimony provided to OIG by NRC senior officials during this investigation.

---

[1] The Commission's primary decisionmaking tool is a written issue paper referred to as a SECY paper.

EXAMPLES OF ONGOING INVESTIGATIVE WORK ARE AS FOLLOWS:

NRC Regulatory Oversight

OIG initiated a special project to proactively monitor NRC technical and regulatory processes, nuclear industry trends, trade press, and other sources to identify potential problematic areas in the agency's regulatory oversight of operating reactors, nuclear materials, and high-level and low-level waste.

NRC Network Intrusion, Computer Misuse, and Computer Forensic Support

The OIG Cyber Crime Unit conducts investigations into internal and external cyber breaches to the NRC's IT infrastructure, conducts cyber investigations involving the NRC and its employees, and works jointly with NRC staff to identify unauthorized or unknown activity on the agency's network. Investigations include computer misuse by NRC employees, targeted spear phishing attacks against NRC employees, attempted network intrusions, unauthorized release of electronic sensitive information, and forensic assistance to the NRC in regard to alleged licensees' violations of regulatory requirements.

Violations of Public Trust

The OIG initiated a project to identify violations of public trust and to develop investigations focused to recognize schemes that may lead to criminal offenses, including bribery, extortion, embezzlement, and illegal kickbacks. This project involves the review of a variety of information sources and deploys innovative methods to focus on restrictions on former employees engaging in postemployment activities that affect the NRC and acts that affect a personal financial interest of current or former employees.

OIG'S STRATEGIC GOALS, STRATEGIES, AND ACTIONS

OIG carries out its mission through its Audits and Investigations Programs. The NRC-OIG 2008-2013 Strategic Plan, which is currently being updated, features three goals and guides the activities of these programs. The plan identifies the major challenges and risk areas facing the NRC and generally aligns with the agency's mission. It also includes a number of supporting strategies and actions that describe OIG's planned accomplishments over the strategic planning period. OIG's strategic plan can be accessed in its entirety at the following address: http://www.nrc.gov/insp-gen/plandocs/strategic-plan.pdf.

Through annual planning activities, audit and investigative resources focus on assessing the NRC's safety, security, and corporate management programs that involve the major challenges and risk areas facing the agency in the given budget year. The work that OIG auditors and investigators perform is mutually supportive and complementary in pursuit of these objectives. Below are OIG's strategic goals and strategies covering this budget cycle.

OIG STRATEGIC GOALS

STRATEGIC GOAL 1: STRENGTHEN THE NRC'S EFFORTS TO PROTECT PUBLIC HEALTH AND SAFETY AND THE ENVIRONMENT.

The NRC faces many safety challenges and an associated increased workload related to nuclear reactor oversight, the regulation of nuclear materials, and the handling of nuclear waste. A significant concern for the agency is regulating the safe operation of the Nation's nuclear power plants through an established oversight process. The NRC also must address an increasing number of license amendment requests to increase the power generating capacity of specific commercial reactors; license renewal requests to extend reactor operations beyond originally set expiration dates; and the introduction of new technology, such as new and advanced reactor designs. Further, the NRC must ensure that its regulatory activities on nuclear fuel cycle facilities and nuclear materials adequately protect public health and safety. Below are OIG's strategies to support the agency's efforts in facing these challenges.

- Strategy 1-1: Identify risk areas associated with the NRC's Reactor Oversight Process and make recommendations, as warranted, for addressing them.

- Strategy 1-2: Identify risk areas associated with NRC efforts to (1) prepare for and manage the review of applications for new power reactors and (2) oversee construction of new power reactors to verify that they are built in conformance with approved designs and in compliance with approved construction standards and make recommendations, as warranted, for addressing them.

- Strategy 1-3: Identify risk areas facing the materials programs and make recommendations, as warranted, for addressing them.

- Strategy 1-4: Identify risk areas associated with low-level waste and the prospective licensing of the high-level waste repository and make recommendations, as warranted, for addressing them.

STRATEGIC GOAL 2: ENHANCE THE NRC'S EFFORTS TO INCREASE SECURITY IN RESPONSE TO AN EVOLVING THREAT ENVIRONMENT.

The NRC continues to face a number of challenges in ensuring that the public is protected from improper use of nuclear materials and technology. The NRC, in concert with other agencies, must maintain a comprehensive assessment of threats and effectively integrate security considerations into its regulatory process. The agency also must ensure that security is adequately incorporated into the design and construction of new facilities. Listed below are OIG's strategies to support the NRC in facing these and other security-related challenges.

- Strategy 2-1: Identify risk areas involved in effectively securing both operating and proposed nuclear power plants, nuclear fuel cycle facilities, and nuclear materials and make recommendations, as warranted, for addressing them.
- Strategy 2-2: Identify risks associated with emergency preparedness and make recommendations, as warranted, for addressing them.
- Strategy 2-3: Identify challenges involved in responding to incidents and make recommendations, as warranted, for addressing them.
- Strategy 2-4: Identify evolving threats to NRC security and make recommendations, as warranted, for addressing them.
- Strategy 2-5: Identify risks associated with nonproliferation of nuclear material and nuclear technology and make recommendations, as warranted, for addressing them.

STRATEGIC GOAL 3: INCREASE THE ECONOMY, EFFICIENCY, AND EFFECTIVENESS WITH WHICH THE NRC MANAGES AND EXERCISES STEWARDSHIP OVER ITS RESOURCES.

The NRC faces significant challenges to efficiently, effectively, and economically manage its resources. Although a number of organizational changes have been implemented in recent years, more changes will occur over the strategic timeframe. The agency will need to continue balancing workloads and priorities to support new reactor licensing efforts. This will create tremendous pressure on all program management areas, including human resources management, information technology, and financial management. Listed below is OIG's strategy to support the agency in mitigating these challenges.

- Strategy 3-1: Identify areas of corporate management risk within the NRC and make recommendations, as warranted, for addressing them.

OIG PROGRAM PERFORMANCE MEASURES

OIG Strategic Goal 1: Strengthen the NRC's Efforts To Protect Public Health and Safety and the Environment						
	2009	2010	2011	2012	2013	2014
Measure 1. Percentage of OIG products/activities[2] undertaken to identify critical risk areas or management challenges[3] relating to the improvement of the NRC's safety programs.						
Target	80%	85%	85%	85%	TBD	85%
Actual	100%	100%	100%	100%	TBD	TBD
Measure 2. Percentage of OIG products/activities that have a high impact[4] on improving the NRC's safety program.						
Target	70%	85%	85%	85%	TBD	85%
Actual	89%	100%	91%	89%	TBD	TBD
Measure 3. Number of audit recommendations agreed to by agency.						
Target	90%	92%	92%	92%	TBD	92%
Actual	60%[5]	60%[6]	80%[7]	91%[8]	TBD	TBD
Measure 4. Final agency action within 2 years of audit recommendations.						
Target	50%[9]	70%	70%	70%	TBD	70%
Actual	67%	80%	80%	80%	TBD	TBD
Measure 5. Agency action in response to investigative reports.						
Target	90%	95%	95%	95%	TBD	95%
Actual	100%	100%	100%	100%	TBD	TBD
Measure 6. Complete active cases in less than 18 months on average.						
Target				90%[10]	TBD	90%
Actual				100%	TBD	TBD

---

[2] OIG products are issued as OIG reports. For the Audits Program, these are audit reports and evaluations. For the Investigations Program, these are investigations, Event Inquiries, and Special Inquiries. Activities are the OIG hotline or proactive investigative reports.

[3] Congress left the determination and threshold of what constitutes a most serious challenge to the discretion of the Inspectors General. As a result, OIG applied the following definition: Serious management challenges are mission-critical areas or programs that have a potential for a perennial weakness or vulnerability that, without substantial management attention, would seriously impact agency operations or strategic goals.

[4] High impact is the effect of an issued report or activity undertaken that results in (1) confirming risk areas or management challenges that caused the agency to take corrective action, (2) achieving real dollar savings or reduced regulatory burden, (3) identifying significant wrongdoing by individuals that results in criminal or administrative action, (4) clearing an individual wrongly accused, or (5) identifying regulatory actions or oversight that may have contributed to the occurrence of a specific event or incident or resulted in a potential adverse impact on public health or safety.

[5] The agency required more than 90 days to review 5 of 6 recommendations on the Agreement State Program audit before resolution. Three of the 5 recommendations were agreed to within 98 days.

[6] The agency required more than 90 days to review 4 recommendations on the Quality Assurance Planning for New Reactors audit before resolution. Subsequently, all 4 recommendations have been closed or resolved.

[7] The agency required more than 90 days to review 3 of 5 recommendations on the Audit of NRC's Implementation of 10 CFR Part 21, "Reporting of Defects and Noncompliance." Subsequently, all 5 recommendations have been resolved.

[8] The agency required more than 90 days to resolve 2 of 5 recommendations on the Audit of the NRC's Management of Licensee Commitments before resolution. Subsequently, all 5 recommendations have been resolved.

[9] The measure will change from final agency action within 1 year on audit recommendations to 2 years on audit recommendations starting in FY 2010.

[10] Starting in FY 2012, OIG will measure the percentage of active cases completed in less than 18 months on average.

OIG Strategic Goal 2: Enhance the NRC's Efforts To Increase Security in Response to an Evolving Threat Environment

	2009	2010	2011	2012	2013	2014
Measure 1. Percentage of OIG products/activities undertaken to identify critical risk areas or management challenges relating to the improvement of the NRC's security programs.						
Target	85%	90%	90%	90%	TBD	90%
Actual	100%	100%	100%	100%	TBD	TBD
Measure 2. Percentage of OIG products/activities that have a high impact on improving the NRC's security program.						
Target	70%	75%	75%	75%	TBD	75%
Actual	100%	100%	100%	100%	TBD	TBD
Measure 3. Number of audit recommendations agreed to by the agency.						
Target	90%	92%	92%	92%	TBD	92%
Actual	82%[11]	97%	100%	96%	TBD	TBD
Measure 4. Final agency action within 2 years of audit recommendations.						
Target	65%[12]	70%	70%	70%	TBD	70%
Actual	40%[13]	80%	100%	88%	TBD	TBD
Measure 5. Agency action in response to investigative reports.						
Target	90%	90%	90%	90%	TBD	90%
Actual	100%	100%	100%	100%	TBD	TBD
Measure 6. Complete active cases in less than 18 months on average.						
Target				90%[14]	TBD	90%
Actual				100%	TBD	TBD

---

[11] The agency took more than 90 days to review 2 recommendations on the National Source Tracking System audit. The agency agreed to both recommendations within 97 days.

[12] The measure will change from final agency action within 1 year on audit recommendations to 2 years on audit recommendations starting in FY 2010.

[13] The agency is taking more than 1 year to complete final action on recommendations related to information security. The agency agreed with all recommendations, and action has been taken to correct identified deficiencies.

[14] Starting in FY 2012, OIG will measure the percentage of active cases completed in less than 18 months on average.

OIG Strategic Goal 3: Improve the Economy, Efficiency, and Effectiveness with Which the NRC Manages and Exercises Stewardship over Its Resources						
	2009	2010	2011	2012	2013	2014
Measure 1. Percentage of OIG products/activities undertaken to identify critical risk areas or management challenges relating to the improvement of the NRC's resources stewardship.						
Target	65%	80%	80%	80%	TBD	80%
Actual	100%	100%	100%	100%	TBD	TBD
Measure 2. Percentage of OIG products/activities that have a high impact on improving the NRC's resources stewardship.						
Target	70%	85%	85%	85%	TBD	85%
Actual	92%	70%[15]	65%[16]	85%	TBD	TBD
Measure 3. Number of audit recommendations agreed to by the agency.						
Target	90%	90%	92%	92%	TBD	92%
Actual	96%	100%	100%	100%	TBD	TBD
Measure 4. Final agency action within 2 years of audit recommendations.						
Target	65%[17]	70%	70%	70%	TBD	70%
Actual	54%[18]	93%	100%	86%	TBD	TBD
Measure 5. Agency action in response to investigative reports.						
Target	90%	90%	90%	90%	TBD	90%
Actual	100%	100%	100%	100%	TBD	TBD
Measure 6. Acceptance by NRC's Office of the General Counsel of OIG-referred Program Fraud and Civil Remedies Act cases.						
Target	70%[19]					
Actual	No referrals					
Measure 7. Complete active cases in less than 18 months on average.						
Target				90%[20]	TBD	90%
Actual				96%	TBD	TBD

---

[15] For FY 2010, a more rigorous standard was applied for the impact of investigations in the corporate management arena.

[16] For FY 2011, a more rigorous standard was applied for the impact of investigations in the corporate management arena.

[17] The measure will change from final agency action within 1 year on audit recommendations to 2 years on audit recommendations starting in FY 2010.

[18] The agency is taking more than 1 year to complete final action on 12 of 17 Training and Development audit recommendations. The agency agreed with all recommendations, and final action has been completed on all 17 recommendations.

[19] The performance measure was determined to be ineffective because another NRC program office was primarily responsible for ensuring completion of action with minimal activity from year to year and because the measure will be removed starting in FY 2010.

[20] Starting in FY 2012, OIG will measure the percentage of active cases completed in less than 18 months on average.

VERIFICATION AND VALIDATION OF MEASURED VALUES AND PERFORMANCE

OIG uses an automated management information system to capture program performance data for the Audits and Investigations Programs. The integrity of the system was thoroughly tested and validated before implementation. Reports generated by the system provide both detailed information and summary data. All system data are deemed reliable.

PROGRAM EVALUATIONS (PEER REVIEWS)

Quality assurance reviews undertaken in FY 2010 and FY 2011 by an NRC OIG consultant determined that audits were conducted in conformance with the Government Accountability Office's Government Auditing Standards. An independent audit peer review performed in FY 2009 by the U.S. Small Business Administration OIG found that the Audits Program's system of quality control provided reasonable assurance that audits were conducted in accordance with applicable professional standards.

In addition, an independent investigative peer review was conducted by the U.S. Department of State OIG in FY 2010 of the OIG Investigations Program. The program was found to be in compliance with the Council of the Inspectors General on Integrity and Efficiency and U.S. Department of Justice investigative standards.

INSPECTOR GENERAL REFORM ACT CERTIFICATION FOR FY 2014

In accordance with the Inspector General Reform Act (Public Law 110-409), the NRC OIG budget request submitted to the NRC Chairman for FY 2014 was for $11.105 million and 58 FTE and was subsequently approved. The Inspector General certifies that NRC's OIG training request of $120,000 satisfies the training requirements for the Inspector General's office. In addition, funds are available for the NRC OIG share of the resources needed to support the Council of the Inspectors General on Integrity and Efficiency.

FY 2014 OFFICE OF THE INSPECTOR GENERAL BUDGET RESOURCES LINKED TO STRATEGIC GOALS

The following table depicts the relationship of the Inspector General program and associated resource requirements to OIG strategic goals.

FY 2014 Office of the Inspector General Budget Resources Linked to Strategic Goals			
Program Links to Strategic Goals	OIG Strategic Goals		
	Strengthen the NRC's Public Health and Safety Efforts	Enhance the NRC's Security Efforts	Increase the NRC's Resource Stewardship Efforts
FY 2014 Programs ($11,105,000; 58 FTE)			
Audits ($7,314,000; 37 FTE)	$3,188,000 18.5 FTE	$1,323,000 6.5 FTE	$2,803,000 12.0 FTE
Investigations ($3,791,000; 21 FTE)	$1,475,000 8.0 FTE	$631,000 3.5 FTE	$1,685,000 9.5 FTE

Numbers may not add due to rounding.

MANAGEMENT AND OPERATIONAL SUPPORT

OIG's Management and Operational Support staff comprises senior managers, the general counsel, and an administrative support staff. OIG's senior managers provide the continued vision, strategic direction, and guidance on the conduct and supervision of audits and investigations. Senior management will also ensure accountability on OIG's established goals and strategies and achievement of intended results.

In furtherance of OIG's mission to promote economy and efficiency and to prevent fraud, waste, and abuse in agency programs and operations, OIG's general counsel, in coordination with cognizant OIG staff, will conduct analyses of existing and proposed legislation, regulations, directives, and policy issues. These objective analyses will result in timely written commentaries to the agency that prospectively identify and prevent potential problems.

The administrative support staff will assist OIG programs by providing independent personnel services; information technology and information management support; financial management, policy, and strategic planning support; training coordination; and the publication of OIG's Semiannual Report to Congress in accordance with the requirements in the Inspector General Act.

To carry out the functions of this program in FY 2014, OIG estimates that its costs will be $1,422,000, which includes salaries and benefits for 8 FTE. The tables below provide a breakdown of the FY 2014 budget estimates for Management and Operational Support by program and a cost comparison by function.

Allocation of Support Costs to OIG Programs

Management and Operational Support Allocation by Program ($K)	FY 2014 FTE	FY 2014 Salaries and Benefits	FY 2014 Program Support
Audits	5	850	39
Investigations	3	510	23
Total	8	$1,360	$62

Numbers may not add due to rounding.

Comparative Costs of Management and Operational Support

Summary	FY 2012 Enacted	FY 2014 Request[21]
Budget Authority by Function ($K)		
Salaries and Benefits	1,322	1,360
Program Support	81	62
Total Budget Authority	$1,403	$1,422
FTE	8	8

Numbers may not add due to rounding.

---

[21] The OIG Management and Operational Support staff comprises senior managers, a general counsel, and administrative support personnel. To carry out the function of this program for FY 2014, OIG estimates its costs to be $1.422 million, which includes salaries and benefits for eight FTE. The associated FTE and salaries and benefits estimates and program support estimates were allocated in proportion to each program's FTE percentage.

Appendix I:
Budget Authority by Function

Appendix I:

Budget Authority by Function

The U.S. Nuclear Regulatory Commission's (NRC's) budget authority is aggregated into the major categories of salaries and benefits, contract support, and travel. Salaries and benefits are estimated based upon full-time equivalent (FTE), pay rates, pay raise assumptions, and effective pay period for pay raise. Benefits costs include the Government's contributions for retirement, health benefits, life insurance, Medicare, Social Security, and the Thrift Savings Plan. Contract support comprises obligations for commercial contracts; interagency agreements; grants; and other nontravel services, such as rent and utility payments. Travel costs primarily comprise expenses for nuclear reactor inspection trips.

Budget Authority by Function (Dollars in Millions)		FY 2014	
NRC Appropriations	FY 2012 Enacted	Request	Changes from Enacted
Salaries and Expenses (S&E)			
Salaries and Benefits	590.3	615.2	24.9
Contract Support	405.1	404.8	(0.3)
Travel	31.9	24.0	(7.8)
Total (S&E)	**1,027.2**	**1,043.9**	**16.7**
Office of the Inspector General (OIG)			
Salaries and Benefits	9.5	9.9	0.4
Contract Support	1.2	1.0	(0.2)
Travel	0.2	0.3	0.0
Total (OIG)	**10.9**	**11.1**	**0.2**
Total NRC Appropriation			
Salaries and Benefits	599.7	625.0	25.3
Contract Support	406.3	405.7	(0.5)
Travel	32.1	24.3	(7.8)
Total (NRC)	**1,038.1**	**1,055.0**	**16.9**

Numbers may not add due to rounding.

Appendix II:
Corporate Support

CORPORATE SUPPORT APPENDIX

The fiscal year (FY) 2014 Congressional Budget Justification identifies the infrastructure and support costs for the U.S. Nuclear Regulatory Commission (NRC) and distributes them to programs as a portion of the total program cost. The allocation methodology is consistent with the methodology used for preparing the agency's financial statements. The business line tables present the associated infrastructure and support funding included in the programmatic funding to provide the full cost of each business line.

	Corporate Support by Business Line (Dollars in Millions)					
Major Programs	**FY 2012 Enacted**		**FY 2014 Request**		**Delta FY 2014–FY 2012**	
	$M	**FTE**	**$M**	**FTE**	**$M**	**FTE**
Operating Reactors	185.4	408.3	198.5	424.9	13.1	16.5
New Reactors	84.1	185.2	83.6	178.9	(0.5)	(6.4)
Nuclear Reactor Safety	**$269.4**	**593.6**	**$282.0**	**603.7**	**$12.6**	**10.1**
Fuel Facilities	20.4	44.9	22.5	48.2	2.1	3.3
Nuclear Materials Users	29.8	65.7	28.8	61.6	(1.1)	(4.1)
Spent Fuel Storage and Transportation	14.6	32.2	16.2	34.7	1.6	2.6
Decommissioning and Low-Level Waste	13.3	29.3	14.0	30.0	0.7	0.8
High-Level Waste Repository	0.0	0.0	0.0	0.0	0.0	0.0
Nuclear Materials and Waste Safety	**$78.1**	**172.0**	**$81.5**	**174.5**	**$3.4**	**2.5**
Corporate Support	**$347.5**	**765.6**	**$363.6**	**778.3**	**$16.0**	**12.6**

Numbers may not add due to rounding.

Corporate Support Budget Authority and Full-Time Equivalents by Product Line
(Dollars in Millions)

Product Line	FY 2012 Enacted		FY 2014 Request		Delta FY 2014–FY 2012	
	$M	FTE	$M	FTE	$M	FTE
Acquisitions	0.0	0.0	19.2	74.3	19.2	74.3
Administrative Services	105.7	106.4	122.0	110.3	16.3	3.9
Financial Management	46.1	167.1	31.7	101.4	(14.5)	(65.7)
Generic HLS	0.9	1.3	0.0	0.0	(0.9)	(1.3)
Human Resource Management	29.4	82.8	25.9	76.2	(3.5)	(6.6)
Information Management	24.8	82.8	26.7	84.7	1.8	1.9
Information Technology	82.2	122.8	89.7	126.7	7.5	3.9
Outreach	19.8	19.3	5.5	19.2	(14.2)	(0.1)
Policy Support	36.7	183.1	36.9	177.4	0.2	(5.8)
Training	0.0	0.0	4.2	8.2	4.2	8.2
Travel	1.9	0.0	1.7	0.0	(0.2)	0.0
Total	**$347.5**	**765.6**	**$363.6**	**778.3**	**$16.0**	**12.6**

Numbers may not add due to rounding.

The agency's infrastructure and support involve centrally managed activities necessary for the staff and agency programs to achieve goals more efficiently and effectively. These activities include acquisitions, administrative services, financial management, generic homeland security, human resource management, information management, information technology, outreach, and policy support. The workload, resource changes from the FY 2012 enacted budget, and significant accomplishments for the product lines listed above are described in the following pages. The outputs of the product lines under Corporate Support contribute to the scoring of the NRC Safety and Security Performance Measures and their contribution to the achievement of its Strategic Outcomes. The above table provides a cost breakdown of infrastructure and support by program.

ACQUISITIONS

The Acquisitions budget provides resources for the implementation of an enterprisewide Acquisition System and support for procurement and strategic sourcing activities. This budget includes support for all aspects of contract operations and oversight necessary to ensure that the U.S. Nuclear Regulatory Commission (NRC) obtains goods and services in an effective manner consistent with mission needs, sound business practices, agency guidance, and Federal regulations. In addition, this budget includes support for implementation of an agencywide streamlined process to (1) achieve alignment among budget formulation, program planning, and execution, (2) eliminate duplication of effort, (3) increase use of enterprise contracts, and (4) improve the agency's ability to effectively respond to emergent requirements. In fiscal year (FY) 2014, resources support the agency's acquisition systems, including the legacy Automated Acquisition Management Solution, and the implementation and interfacing of the new Strategic Acquisition System (STAQS) with the core Financial Accounting and Integrated Management Information System (FAIMIS).

CHANGES FROM FY 2012 ENACTED BUDGET

In FY 2014, resources increase to reflect realignment to the new Acquisitions Product Line that will support the implementation of a 21st century strategic acquisition program, including a process to improve the agency's procurement activities and related reporting, and an enterprisewide acquisition system that will be integrated with FAIMIS.

SIGNIFICANT ACCOMPLISHMENTS IN FY 2012

The NRC continued to make progress in implementing a 21st century strategic acquisition program, an integrated financial and acquisition planning, execution, and reporting methodology based on business process improvements through implementation of leading practices and system modernization. The approach is based on enterprise spending management and strategic sourcing principles that have a proven track record of success in industry and Federal agencies. In FY 2012, the agency completed its second spending analysis and established four additional Portfolio Councils. In addition, eight enterprisewide contracts were awarded—three under the Portfolio Council for Education and Training and five under the Portfolio Council for Meetings and Conferences. The agency also conducted a thorough planning assessment to determine the most cost-effective approach to implement an acquisition system that will be integrated with FAIMIS. In June 2012, the agency selected a shared service provider to implement STAQS.

The NRC performed contract management necessary to ensure that it obtains goods and services in an efficient and effective manner consistent with mission needs and sound business practices. Contract management tasks included contract negotiation, award, administration, and closeout; grants award and administration; and administration of the NRC Purchase Card Program and the Agency Acquisition Certification and Training Program. The agency also provided oversight for commercial contracts; grants; and interagency agreements, including those with U.S. Department of Energy laboratories. During FY 2012, the agency maintained an Acquisition Professional Development Program to support the training and development of entry-level contracting specialists and initiated implementation of defined strategic sourcing processes with expanded use of enterprisewide contracts.

ADMINISTRATIVE SERVICES

The Administrative Services budget provides resources for rent and utilities for headquarters (HQ), regional, and Technical Training Center space; corporate rulemaking; Information Technology (IT) systems that support security, space planning, and administrative services for the U.S. Nuclear Regulatory Commission (NRC); facilities management, including operation and maintenance services, systems and office furniture, property management, labor services, custodial services, operation and maintenance services, and building alterations; support services, including fleet management, transit subsidies, supplies, and multimedia services; physical and personnel security services, including security equipment and investigations, drug testing, and guard services; and support and guard services in the regions.

CHANGES FROM FY 2012 ENACTED BUDGET

In FY 2014, resources increase for rent and utilities and for physical and personnel security to comply with mandatory security requirements throughout the agency. The increase is partially offset by decreases associated with the work on the Three White Flint North building and an agency-wide effort to reduce overhead resources through increased efficiency and effectiveness. Additional resource increases are associated with required One White Flint North (OWFN) facility rehabilitation, including the initial phase of the modernization to the heating, ventilation, and air conditioning systems.

SIGNIFICANT ACCOMPLISHMENTS IN FY 2012

In support of Executive Order 13514, "Federal Leadership in Environmental, Energy, and Economic Performance," the NRC installed additional upgrades to the energy management system in Two White Flint North (TWFN) and variable frequency drives on the chillers in OWFN, replaced two cooling towers in TWFN, and installed new LED lighting in the elevator lobbies of TWFN. All of these projects resulted in a reduction of electrical consumption. The cooling tower replacement also resulted in a reduction in water consumption. In addition, for the third consecutive year, the NRC was recognized for outstanding achievement in recycling by Montgomery County, MD.

On June 29, 2012, the developer, LCOR, received notice of substantial completion and certificate of Use and Occupancy from Montgomery County for the 3WFN base building. This was a significant milestone. LCOR delivered completed floors in five phases over a 6-month period.

FINANCIAL MANAGEMENT

The fiscal year (FY) 2014 Financial Management budget supports the modernization and operation of the U.S. Nuclear Regulatory Commission's (NRC's) financial systems, budget development and execution, agency financial services, accounting and reporting activities, administration of a robust internal control program, and strategic and performance planning to achieve the effective and efficient use of the agency's financial resources.

Resources for financial systems modernization will be used to provide steady-state operational support for the new core financial system, Financial Accounting and Integrated Management Information System (FAIMIS), and transition to the Governmentwide e-Travel contract.

CHANGES FROM FY 2012 ENACTED BUDGET

In FY 2014, resources decrease due to the decommissioning of two financial systems and to reflect realignment to the new Acquisitions product line that will support the implementation of a 21st century strategic acquisition program, including a process to improve the agency's procurement activities and related reporting, and an enterprisewide acquisition system that will be integrated with FAIMIS.

SIGNIFICANT ACCOMPLISHMENTS IN FY 2012

The NRC took a number of actions to improve financial management in the agency during FY 2012. Significant accomplishments in this area include progress toward the modernization of financial systems, augmentation of the agency's contracting and procurement practices, enhancements to the Budget Formulation System (BFS), implementation of new budget execution and funds utilization processes, receipt of an unqualified opinion on the FY 2012 Financial Statements Audit, and continued improvement in the agency's business processes.

Sustained emphasis on modern Web-enabled technology, automated processes, and extensive user support has improved the financial information available to the NRC. This has allowed for better-informed decisionmaking.

On June 15, 2012, the NRC published a final rule in the *Federal Register* amending the licensing, inspection, and annual fees charged to its applicants and licensees. The amendments are necessary to implement the Omnibus Budget Reconciliation Act of 1990 (OBRA-90), as amended, which requires the NRC to recover, through fees, approximately 90 percent of its budget authority in FY 2012, not including amounts appropriated for waste incidental to reprocessing and amounts appropriated for generic homeland security activities. Based on the Consolidated Appropriations Act of 2012, the NRC's required fee recovery amount for the FY 2012 budget was $1,038.1 million. After accounting for billing adjustments, the total amount to be billed as fees to licensees was $901 million. The *Federal Register* notice can be accessed at http://www.gpo.gov/ fdsys/pkg/FR-2012-06-15/pdf/2012-14589.pdf.

For the ninth consecutive year, an independent auditor has rendered an unqualified opinion on the NRC financial statements. The auditor also rendered an unqualified opinion on the agency's internal controls, concluding that the NRC had no reportable conditions or significant deficiencies.

The NRC continued to make substantial progress in modernizing its financial systems throughout FY 2012. The NRC enhanced system performance, data integrity, business processes, user expertise, and reporting in FAIMIS. On July 31, 2012, the NRC completed a FAIMIS re-hosting initiative and successfully transferred hosting and customer Helpdesk support services for FAIMIS from the U.S. Department of the Interior's National Business Center to CGI Federal's Phoenix Data Center. As a result of the FAIMIS re-hosting initiative, the NRC is hosted within a Federal cloud environment and has direct access to the technical and business expertise of the Momentum System owners (Momentum is the commercial-off-the-shelf (COTS) system upon which FAIMIS is based). In FY 2012, the NRC upgraded its COTS HRMS for time and labor. The new HRMS system not only strengthened data security, implemented electronic workflows, and reduced yearly costs, but is more user-friendly and expanded analytical capabilities for better management of the agency's payroll. The NRC also added a salary and benefits projection application to its BFS. This BFS enhancement facilitates the analysis of employee compensation and benefits scenarios for future years and improves budget forecasting. Sustained emphasis on modern Web-enabled technology, automated processes, and extensive user support has improved the financial information available to the NRC, which has allowed for better-informed decisionmaking.

Because of continued enhancements made to the agency's financial management processes, the NRC has once again achieved operational excellence in FY 2012 and has completed all other FY 2012 external reporting submissions to the U.S. Department of the Treasury and Office of Management and Budget on time. In addition, for the 11th consecutive time, the NRC received the Certificate of Excellence in Accountability Reporting award from the Association of Government Accountants.

NRC staff successfully completed nine business process improvement (BPI) projects and started ten others, including projects that will reduce agency overhead, as the result of increased efficiency and effectiveness. In addition, reliance on contractors for process improvement has continued to diminish as the expertise of the agency's BPI team has continued to increase. The NRC's BPI team regularly interacts with the Federal Improvement team to share BPI best practices with the 300 members who represent 33 different Federal improvement organizations. Further, the NRC performed a comprehensive review of agency overhead functions (e.g., administrative services, human capital, financial management (including contract management), and information technology) to identify effective, efficient and cost-conscious business solutions and to eliminate duplicative processes and functions.

GENERIC HOMELAND SECURITY

There are no resources in the Generic Homeland Security budget in fiscal year (FY) 2014 because the requirements under Homeland Security Presidential Directive 12 will be fully implemented by FY 2013. Any resources supporting maintenance of security equipment and physical access control systems are budgeted with other recurring costs in the Administrative Services Product Line.

HUMAN RESOURCE MANAGEMENT

In fiscal year (FY) 2014 resources provide for recruitment and staffing activities; work-life services, including employee counseling; employee and labor relations; and agencywide policy development and strategic workforce planning. In addition, resources provide for Permanent Change of Station (PCS) Program activities, including resident inspector moves; oversight of the Open Collaborative Work Environment (differing professional opinions, nonconcurrence process, and open door policy); and Internal Safety Culture Program activities.

CHANGES FROM FY 2012 ENACTED BUDGET

In FY 2014, resources decrease as a result of anticipated reduction of program requirements for PCS activities. In addition, resources for agency Training and Development were realigned to the newly added Training Product Line for FY 2014.

SIGNIFICANT ACCOMPLISHMENTS IN FY 2012

For several years, the U.S. Nuclear Regulatory Commission (NRC) experienced growth resulting from an increased interest in nuclear power. As the NRC moved toward the future, staff levels stabilized, and any growth over the next several years is unlikely. In response, the NRC adjusted its human capital strategies to ensure an approach that focuses on the mission of protecting public health and safety while remaining mindful of staff needs.

The NRC's human capital approach supported increasing mandates within a no-growth budget environment. The NRC's strategy was to transform workforce centers by reducing inefficiencies and overhead and by centralizing and streamlining processes. The NRC viewed work in a context of budgeted priorities and strategically focused on not only replacing employees who depart but also fine-tuning available skills sets to meet future mission needs while it still emphasized Governmentwide programs, such as hiring of the disabled, employing veterans, enhancing diversity management, and supporting the agency's Comprehensive Diversity Management Plan. Steps included individual offices developing detailed plans for efficiencies and consolidation; developing a detailed approach and framework for the staff transition aspects of the plan, including transitioning affected employees to newly defined positions; and developing a communication plan that included employee meetings, frequently asked questions, and career counseling. Additionally, the NRC conducted a limited buyout early in FY 2012.

Over the past 18 months, the NRC used a variety of methods and measures to regulate hiring. These methods refined the hiring process and helped control the use of full-time equivalents (FTE). During the first three quarters of FY 2012, these hiring controls resulted in the attainment of FTE targets that allowed the NRC to expand entry-level hiring for engineers and scientists. The NRC worked to institutionalize a workforce planning process using a mission-critical occupation framework that ensured that the agency has the appropriate number of staff with the right skills, competencies, and experience to ensure successful job performance and realization of organizational objectives. The NRC continued to model a recruitment program that attracted a diverse group of candidates and continued to recruit externally, as appropriate. The NRC developed and implemented a recruitment program that would attract a diverse group of candidates. The agency continued to recruit externally for targeted critical skills, while also focusing on ensuring that the current workforce was engaged and motivated to maximize efficiency of the existing staff.

The NRC also adapted its training and development programs to meet the changing needs of the agency staff and changes in technology to ensure that critical skills and competencies were available for the future. The NRC continued to focus on a competency-based approach to training to ensure a line-of-sight alignment between employees' learning experiences and the agency's mission. Training and development programs were designed to shorten the time to competency. As the staff matured, the NRC's learning and development programs continued to evolve to support the needs of the next generation of regulatory experts. For instance, the NRC continued the successful development of new reactor simulators and technical training courses to coincide with the building of a new generation of nuclear reactors. The agency also completed and expanded the pilot use of paperless technical subject matter classroom training using tablet-based training and has implemented the use of selected training courses through new enterprisewide contracts. By using these approaches, the NRC ensured effectiveness of training with the added benefits of a reduction in costs and schedule convenience for the learner.

The NRC recognizes the need to capture and maintain the knowledge and skills of senior staff and management as they become eligible for retirement. The agency maintains a knowledge management program to support effective approaches to knowledge collection, transfer, and use. This program includes strategic hiring and training to fill knowledge gaps, establishing an IT infrastructure to facilitate knowledge transfer, and fostering a culture of knowledge transfer and retention.

The NRC continued to be one of the best places to work in the Federal Government according to Federal Human Capital Survey results. The agency excelled in areas, such as matching employees' skills to the agency's mission, strategic management, effective leadership, performance-based advancements, training and development, support for diversity, and work-life balance. The NRC realized that the success of the agency depends on the talent and commitment of its employees and strived to create a workplace rich in work-life balance where employees were engaged in meaningful and challenging work.

INFORMATION MANAGEMENT

The Information Management (IM) program develops and implements the framework and technologies for managing and protecting information to ensure it is available to support a stable and predictable regulatory environment. In fiscal year (FY) 2014, IM resources will provide document and records management services, such as the operation of the Public Document Room; electronic document intake, profiling, indexing, and retrieval; modernization of internal and external Web sites; and compliance with the Freedom of Information Act (FOIA) and the Privacy Act.

Information security activities support secure communications and information security, policy and procedures, maintenance/services and supplies, classification management, and management of Sensitive Unclassified Nonsafeguards Information. FY 2014 resources will fund implementation of a new Governmentwide policy on Controlled Unclassified Information and Universal Content Management.

Central management of the U.S. Nuclear Regulatory Commission's (NRC's) subscriptions to technical journals and databases, online codes and standards, and electronic newsletters journals supports the scientific and research work of the agency staff and the regulatory mission of the agency. Electronic newsletters are an integral component of communication within the energy industry, and these subscriptions ensure that the Commission, management, and staff maintain currency with industry developments, political decisions, and stakeholder concerns. Subscriptions to industry codes and standards are necessary to support the staff's determinations of compliance with Commission regulations. The codes and standards are cited in the regulations, and staff members require access to cited codes and standards to conduct the necessary inspections and reviews to determine compliance with NRC requirements.

CHANGES FROM FY 2012 ENACTED BUDGET

In FY 2014, resources increase to support Universal Content Management, which will allow the NRC Legacy Systems to share data in a more streamlined manor. The increase is partially offset by decreases to the Agencywide Documents Access and Management System (ADAMS) and Document Records Management.

SIGNIFICANT ACCOMPLISHMENTS IN FY 2012

Effective IM ensures that needed information is available to the staff to help support planned regulatory programs and policies. It also allowed the NRC to meet its openness objective related to informing and involving stakeholders in the regulatory process by providing timely access to accurate agency information. FY 2012 accomplishments in this area included (1) improvement of the efficiency of the agency's FOIA program through the use of e-mail de-duplication software, (2) modernization of the NRC's public document publishing technologies to ensure the timely and accurate dissemination of information to the agency's public Web site, (3) deployment of Internet Protocol Version 6 to the agency's public Web site to ensure worldwide compatibility, (4) consolidation of the agency's Web publishing services to ensure effective and timely delivery of information to the staff and stakeholders, (5) completion of the migration of the agency's legacy forms management system to a new Portable Document Format (PDF)-based system, (6) continuation of personal interactions with stakeholders through the Public Document Room where stakeholders can work directly with a person to retrieve information, and (7) dissemination of key information through the issuance of timely public meeting notices, FOIA responses, and documents made publicly available in ADAMS.

INFORMATION TECHNOLOGY

In fiscal year (FY) 2014, resources will fund the U.S. Nuclear Regulatory Commission's (NRC's) information technology (IT) infrastructure, enduser support services for IT applications, database and application support for agency systems, and configuration management and IT project management support. Funded programs include Capital Planning and Investment Control (CPIC) processes, IT strategic management and enterprise architecture planning, and agencywide IT procurement management.

The budget will fund the following ongoing activities:

- IT infrastructure enduser support services, telecommunications services, network and production operations, and central management of all desktop, laptop, and network resources and services at headquarters (HQ), regional offices, and resident inspector sites. Resources support the Network Operations Center, Customer Support Center, the Consolidated Testing Facility, and seat management and desktop support for more than 5,800 desktop workstations and the supporting infrastructure. Also included are the managed public key infrastructure and production operations support, including systems administration and data center operations.
- Identification of the best technologies to fill gaps associated with strategic goals, such as "Working from Anywhere" and "Working with Anyone," and the identification, testing, and piloting of new technology needed to support specific agency business needs. Recent examples include technologies to support the NRC's Open Government flagship initiative, such as enhancing stakeholder engagement using innovative and cost-effective collaboration technologies, defining common strategies to support mobility and universal access, consolidating systems into enterprise solutions, and increasing the number of devices that can access agency systems through a Bring Your Own Device program.
- The NRC's Legacy System modernization and transformation program. Resources will be used to support an effective CPIC program for enterprisewide configuration management and maintenance and operational support of approximately 120 application systems. In addition, resources will support project management, business analysis, and applications development for office-specific and enterprisewide applications.
- Compliance with the Federal Information Security Management Act, IT security policy, standards, training, cyber situational awareness and response, and security authorization of all NRC IT systems. Resources support the use of distinctive IT security tools and expertise to provide a robust cyber program for the protection of NRC cyber assets. Efforts support infrastructure operations, including system authorization activities, penetration testing and system scanning, development of policies and standards, and development and delivery of computer security training and awareness. Also employed are automated forensic software and hardware products used in responding to security incidents. The cyber-security experts also review new technologies and work with system owners to ensure those technologies are implemented in a way that is safe and meets Federally mandated and NRC-defined security requirements.
- Cyber Situational Awareness Program for penetration testing, vulnerability and threat assessments, real-time monitoring, visibility and reporting, and computer security incident response, along with providing insight into the security impact that new technologies will have on the NRC infrastructure and enabling continuous cyber-security reporting.

- Reduction of the NRC's data center footprint. Efforts include leveraging a combination of strategies to lower energy consumption and operation costs through increased use of cloud computing alternatives, managing the NRC's application system modernization initiatives, strengthening server and desktop virtualization, and setting other green IT technologies into operation across the enterprise. As a part of the NRC HQ building, the agency will build an energy-efficient modern data center that uses green technologies in space, design, power, heating, ventilation, and cooling to support energy-efficient 24/7 data center operations.
- Outsourcing data center services, which is a major step to achieving cloud computing initiatives at the NRC.
- Enterprisewide e-mail encryption will ensure compliance with the Executive Order mandating all Government agencies encrypt all out-going email.

CHANGES FROM FY 2012 ENACTED BUDGET

In FY 2014, resources increase because of infrastructure costs, enhancement of the IT security program, modernization of the NRC Legacy Systems, and support of the centralization of the IT infrastructure and application support activities. These increases are offset by reductions and reinvestments that reflect reduced maintenance needs of older Legacy systems, delaying system modernization where possible, reducing support levels for some systems, and migration to shared service platforms (therefore reducing data center requirements).

SIGNIFICANT ACCOMPLISHMENTS IN FY 2012

Effective IT infrastructure ensured that the NRC had a reliable and responsive foundation of technology to support business needs and agency operations to advance the agency's mission. Several objectives were achieved in this area. The agency migrated its Internet service to a Managed Trusted Internet Protocol Service through the General Services Administration Networx contract. Other key successes included IT infrastructure move support in one of the agency's regional offices and significant preparation for a planned move to the agency's new HQ office building. The agency enhanced services available to its mobile workforce by making WiFi access available to mobile desktop users and successfully piloted a Bring Your Own Device solution for e-mail and calendaring functions.

The NRC developed a plan to map strategic programs and business objectives to the agency security architecture to provide a prioritized blueprint for secure IT capability. The NRC implemented an Automated Plan of Action and Milestone process that uses an automated tool to improve quality assurance and timely reporting by system owners.

Another primary focus area was service, a key component of operational excellence across the agency. In a continuing effort to evaluate the effectiveness of its information technology/information management (IT/IM) services, the NRC solicited feedback from employees on its IT/IM program by adding questions on this topic to the employee viewpoint survey conducted in FY 2011. The agency is also conducting an independent validation and verification of its IT/IM services to assess the costs of existing services and to establish clear service expectations. The NRC also conducted a facilitated process to update its IT/IM Strategic Plan in coordination with ongoing efforts to update the NRC Strategic Plan. The IT/IM Roadmap also contributed to planning and budget formulation by providing a view of current IT/IM capabilities and agency transition plans through 2013. The procurement to establish a new enterprisewide contract for maintenance, operation, and modernization of agency IT systems was initiated in FY 2011.

Maintenance, Operation, and Modernization (MOM) Functional Area 2 (FA2) Maintenance and Operations of Legacy Systems contract task orders were awarded in FY 2012 to procure continuous maintenance and operational IT support services for current NRC automated computer systems. The MOM FA2 contract included 24 task orders and provided maintenance and operations support to 11 NRC program offices.

OUTREACH

In fiscal year (FY) 2014, resources provide for outreach activities, which include maintaining the civil rights complaints process; promoting affirmative employment, diversity, and inclusion; ensuring compliance with small business laws, conducting business development assistance, and providing the maximum practicable prime and subcontract opportunities for small businesses; and continuing efforts to implement the U.S. Nuclear Regulatory Commission's (NRC's) Outreach and Compliance Coordination Program, in accordance with applicable Federal civil rights statutes and NRC regulations.

Resources also provide for grants to Minority Serving Institutions (MSI) to assist them in producing a skilled diverse Science, Technology, Engineering, and Mathematics (STEM) workforce.

Resources also support hosting of the annual Regulatory Information Conference (RIC) with the nuclear industry to discuss safety and regulatory issues of mutual interest. The objective of the RIC is to provide a communication forum for senior NRC and industry management on current and future safety initiatives and regulatory issues.

CHANGES FROM FY 2012 ENACTED BUDGET

In FY 2014, resources decrease because of the elimination of the Integrated University Program and education Grants Program.

SIGNIFICANT ACCOMPLISHMENTS IN FY 2012

The NRC's Small Business Program conducted more than 100 acquisition compliance and subcontracting plan compliance reviews totaling over $300 million in products and services, which led to the agency's highest level of small business contract performance to date. As a result, the NRC is currently one of only two Federal agencies exceeding all of its small business prime contract goals. The NRC held a Small Business Seminar and Matchmaking Event in FY 2012, which represents the first NRC small business event that included collaboration with the Montgomery County Chamber of Commerce, Webstreamed content from agency headquarters, and senior-level participation from the Executive Director of Operations and the Commission.

The NRC received accolades from private and public sector entities, including the White House Initiative on Historically Black Colleges and Universities (HBCU), for "Best Practices" related to its compliance and MSI programs. The NRC conducted significant preaward compliance reviews and postaward monitoring; provided outreach, technical assistance, coordination, and training to ensure civil rights compliance; and monitored grantees (through desk and onsite audits) to ensure funding objectives and compliance requirements were met.

NRC cosponsored numerous MSI activities, including experiential learning opportunities and STEM summer camps and symposiums for K-12 students. The agency participated in major conferences and symposiums that were attended by over 1,000 participants related to (1) guidance for educators administering K-12 summer camps and symposiums, (2) careers in the nuclear industry, (3) emergency management preparedness, (4) environmental justice, (5) the transition of veterans into STEM and civilian occupations, (6) contracts and grants skill building, (7) MSI Capacity Building and Technical Assistance Conference, and (8) the White House Initiatives on HBCU. These efforts resulted in the designation of the NRC as a "Top Supporter" of HBCU engineering programs for the fifth consecutive year.

The agency issued its annual No FEAR Act training, which achieved an employee completion rate of 99 percent. The agency processed 30 informal and 15 formal Equal Employment Opportunity complaints, completed investigations, issued final agency decisions, and conducted mediations. The agency held numerous informational "lunch and learn" sessions and a Diversity Day Program.

In FY 2012, the agency awarded 75 education-related grants, which included 25 grants for curriculum development, 15 grants for faculty development, 9 grants for scholarships, 13 grants for fellowships, and 13 grants to Trade Schools and Community Colleges for scholarships. These grants assist in expanding the workforce in nuclear safety and nuclear-related disciplines and in developing the next-generation nuclear workforce.

POLICY SUPPORT

Resources in fiscal year (FY) 2014 will provide for additional policy and adjudicatory support to the Commission. Specifically, the budget provides resources for the following:

- U.S. Nuclear Regulatory Commission (NRC) policy formulation and guidance
- legal advice and adjudicatory review to the Commission
- independent evaluations of NRC programs and implementation of the Commission's policy directives
- interaction with the Executive Branch on matters of international nuclear safety and security issues and developments
- work with the International Atomic Energy Agency, the Nuclear Energy Agency, and other international partners
- advice and assistance to the Commission on congressional and protocol issues and on public affairs activities leading to openness and increased public confidence
- management and oversight of agency programs

CHANGES FROM FY 2012 ENACTED BUDGET

In FY 2014, resources decrease is due to a change in strategy for capturing the FTE resources for the Commission Adjudicatory Technical Support Program, and is a result of an agencywide effort to reduce overhead resources through increased efficiency and effectiveness.

CORPORATE SUPPORT OUTPUT MEASURES

ACQUISITION

Percent of Eligible Service Contracting Dollars (Contracts over $25,000) That Use Performance-Based Contracting Techniques during the Fiscal Year						
	FY 2009	FY 2010	FY 2011	FY 2012	FY 2013	FY 2014
Target	Not less than 65%	Not less than 65%	Not less than 65%	Not less than 65%	TBD	Not less than 65%
Actual	89%	79%	69%	60.50%		

OMB-Directed Acquisition Reform Initiative Measure—Percent of Required Synopses for Acquisitions Posted on the Governmentwide Point-of-Entry Web Site (www.FedBizOpps.gov) during the Fiscal Year*						
	FY 2009	FY 2010	FY 2011	FY 2012	FY 2013	FY 2014
Target	100% of all required synopses.	100% of all required synopses.	100% of all required synopses.	100% of all required synopses.	TBD	100% of all required synopses.
Actual	100%	100%	100%	100%		

*Percent of required synopses for acquisitions posted on the Governmentwide point-of-entry Web site (www.FedBizOpps.gov) during the fiscal year. Synopses for acquisitions are those valued at over $25,000 for which widespread notice is required, including all associated solicitations except for acquisitions that are covered by an exemption in the Federal Acquisition Regulations.

FINANCIAL MANAGEMENT

Meets Statutory Fee Collection Requirement						
	FY 2009	FY 2010	FY 2011	FY 2012	FY 2013	FY 2014
Target	Achieve approximately 100% actual collections when compared with projected collections. Maintain past due accounts receivable at 1% or less of annual billings for the fiscal year.	Achieve approximately 100% actual collections when compared with projected collections. Maintain past due accounts receivable at 1% or less of annual billings for the fiscal year.	Achieve approximately 100% actual collections when compared with projected collections. Maintain past due accounts receivable at 1% or less of annual billings for the fiscal year.	Achieve approximately 100% actual collections when compared with projected collections. Maintain past due accounts receivable at 1% or less of annual billings for the fiscal year.	TBD	Achieve approximately 100% collections when compared with projected collections. Maintain past due accounts receivable at 1% or less of annual billings for the fiscal year.
Actual	98% collected. Maintained past due amounts receivable at less than 1% of annual billings.	Target met.	99.5% collected. Past due amounts receivable were 1.34% of annual billings.	99.3% collected. Past due amounts receivable were 1.0% of annual billings.		

Percentage of Non-Salary Payments Made Electronically and Accurately within Established Schedule						
	FY 2009	FY 2010	FY 2011	FY 2012	FY 2013	FY 2014
Target	98%	98%	98%	98%	TBD	98%
Actual	96%	98%	98%	98%		

HUMAN RESOURCE MANAGEMENT

	FY 2009	FY 2010	FY 2011	FY 2012	FY 2013	FY 2014
Percentage of Professional Hires Retained for a Minimum of 3 Years after Initial Employment						
Target	85%	85%	85%	85%	TBD	85%
Actual	87%	89%	91%	86.50%		

INFORMATION MANAGEMENT

	FY 2009	FY 2010	FY 2011	FY 2012	FY 2013	FY 2014
Information Dissemination Timeliness—Meets Agency Targets for Key Information Dissemination Channels, including Public Meeting Notices and Freedom of Information Act*						
Target	New measure in FY 2009	Timeliness targets met for FOIA responses, public meeting notices, and NRC documents made publicly available (1)	Meet 3 out of 4 targets.	Meet 3 out of 4 targets.	TBD	Meet 3 out of 4 targets.
Actual	86%	4 out of 4	4 out of 4	3 out of 4		

Targets include the following: (1) Percent of the time NRC responds to FOIA requests within 20 working days (75%), (2) percentage of category 1,2, and 3 meetings on regulatory issues for which the NRC posted a meeting notice on the public meeting notice Web site at least 10 days in advance of the meeting (90%), (3) percent of nonsensitive, unclassified regulatory documents generated by the NRC and sent to the agency's Document Processing Center that are released to the public by the sixth working day after the date of the document (90%), (4) percent of nonsensitive, unclassified regulatory documents received by the NRC that are released to the public by the sixth working day after the document is added to the Agencywide Documents Access and Management System main library (90%).

	FY 2009	FY 2010	FY 2011	FY 2012	FY 2013	FY 2014
Public Score for Information Access—The NRC's Score on the Annual American Customer Satisfaction Index for Federal Web Sites						
Target	New measure in FY 2013				TBD; target to be baselined in FY 2012.	73
Actual						

INFORMATION TECHNOLOGY

Percent of Time That Key Information Technology (IT) Infrastructure Services Are Available						
	FY 2009	FY 2010	FY 2011	FY 2012	FY 2013	FY 2014
Target	New measure in FY 2009	99.50%	99.50%*	99.50%	TBD	Measure replaced with use of NRC Badge for sign-on measure.
Actual	100%	99.90%	99.90%	99.7%		

This measure is calculated based on statistics gathered each month from a network-monitoring tool that constantly monitors the availability status of key infrastructure components. It shows the amount of time, in minutes, that all (any) infrastructure components were unavailable. That information is then used to calculate the overall availability percentage based on the number of working days in each month (the total hours of operation) and the number of people supported by each component.

*Target previously reported as 100% in error.

IT Security Risk Management—Percent of Operational Applications and General Support Systems That Have Met the NRC's Annual Risk Management Activities Requirements in Accordance with Guidance from the Chief Information Officer (CIO)*						
	FY 2009	FY 2010	FY 2011	FY 2012	FY 2013	FY 2014
Target	New measure in FY 2010.		95%	95%	TBD	Measure to be replaced with Cyber Security Program Effectiveness measure.
Actual		96%	97%	96%		

*This measure replaced the output measure "Systems Certification and Accreditation—Percent of Major Applications and General Support That Have Been Certified and Accredited" from the FY 2011 budget. The measure includes certification and accreditation along with other risk-management activities.

IT Investment Management—Average Score on a Scale of 1 to 10 for All NRC IT Investments on the OMB IT Dashboard						
	FY 2009	FY 2010	FY 2011	FY 2012	FY 2013	FY 2014
Target	New measure in FY 2010.		>7.5	80% of agency investments are green at the end of the fiscal year.*	TBD	> 7.5
Actual		6.38	7.53	Green		

*The OMB Exhibit 300 Score measure has been replaced by the IT Dashboard Score. The measure target was changed in FY 2012 to reflect OMB's revised approach to IT Dashboard scoring.

Use of NRC Badge for Sign-On—Percent/Number of Federal Information Security Management Act (FISMA)-Reportable, NRC-Hosted Applications That Use the NRC Badge (Personal Identity Verification Card) for Sign-On*						
	FY 2009	FY 2010	FY 2011	FY 2012	FY 2013	FY 2014
Target	New measure in FY 2013.				TBD; measure to be baselined in FY 2012.	Preliminary target to be established.
Actual						

*This measure replaces the output measure "Percent of the Time That Key IT Infrastructure Services Are Available" from the FY 2012 budget.

	Cyber Security Program Effectiveness—Rating of the NRC's Cyber Security Program Effectiveness Based on the Annual Inspector General FISMA Audit*					
	FY 2009	FY 2010	FY 2011	FY 2012	FY 2013	FY 2014
Target	New measure in FY 2013.					Satisfactory in all areas.
Actual						

This measure replaces the output measure "IT Security Risk Management—Percent of Operational Applications and General Support Systems That Have Met the NRC's Annual Risk Management Activities Requirements in accordance with Guidance from the CIO" from the FY 2011 budget.

Appendix III:
Reimbursable Work

Summary of Reimbursable Work
(New Budget Authority in Thousands of Dollars)

	FY 2012 (Actual)	FY 2014 (Projection)
TECHNICAL ASSISTANCE TO OTHER FEDERAL AGENCIES		
Employee Detail to Domestic Nuclear Detection Office (DHS)	197	174
Employee Detail to National Counterterrorism Center (NCTC)	0	162
Fuel Cycle Research and Development (DOE)	500	500
Gerald R. Ford Class Aircraft Carrier Safety Review (DOE)	1,000	0
Joint Funding of ICRP Activities (EPA)	25	25
Navy Reviews (U.S. Navy)	12	12
Next Generation Nuclear Plant (NGNP) Cooperative Activities (DOE)	0	0
Review/Approval of Selected Foreign Certificates for Packages (Casks) (DOE)	0	100
Review of Alternate Transportation Security Protocol (DOE)	0	0
Route Reviews (DOE)	0	0
Waste Actions for Hanford (DOE)	0	100
Waste Review for West Valley (DOE)	120	0
INTERNATIONAL ASSISTANCE		
International Invitational Travel (IAEA & various foreign governments and international organizations)	156	200
Invitational Travel - American Institute in Taiwan	14	20
COOPERATIVE RESEARCH		
Environmentally Assisted Fatigue Effects (EPRI)	200	0
Sandia Fuels Project - Phase 2 (EPRI)	250	0
Foreign Cooperative Research Agreements (Multiple)	2,246	2,100
SECURITY RELATED ACTIVITIES		
Criminal History Program (Licensees)	2,578	2,500
Information Access Authorization Program (Licensees)	903	880
Material Access Authorization Program (Licensees)	1	0
TOTALS	**$8,202**	**$6,773**

*Does not include classified reimbursable work agreements

Appendix IV:
Estimated Fee Recovery

Agency Fee Recovery
(Dollars in Millions)

	FY 2012 Final Fee Rule 1	FY 2014 Projection
Total Appropriation 2	**1,038.1**	**1,055.0**
Less Non-Fee Items 3	(27.5)	(20.9)
Base	1,010.6	1,034.1
Fee Recovery Rate - 90% of Base	909.5	930.7
Billing & Carryover Adjustments 4	(8.5)	(0.2)
Amount to be Recovered through Fees	**$901.0**	**$930.5**
Estimated Part 170 Fees	**$371.4**	**$375.0**
Percent of total recovered amount	41.2%	40.3%
Estimated Part 171 Annual Fees	**$529.6**	**$555.5**
Percent of total recovered amount	58.8%	59.7%
Total Net Appropriated	**$128.6**	**$124.3**

Numbers may not add due to rounding.

Note: As a fee based agency, reduction to agency base budget yields a 10% reduction in net budget auhtority for every dollar of those reductions

Waste Incidental to Reprocessing (WIR) 3,5	0.8	1.4
Generic Homeland Security 3	26.7	19.5
Total Non-Fee Items	**$27.5**	**$20.9**

1 Published in the Federal Register (76 FR 36780; June 15, 2012)
2 Includes both Salaries and Expenses and Inspector General Appropriations
3 Non Fee Items
4 Includes estimated unpaid invoices and payments of prior year invoices.
5 Prior year Waste Incidental to Reprocessing (WIR) appropriations totaling $2.6 million were allocated in FY 2011 and FY 2012. No significant prior year WIR appropriations are expected to be available in FY 2014.

Appendix V:
Report on Drug Testing

Appendix V: Report to Congress on Drug Testing

Congress and the U.S. Department of Health and Human Services (HHS) initially approved the U.S. Nuclear Regulatory Commission's (NRC's) Drug Testing Program in August 1988, and the agency subsequently updated the program in November 1997. The program was revised again and received approval from HHS on August 23, 2007. The NRC's drug testing requirements for the nuclear industry (licensees), as imposed by agency regulations, are separate and distinct from this program and are not covered by this report. The NRC's Drug Testing Program under Executive Order (E.O.) 12564 includes random, applicant, voluntary, followup, reasonable suspicion, and accident-related drug testing. Testing was initiated for nonbargaining unit employees in November 1988, and for bargaining unit employees in December 1990 after an agreement was negotiated with the National Treasury Employees Union. On August 25, 2008, the NRC's testing program was expanded to include all NRC sensitive positions as testing designated; therefore, all employees became subject to random drug testing.

During fiscal year 2012, the NRC conducted approximately 2,093 tests of all types between October 1, 2011, and September 30, 2012. There were two positive drug test results (both for marijuana). These individuals completed the required outpatient treatment programs. One employee has since retired while the second continues to be subject to followup drug testing.

The NRC also completed internal quality control reviews during the past year to ensure that the agency's program continues to be administered in a fair, confidential, and effective manner.

The NRC's drug testing program is based on the principles and guidance according to E.O. 12564, Public Law 100-71, HHS guidelines, and Commission decisions.

Acronym List

Acronym List

3WFN. Three White Flint North

ABWR. An advanced boiling-water reactor is a Generation III boiling-water reactor.

ACP. American Centrifuge Plant is a future USEC plant to be built in Oak Ridge, TN.

ADAMS. The Agencywide Documents Access and Management System is the U.S. Nuclear Regulatory Commission's (NRC's) official recordkeeping system that provides access to vast "libraries" or collections of documents related to the agency's regulatory activities.

ADR. The Alternative Dispute Resolution Program supports the NRC's commitment to promote and maintain a discrimination-free work environment.

AEA. The Atomic Energy Act refers to a number of different laws on the governance of nuclear power and nuclear weapons production.

AIT: Augmented inspection team

ALARA. As low as is reasonably achievable

ASLB. Atomic Safety and Licensing Board

ASME. The American Society of Mechanical Engineers is a not-for-profit professional organization that enables collaboration, knowledge sharing, and skill development across all engineering disciplines.

ASP. Accident Sequence Precursor

BFS. Budget Formulation System

BWR. A boiling-water reactor is a type of nuclear reactor. It is the second most common type of nuclear reactor after the pressurized-water reactor.

C&A. Certification and Accreditation is a process that ensures that Information Technology (IT) systems and major applications adhere to formal and established security requirements that are well documented and authorized. The Federal Information Security Management Act of 2002 requires C&A.

CAL. Confirmatory action letter

CCDP. Conditional core damage probability

CE. Current estimates are fact-of-life changes in the budget between the President's Budget and the enacted budget.

CFR. The *Code of Federal Regulations* is the codification of the general and permanent rules and regulations published in the *Federal Register* by the executive departments and agencies of the Federal Government of the United States.

CoCs. A certificate of compliance for a cask model is issued by the NRC for findings that meet the requirements in Title 10 of the *Code of Federal Regulations* (10 CFR) 72.236, "Specific Requirements for Spent Fuel Storage Cask Approval and Fabrication."

COL. A combined operating license is the NRC's simultaneous issuance of a nuclear power plant construction permit and operating license.

COTS. Commercial-off-the-shelf (software)

CPIC. Capital Planning and Investment Control compares actual results with expected results after an IT investment has been fully implemented. This is done to assess the IT investment's impact on program performance, to identify any changes or modifications that may be needed, and to revise the IT investment management process based on lessons learned through its application.

DBT. Design-basis threats characterize the adversary against which nuclear plant owners must design physical protection systems and response strategies.

DC. Design certification is the NRC approval of a nuclear power plant design, independent of an application to construct or operate a plant.

DEIS. A draft environmental impact statement is a draft of the document required by the National Environmental Policy Act for Federal Government agency actions "significantly affecting" the quality of the human environment. A decisionmaking tool, an EIS describes the positive and negative environmental effects of proposed agency action and cites alternative actions.

DOE. U.S. Department of Energy

DTTS. The Defense Transportation Tracking System is a satellite-enabled computerized tracking system that supplies information to provide emergency response assistance.

ECM. Enterprise content management includes processes and technologies that support the full lifecycle of the NRC's information.

EIS. An environmental impact statement is a document that the National Environmental Policy Act requires for Federal Government agency actions "significantly affecting the quality of the human environment." A decisionmaking tool, an EIS describes the positive and negative environmental effects of proposed agency action and cites alternative actions.

EPA. Environmental Protection Agency

EPR. Evolutionary Power Reactor

ESBWR. An economic simplified boiling-water reactor is a 4,500-megawatt-thermal (MWt) reactor that uses natural circulation for normal operation and has passive safety features.

ESP. An early site permit is the NRC approval of one or more sites for a nuclear power facility, independent of an application for a construction permit or combined license.

EST. Extended storage and transportation refers to the extended storage and transportation of spent nuclear fuel and high-level waste.

FAIMIS. The Financial Accounting and Integrated Management Information System is part of the NRC's financial systems upgrade.

FCOP. Fuel cycle oversight process

FEIS. Final environmental impact statement

FEMA. Federal Emergency Management Agency

FERC. Federal Energy Regulatory Commission

FFD. The Fitness-for-Duty Program is required for all NRC licensees by 10 CFR Part 26, Subpart K, "FFD Programs for Construction." FFD includes drug testing, behavioral observation, and fitness monitoring programs.

FISMA. The Federal Information Security Management Act is a U.S. Federal law enacted in 2002 as Title III of the E-Government Act of 2002. The act requires each Federal agency to develop, document, and implement an agencywide program to provide information security for the information and information systems that support the operations and assets of the agency, including those that another agency, contractor, or other source provides or manages.

FOF. Force-on-Force exercises assess a nuclear plant's physical protection to defend against the so-called design-basis threat.

FOIA. The Freedom of Information Act is a law ensuring public access to U.S. Government records. Upon written request, agencies of the U.S. Government are required to disclose those records unless they can be lawfully withheld from disclosure under one of nine specific exemptions in the FOIA.

FTE. Full-time equivalent is a way to measure a worker's involvement in a project. An FTE of 1.0 means that the person is equivalent to a full-time worker, whereas an FTE of 0.5 signals that the worker is only half time.

FY. Fiscal year is a period used for calculating annual financial statements in businesses and other organizations.

GE-Hitachi. GE-Hitachi is a joint venture between General Electric, Hitachi, and Toshiba. GE-Hitachi operates the fuel fabrication facility in Wilmington, NC.

GWd/MTU. The measurement of actual energy released per mass of initial fuel is gigawatt days/metric ton of heavy metal (GWd/MTHM), or similar unit (uranium), used in the calculation of burnup or fuel utilization.

HAB. Hostile-action-based emergency preparedness drills are required by NRC regulations. All NRC commercial nuclear power plant licensees are required to participate in emergency preparedness exercises. These exercises are evaluated to ensure the skills of emergency responders are maintained and to identify and correct any weaknesses.

HCU. Historically Black Colleges and Universities

HLS. Homeland security is a concerted national effort to prevent terrorist attacks within the United States, reduce America's vulnerability to terrorism, and minimize the damage and recover from attacks that do occur.

HLW. High-level waste is the highly radioactive material produced as a byproduct of the reactions that occur inside nuclear reactors. High-level wastes are either in the form of spent reactor fuel when it is accepted for disposal or waste materials remaining after spent fuel is reprocessed.

HOC. Headquarters Operations Center

HQ. Headquarters refers to the NRC headquarters campus in the Washington, DC, metropolitan area.

I&C. Instrumentation and control systems use digital devices in safety systems in nuclear facilities. The deployment of digital technology in nuclear facilities has the potential to improve safety and operational performance.

IAEA. International Atomic Energy Agency

IM. Information Management is an NRC-wide initiative to collect and manage agency information; to improve the productivity, effectiveness and efficiency of agency programs; and to enhance the availability and usefulness of information to users inside and outside the agency.

IMPEP. The Integrated Materials Performance Evaluation Program is a program that the NRC designed and piloted as a review process for Agreement State and NRC regional radioactive materials programs.

INIS. International Isotopes

iPWR. Integral pressurized-water reactor

ISFSI. An independent spent fuel storage installation is defined as a complex designed and constructed for the interim storage of spent nuclear fuel, solid reactor-related greater than Class C (GTCC) waste, and other radioactive materials associated with spent fuel and reactor-related GTCC waste storage.

ISA. Integrated safety analysis

ISG. Interim staff guidance refers to documents that the NRC issues to clarify or address issues not discussed in a Standard Review Plan.

ISMP. An Integrated Source Management Portfolio is a secure and effective set of automated tools to house and maintain information on licensees, nationally tracked sources possessed by licensees, and licensee transactions.

IT. Information technology deals with the use of computers and software.

ITAAC. The inspections, tests, analysis, and acceptance criteria process is designed to verify that a new nuclear facility has been constructed and will operate in compliance with the COL, NRC regulations, and the Atomic Energy Act.

IV&V. Independent verification and validation is the process of a third-party check that the NRC performance measures meet the requirements and fulfill their intended purpose.

KEPCO. Korea Electric Power Corporation

LAR. License amendment request

LER. License event report

LER Search. License Event Report Search System

LES. Louisiana Energy Services is a group of some of the largest companies in the nuclear power field and is a supplier of enriched uranium for commercial atomic power reactors.

LLW. Low-level waste includes items that have become contaminated with radioactive material or have become radioactive through exposure to neutron radiation.

LSN. The Licensing Support Network is an electronic system that the NRC's Atomic Safety and Licensing Board Panel operates to provide free Web-based access to documents that may be used as evidence in the NRC's review process and licensing proceedings associated with the application that DOE submitted to seek authorization to construct a high-level radioactive waste repository at Yucca Mountain, NV.

LVS. The License Verification System is a national verification system that would be used to detect and prevent unauthorized parties with malicious intent from obtaining nuclear materials.

MC&A. Material control and accounting means the use of control and monitoring measures to prevent or detect loss of special nuclear materials. Material accounting is defined as the use of statistical and accounting measures to maintain knowledge of the quantities of special nuclear materials present in each area of a facility. It includes the use of physical inventories and material balances to verify the presence of material or to detect the loss of material through theft.

MDEP. The Multinational Design Evaluation Program is a multinational initiative taken by national safety authorities to develop innovative approaches to leverage the resources and knowledge of the national regulatory authorities who will be tasked with reviewing new reactor power plant designs.

MILES. The Multiple Integrated Laser Engagement System is used by the U.S. military and other armed forces around the world for training purposes. It uses lasers and blank cartridges to simulate actual battle.

MOM. Maintenance, Operation, and Modernization

MOX. Mixed oxide is nuclear fuel containing more than one oxide of fissile or fertile materials.

MSI. Minority Serving Institution

NEA. Nuclear Energy Agency

NEPA. National Environmental Policy Act

NERC. The North American Electric Reliability Council is the organization of U.S. electrical grid operators.

NFPA. National Fire Protection Association

NFS. Nuclear Fuel Services, Inc., is a company that supplies fuel for the U.S. Navy's fleet of nuclear-powered vessels. It has also processes weapons-grade uranium into nuclear reactor fuel.

NGNP. A Next Generation Nuclear Plant is a Generation IV version of the very high temperature reactor.

NIST. National Institute of Standards and Technology

NMED. Nuclear Materials Event Database

NMIP. The Nuclear Materials Information Program is an interagency effort that DOE manages to consolidate information from all sources pertaining to worldwide nuclear materials holdings and their security status into an integrated and continuously updated information management system.

NMMSS. The Nuclear Materials Management and Safeguards System is a centralized U.S. Government database that tracks and accounts for source and special nuclear material to ensure that it has not been stolen or diverted to unauthorized users.

NMP. The National Materials Program is a term that has been applied to the broad collective frameworks within which both the NRC and the Agreement States function in carrying out their respective radiation safety regulatory programs.

NRC. U.S. Nuclear Regulatory Commission

NSTS. The National Source Tracking System is a major security initiative of the NRC that tracks high-risk radioactive sources from the time that they are manufactured or imported through their disposal or export, or until they decay enough to no longer be of concern.

NUREG. Nuclear Regulatory Commission regulation. The NRC issues NUREGs.

NWPA. The Nuclear Waste Policy Act of 1982 created a timetable and procedure for establishing a permanent, underground repository for high-level radioactive waste by the mid-1990s. The Act provided for some temporary Federal storage of waste, including spent fuel from civilian nuclear reactors.

OE. Office of Enforcement

OECD. Organisation for Economic Co-operation and Development

OIG. Office of the Inspector General

OIP. Office of International Programs

OMB. Office of Management and Budget

OPM. Office of Personnel Management

ORR. An operational readiness review inspection is conducted by the NRC when construction nears completion for the facility's most safety-significant features, including but not limited to, chemical safety, fire protection, radiological control procedures, emergency preparedness, training, and qualification of facility personnel and criticality safety.

OWFN. One White Flint North

PACS. The Physical Access Control System refers to an NRC infrastructure upgrade.

PB. The President's Budget is the President's proposal to the U.S. Congress, which recommends funding levels for the next fiscal year, beginning October 1.

PBPM. Planning, Budgetary, and Performance Measurement

PDF. Portable Document Format

PCS. Permanent Change of Station is an NRC program that assists with employee relocations.

PII. Personally Identifiable Information

PMM. Project Management Methodology is a tool that describes every step in the project lifecycle in depth, so that project managers know exactly which tasks to complete, when, and how.

PRA. Probabilistic risk assessment

PRM. A petition for rulemaking is the mechanism by which individuals, public interest groups, and private enterprise can argue in favor of changes or new rules for ensuring the general welfare of the Nation.

PSSC. Principle structures, systems, and components

PWR. Pressurized-water reactors keep water under pressure so that it heats but does not boil. The water from the reactor and the water that is turned into steam in the steam generator do not mix.

RAMQC. Radioactive material(s) in quantities of concern include americium-241, cobalt-60, cesium-137, plutonium-238, and strontium-90, among others, in specific quantities. It does not include spent nuclear fuel.

RASCAL. Radiological Assessment System for Consequence Analysis

RIC. The Regulatory Information Conference is an annual conference that brings together over 3,000 participants from 32 countries to provide an opportunity for Government, industry, international agencies, and other interested stakeholders and members of the public to meet and discuss safety initiatives and regulatory trends.

ROP. The Reactor Oversight Process is the process by which the NRC monitors and evaluates the performance of commercial nuclear power plants. Designed to focus on plant activities most important to safety, the process uses inspection findings and performance indicators to assess each plant's safety performance.

RPS. The Reactor Programs System provides an integrated methodology for planning, scheduling, conducting, reporting, and analyzing inspection activities at the nuclear power reactor and fuel facilities in the United States.

RTR. Research and test reactors

SAPHIRE. The System Analysis Programs for Hands-On Integrated Reliability Evaluation is a software application developed for performing a complete probabilistic risk assessment.

SDP. The significance determination process assigns risk characterization to inspection findings based on large early release frequency considerations.

SER. The safety evaluation report documents the NRC staff's technical reviews.

SGI. Safeguards Information is a special category of sensitive unclassified information that must be protected. Safeguards Information concerns the physical protection of operating power reactors, spent fuel shipments, strategic special nuclear material, or other radioactive material.

SIDS. Suspicious Incidents Data System

SLES. The Secure LAN/Electronic Safe is an electronic document management system for sensitive Safeguards Information.

SMR. A small modular reactor design is less than one-third the size of a current nuclear plant and can create approximately a quarter of the energy output.

SNF. Spent nuclear fuel

SNM. Special nuclear materials are defined by Title-I of the Atomic Energy Act of 1954 as plutonium, uranium-233, or uranium enriched in the isotopes uranium-233 or uranium-235. The definition includes any other material that the NRC determines to be special nuclear material, but it does not include source material. The NRC has not declared any other material as SNM.

SRP. Standard Review Plan

STAQS. Strategic Acquisition System

STEM. Science, Technology, Engineering, and Mathematics

STP. The South Texas Project is a nuclear power station southwest of Bay City, TX.

TAPIS. The Transportation Approval Package Information System is one of several applications that use National Institutes of Health IBM mainframe timesharing services. Although the hardware for these applications resides outside of the NRC, the agency still supports them.

UNC. The United Nuclear Corporation site is located in New Mexico. It includes a former uranium ore processing mill and tailings disposal area.

US-APWR. The U.S.-Advanced Pressurized-Water Reactor is a standard design for a 4,451-MWt pressurized-water reactor.

USEC. The U.S. Enrichment Corporation supplies enriched uranium fuel for commercial nuclear power plants.

U.S.-EPR. The U.S. Evolutionary Power Reactor is third generation pressurized-water reactor design.

WASSC. The Waste Safety Standards Committee is an IAEA safety committee.

WBL. Web-Based Licensing is a materials licensing system that the NRC uses for managing licensing information for businesses using radioactive materials.

WIR. Waste incidental to reprocessing is the waste byproduct that comes from reprocessing nuclear fuel.

WVDP. The West Valley Demonstration Project is operated by DOE and was created in 1980 by the West Valley Demonstration Project Act.